SEVEN SYSTEMS OF INDIAN PHILOSOPHY

SEVEN SYSTEMS OF INDIAN PHILOSOPHY

Pandit Rajmani Tigunait, Ph.D.

The Himalayan International Institute of Yoga
Science and Philosophy of the U.S.A.
Honesdale, Pennsylvania

RR 1, Box 400
Honesdale, Pennsylvania 18431

04 03 02 01 00 99 98 8 7 6 5

The paper used in this publication meets the minimum requirements of American National Standard for Information Sciences—Permanence of Paper for Printed Library Materials, ANSI Z39.48-1984.

Library of Congress Cataloging in Publication Data:
Tigunait, Rajmani
Seven systems of Indian philosophy.

Includes index.
1. Philosophy, Indic. I. Title.
B131.T53 1983 181'.4 83-4327
ISBN 0-89389-076-6

समर्पणम्

श्रीकराय श्रीरूपाय गुरुचक्रविहारिणे ।
श्रीस्वामिपदयुक्ताय रामाय सततं नमः ।।

अये गुरो पूज्य दयानिधे मुदा चकार बाले मयि सौम्यवीक्षणम् ।
तथा तमो दूरमपाकृतं त्वया कृतार्थकामः खलु याचते पुनः ।।

सद्वासद्वा किमपि विदितं त्वत्प्रसादानुभावात्
सर्वज्ञत्वं सकलविषये वर्तते लोकमातुः ।
वाचां गुम्फञ्चरणकमले तावके पुष्पमालाञ्चाङ्-
गीकृत्य प्रकटय ममानन्दसाम्राज्यलक्ष्मीम् ।।

To my Gurudeva:
Thy own flowers of blessing and inspiration are
returned to thy lotus feet.

Contents

Foreword

The search and love for knowledge are as intrinsic to human nature as the drives for self-preservation and social interaction. From the time we first wonder at the colors and sounds about us to the moment we finally confront eternity with our last breaths, we are occupied with the pursuit of understanding our environment, ourselves, and the nature of whatever reality may exist beyond. People essentially want to *know*, and the basic questions of life—why, who, whence, whither, and how—tease even the staunchest materialist in the quiet moments of awe or the times of pressing injustice. To answer these questions, there have evolved two great philosophies, which are usually designated by the geographical divisions of East and West. The modern Western approach addresses the problem from an objective, theoretical, and pluralistic standpoint, whereas the ancient Eastern approach is more subjective, experiential, and holistic. The West looks outward to external data, and the East turns inward to internal experience; one method is based primarily on dialectics and discursive deductive speculation, while the other is based on introspection and direct intuitive insight.

The Eastern orientation is becoming increasingly important in the West as we begin to realize that there are more things in heaven and earth than are dreamt of in most Western philosophies. As proponents of the Western approach investigate increasingly subtle aspects of reality, the basic assumptions of the two philosophies are becoming less divergent. The philosophy of Vedānta long ago declared that the whole universe is Brahman—all-pervading Consciousness—and modern science is now beginning to come to the same conclusion, based on empirical data and inferential methodology. Quantum field theory and the theory of relativity are pointing toward the essential unity of all things, and the disciplines of physics and metaphysics are thus finding common ground. In their search for an intellectually satisfying explanation of the nature of reality, modern Western scientists and philosophers are discovering and exploring the wisdom of the Asian world view. A similar transition from materialism to idealism is evident in the arts. The modern artist has shifted from literal replication to abstract interpretation and finally to nonobjective conceptualization. Many present-day creations bear a marked likeness to ancient yogic works of art in essence and in appearance because both are attempts to convey visual philosophical statements about the nature of certain aspects of reality. Psychology has of course also been in the forefront of the exploration into the nature of reality, and new subdisciplines—such as transpersonal psychology, the psychology of consciousness, and parapsychology—investigate subtleties of life beyond the mind. Studies such as these find few prototypes except in Eastern philosophy. As psychologists attempt to find solutions to the mental problems of life on deeper levels, large numbers of them are coming to esteem the ethical systems, practical techniques, and positive cosmology of Eastern philosophy.

Thus it is becoming increasingly apparent to Western

thinkers that, as Mahatma Gandhi said, "Much that we hug today as knowledge is ignorance pure and simple." In the effort to discover what is true, more and more Westerners are investigating the Eastern approach as well as the Western approach. When one turns to Eastern philosophy as an aid to explore the nature of reality and consciousness, it is the Indian systems of philosophy that stand out as paramount, because Eastern philosophy essentially is Indian philosophy. The novice student may feel a bit perplexed, however, in beginning to study this different orientation due to the unfamiliar perspective it provides. This is understandable, because only a few Western philosophers (such as Plato, Augustine, and Berkeley) have described an idealistic framework such as that found in Indian philosophies. Foreign words and unique concepts may further puzzle beginners until they become more acquainted with the new territory.

Although many scholarly descriptions of Indian philosophy are available to clarify the philosophical models and explain the details of each school, the vast bulk of the subject matter and its precise intricacies are nonetheless difficult to assimilate. In response to this problem, the present text provides a concise yet comprehensive basic outline of the major systems of Indian philosophy in a manner that is highly accurate and yet easily understandable. Sanskrit terms are provided for academic purposes, but one need not have any prior understanding of the field to comprehend the basic outlooks and tenets described in each school of philosophy.

The respect and interest that the learned author has for each system is apparent in the skill and enthusiasm with which he explains them. Having been trained in the scholarly Brahmin tradition since early childhood and having studied with various adepts and scholars, Pandit Doctor Tigunait has also attained an estimable academic reputation in his years of formal schooling. But he is not a mere scholar, for the practical results of his love for knowledge and his ardent quest for truth are apparent in his life and personality. He is a devoted meditator and thinker as well as a learned scholar, and the teachings of the scriptures have been assimilated in their essence into the depths of his being. Thus he is eminently well-suited to accomplish the difficult task of writing such a text, which states profound philosophical concepts in a manner understandable to a novice while remaining in accord both with tradition and with strict academic standards. This text is a straightforward and definitive review that will satisfy the reader's initial curiosity and eliminate confusion while piquing interest in and paving the way for further in-depth study. This handbook will prove an invaluable introduction and basic reference for any student of Eastern philosophy.

My heartfelt thanks go to Panditji for requesting my assistance in preparing the manuscript of this book, for in so doing I have gotten a glimpse of the profound depths of Indian philosophy and have identified areas of particular interest about which I am inspired to learn more and more. I am sure readers of this book will enjoy a similar experience.

Arpita, Ph.D.

Preface

A year ago my Gurudeva asked me to write a book on Indian philosophy. This book was originally written as a textbook for the graduate students in the Himalayan Institute's Program in Eastern Studies and Comparative Psychology. The purpose is to present the major systems simply and clearly so that beginning students can comprehend the concepts while at the same time offering a depth of understanding that will be useful to scholars as well. I have tried my best to make this textbook a stepping-stone to prepare students for further study of Indian philosophy as presented in more complex texts, such as those by Radhakrishnan and Dasgupta.

In this review I have not included Cārvāka and Jainism since their philosophical value is not as great as the other systems. Śaivism, Śaktism, and Tantra will be covered separately in a later text. It should also be mentioned that I do not follow the footsteps of English writers in describing the Mīmāṃsā system. Rather I directly present the theories and practices of this system from the original scriptures of the Mīmāṃsā school. The methodology applied in this

book is simple and explanatory; it does not follow the traditional śāstrārtha style of prior and subsequent views.*

I thank Dr. Arpita for looking into the manuscript carefully. Thanks are also due to Dr. Sudha Thornburg for giving her valuable time in taking dictation, John Miller for the index to the book, Larry Clark for editing, Bandana (Barb Bova) for typing, Janet Zima for design and illustration, and Darlene Clark for typesetting. I also express my affection and love to the students for whom this book was originally written.

Heart-touching feelings are offered to my beloved wife, Meera, for preparing the rough draft of the manuscript and helping me to put together the manuscript.

*In the traditional style of philosophical writing, scholars would first critique other systems, pointing out their errors and lack of completion. They would then offer a subsequent interpretation which they believed corrected for these deficiencies.

The Spelling and Pronunciation of Sanskrit Letters and Words

Sanskrit vowels are generally the same pure vowel sounds found in Italian, Spanish, or French. The consonants are generally pronounced as in English.

a	org*a*n, s*u*m
ā	f*a*ther
ai	*ai*sle
au	s*au*erkr*au*t
b	*b*ut
bh	a*bh*or
c	*ch*ur*ch*
ch	chur*chh*ill
ḍ	*d*ough
d	*d*ough (slightly toward the *th* sound of *th*ough)
ḍh	a*dh*ere
dh	a*dh*ere (slightly toward the *theh* sound of brea*the h*ere)
e	pr*ey*
g	*g*o
gh	do*gh*ouse
ḥ	[slight aspiration of preceding vowel]
h	*h*ot
i	*i*t
ī	pol*i*ce
j	*j*ump

jh	lo*dgeh*ouse
k	*k*id
kh	wor*kh*orse
ḷ	no English equivalent; a short vowel pronounced somewhat like the *lry* in reve*lry*
l	*l*ug
ṃ	[resonant nasalization of preceding vowel]
m	*m*ud
ṅ	si*ng*
ṇ	u*n*der
ñ	pi*n*ata
n	*n*o
o	n*o*
p	*p*ub
ph	u*ph*ill
ṛ	no English equivalent; a simple vowel *r*, such as appears in many Slavonic languages
ṝ	the same pronunciation as *ṛ*, more prolonged
r	*r*um
ś	*sh*awl (pronounced with a slight whistle; German *sp*rechen)
ṣ	*sh*un
s	*s*un
ṭ	*t*omato
t	wa*t*er
ṭh	an*th*ill
th	*Th*ailand
u	p*u*sh
ū	r*u*de
v	*v*odka (midway between *w* and *v*)
y	*y*es

Vowels. Every vowel is either long or short. The dipthongs *e, ai, o,* and *au* are always long; *ḷ* is always short. Long *a, i, u,* and *ṛ* are indicated by a horizontal line over the vowel. The long form of a vowel is pronounced twice as long as the short form.

Consonants. Sanskrit has many aspirated consonants, that is, consonants pronounced with a slight *h* sound: *bh ch ḍh dh gh jh kh ph ṭh th.* These aspirated consonants should be pronounced distinctly. The retroflex consonants, *ḍ ḍh ṇ ṣ ṭ ṭh,* are pronounced with a hitting sound, as the tip of the tongue is curled back to the ridge of the hard palate. The dentals, *d dh n t th,* are pronounced with the tip of the tongue touching the upper teeth.

Accentuation. There is no strong accentuation of syllables. The general rule is to stress the next-to-last syllable of a word, if that is long. A syllable is long if (*a*) it has a long vowel or (*b*) its vowel is followed by more than one consonant. If the next-to-last syllable of a word is short, then the syllable before that receives the stress.

chapter

1

What Is Indian Philosophy?

To understand the basic tenets of Indian philosophy, the Western reader must be willing to entertain a new definition of the term philosophy. The Sanskrit word for philosophy is *darśana*, which means direct vision. This word highlights a major difference between modern Western philosophy, which predominantly relies on intellectual pursuit, and Indian philosophy, which relies on the direct vision of truths and pure Buddhi (pure reasoning). With the exception of a few Christian and Jewish mystics, not many modern Western philosophers would agree with Plato's definition of a philosopher as one who loves the "vision" of truth. But it is precisely this vision of truth that forms the foundation of all but the most materialistic schools of Indian philosophy.

A second difference between Western and Indian philosophies is that the latter are much more comprehensive. Western philosophies and sciences tend to compartmentalize the various aspects of life into distinctly separate disciplines. Only the Aristotelian and medieval Catholic philosophies begin to approach the scope and integration of ideas found in Indian philosophy. The major Indian schools integrate into a single framework metaphysics, epistemology, logic, axiology, aesthetics, ethics, sociology, psychology, and physiology. To Indian thinkers, these disciplines are so interrelated that they are looked upon as if residing in a single body whose members cannot be severed from the whole without losing their vitality. Indian philosophy is so comprehensive that it includes not only theoretical but also practical aspects. In fact, to the Indian mind, philosophy is not divorced from practical life. Theoretical knowledge that has no application in daily life is not philosophy at all, but is mere metaphysical speculation. The conclusions and beliefs that grow out of Indian philosophy form the foundation for all the other sciences and arts, including the natural sciences, medicine, political science, law, literature, sculpture, dance, music, and theatre, as well as interpersonal relationships at the levels of nation, community, and family. Indian philosophy addresses all the natural and spiritual needs of man, from knowledge of Supreme Consciousness in the *Brahmavidyā* to the science of medicine in the *Āyurveda*.

The term *Indian* is also subject to further clarification. It is used here to describe those philosophical schools that originated, developed, and flourished in the area that today comprises the whole of Southeast Asia. The word *Indian* should not, however, be used interchangeably with the term *Hindu*, with which it is closely related etymologically. The term Hindu is not only a misnomer, but is also misleading because it carries with it the connotation of religion. The terms Indian and Hindu have never been used in India itself to refer to nationality, culture, religion, or philosophy. Indians actually call their subcontinent *Bhārata*, after the ancient king Bharata, whose name means "one who is capable of nourishing and protecting." King Bharata was capable of nourishing and preserving the "Golden Bird" of India when it was the flourishing international center of wealth and culture. *Bhārata* also means "lover of knowledge," or in this case, "the land that loves knowledge."

Furthermore, the current popular usage of the term Hinduism does not correspond to its original meaning. When Alexander the Great invaded the subcontinent around 325 B.C., he crossed the River Sindhu and renamed it Indus, which was easier for the Greek tongue to pronounce. Alexander's Macedonian forces subsequently called the land to the east of this river *India*. Later, the Moslem invaders called the Sindhu River the Hindu River because in their language, Parsee, the Sanskrit sound *s* converts to *h*. Thus, for the Persians, Sindhu became Hindu, and the land east of that river became known as Hindustan. In more recent times, the land was again called India, but during the British regime, politicians frequently used the terms *Hindu* and *Hinduism*, emphasizing the religious and political overtones of these words. This was done to differentiate the Hindus from the Moslems, thus aiding the British policy of "divide and rule." Western writers then adopted these terms for the sake of convenience, and Eastern writers conformed to the norms set by those in power.

Confusion spread as the word *Hinduism* increasingly came to be used to designate the so-called religion of the Indian people. In actuality, however, it is more properly used to describe the entire culture of a geographic region that, though apparently quite diverse, holds many underlying characteristics in common. The misconceptions surrounding the term Hinduism now make it a virtually useless word. Its usage is roughly analagous to the hypothetical case of invaders occupying the United States and referring to the native way of life as *Yankee-ism* and then purporting this to be the "American religion." In India, no religion called Hinduism ever existed, and even today the learned and well-informed spiritual and religious leaders of India do not use this term. They use instead the term *sanātana dharma*, which means "eternal law," to refer to their systems of religious belief.

Indian philosophy, then, is more appropriately referred to as *darśana*, and Indian religious beliefs as *sanātana dharma*. Both terms refer to philosophical insights directly experienced by ancient sages who lived in the Indus Valley, the Himalayas, and other corners of India. Knowledge gained through the senses and through reason forms only a small part of these systems. The direct transcendent experience of the reality beyond the material and logical domains is both the source and the ultimate goal of these systems. The mind and its senses are the necessary tools initially used in the process of attaining this highest state, but they are not competent means to attain the final goal. Transcendent insight alone provides the whole truth. The theories and procedures described in the systems of Indian philosophy—though originating in certain places and times and propounded by specific enlightened founders or codifiers—are not limited to any particular era, culture, or group. Rather they address the universal and ongoing concerns of humanity and are meant for all.

In the West, the answers to ultimate questions are usually provided by religion, but this is not the case in India. That which is known in the West as religion is in India merely a set of social laws including ethics, custom, and ritual. India has always held a holistic approach toward life, which is seen as being composed of two inseparable aspects. Life related to the outer world (family, society, nation, humanity) is regulated by religion, and life related to the inner world is studied and guided by philosophy. Philosophy itself is viewed as having two different aspects, one theoretical and the other practical. Theory without practice cannot bring one to the desired goal, and practice without theory is meaningless and subject to distortion. For these reasons the holistic approach, which combines all the sciences related to both internal and external life, has always been employed in India. No wall stands between philosophy and religion because both are inextricably interwoven.

In the West, this comprehensive approach, including both darśana and sanātana dharma, does not exist. It is therefore frequently misunderstood by Occidental readers. The great Indian systems that address the problems of life are often mistakenly regarded as being either mere philosophy or religion. Actually, however, the Indian systems are both of these—and neither of these. Thus, these systems represent a totally unique approach for the Western mind. Likewise, the Indian mind has difficulty understanding the circumscribed notions of religion and philosophy as they are known in the West. In India, seeking the truth by blind adherence to dogma or by reliance on logic and observation alone is very seldom pursued. Rather, the liberty to think freely and to search for the truth personally, independently, and experientially are traditional in Indian culture. Westerners live freely and think in structured ways, while Easterners think freely and live in structured ways. The West focuses on external nature, as is witnessed by its material comforts and technology, while the East is proficient in dealing with inner nature, as its rich tradition of spiritual achievement proclaims. Although tradition is respected in India, only direct experience is thought to bring the answers to the questions of life. As the Upaniṣads say, "Follow that advice of mine which is good and helpful for your progress, and neglect even my own advice which is not."

It is apparent that these common misunderstandings about Indian philosophy must be resolved in order to understand completely the concepts and sciences involved. When one uses the term *Indian philosophy*, he should keep in mind that these concepts and sciences result from the personal experiences of great sages whose ideas do not belong to any particular place or time. The teachings passed on by the sages are universal and highly practical systems that are provided for the benefit of all humanity. Dealing with the basic problems of human life, these teachings point out avenues for solving life's questions and problems and for attaining contentment and wisdom here and now.

Indian philosophy is a way of life, a comprehensive system

for attaining direct experience of the Ultimate Reality and Truth. It is not a religion, for it has nothing to do with the confines of ritual, dogma, institutions, blind faith, or anthropomorphic deities. Nor is it mere intellectual speculation, for it extends beyond the limits of the senses and the rational mind, and it provides methods for attaining experiences of the transcendent Reality. The founders of these great systems are the carriers of large candles aflame with the brilliant and eternal light of truth. Their light is not meant only for those born in the East, but it shines for all humanity. These sources can provide inspiration and guidance to set many individual candles aflame and to enlighten the dark chambers of seeking hearts.

Why Is Philosophy Needed?

A human being is not only a physical being. He is a thinking being, too. Most of the time, people suffer within their own mental worlds, but this suffering can be overcome by making thoughts pure and positive. Such thoughts and attitudes result from a disciplined mind that is not unduly involved with external objects, for problems arise from misunderstanding one's relationship with this external world. If the real nature of the external world and its relationship with body, mind, and soul is analyzed and utilized properly, then it can become a great source of enjoyment within and without. In today's world most people try to attain permanent peace and happiness through external objects, but these are in themselves temporary and subject to decay and change.

Modern man is ambivalent. On the one hand he is not sure about himself and is constantly dwelling in the darkness of ignorance; on the other hand he thinks he possesses a great intellect and is a member of a highly advanced technological society. He is proud to fly in space, yet he is suffering in his relationships and constantly running to psychiatrists, psychologists, priests, teachers, doctors, and friends for solace. This confusion is due to the lack of a philosophy of life. Life without a concrete philosophy is like a castle built on the sand; it is always ready to crumble with every tiny ripple of water. Without understanding the omniscience, omnipresence, and omnipotence of eternal life, one is bound to feel insecure, living in a world of fear. One's entire consciousness and energy is then involved in self-preservation, and thus one is not free to explore other avenues of life. Philosophy is the body of knowledge that frees one from fear and from the primitive instinct of self-preservation. It leads one "from the unreal to the real; from the darkness to the light; from mortality to immortality." This philosophy is beyond the grasp of religion and is not the personal viewpoint of any sect or group. It is universal.

All schools of Indian philosophy are designed to provide a systematic method for exploring one's inner potentials and ultimately reaching the center of bliss, happiness, and consciousness hidden in the innermost chamber of every human heart. In Eastern philosophy, the external world is not ignored but is considered to be a means to higher attainment. Thus, this philosophy is helpful not only for those who are complete renunciates, but also for those who are active in the world. Indian philosophy quenches the thirst of desires, thoughts, emotions, memories, and anxieties through its skillful techniques, which are designed within a variety of different frameworks. Philosophy teaches one how to train the mind to think logically, and how to reform one's inner attitudes toward the external world. The great philosophical thoughts of India somehow could not integrate into the various Indian cultures, and therefore many Indians were not benefited by the vast literature of the philosophy that exists even today.

There was a time when people were not so materialistic, when they were free from psychosomatic diseases. Now some medical professionals think that seventy to eighty percent of diseases are psychosomatic—and there is no permanent remedy for these diseases except an effective philosophy of life. The body is a great instrument for the worldly and spiritual journey. Eastern philosophy offers remarkable and highly scientific techniques for studying its various aspects, for dealing with them, and for gaining voluntary control over them so that the body will not be a stumbling block on the path. Eastern philosophy provides for a complete understanding of all levels of the personality. For psychophysiological and spiritual well being, philosophy is an essential foundation. Materialism without a sound philosophy is a terrible curse afflicting modern society. For lack of philosophy modern man has become selfish. It seems that there is no way for humanity to attain the next step of civilization and live peacefully except by going back to the path of the sages.

The Veda and Its Contribution to Indian Philosophy

In Indian philosophy and culture, the Veda is of paramount importance. It constitutes the most ancient scripture known to man. It was transmitted orally, possibly as early as 4,000 B.C., before it was compiled. Sanskrit, the language of the Veda, is ancient and is the richest of all the languages of the world, but alas, only a fortunate few know this language. Even when Sanskrit was in its full bloom it was probably known only to a limited number of scholars. That is why it was called *devavāṇī*, "language of the bright beings." The Sanskrit language is tough, terse, and abstruse, but every word and sound explains its origin in its root form. It is the most poetic language of the world. Vedic Sanskrit is more ancient than classical Sanskrit. Long before Pāṇini systematized classical Sanskrit grammar, Niruktam used to interpret Vedic Sanskrit words.

The Veda has four sections: Ṛg, Yajur, Sāma, and Atharva. In their present form, they contain approximately 20,000 verses. The Ṛg Veda is a collection of poetic hymns in which numerous gods and goddesses—who are the personifications of different aspects of the forces of nature—are invoked and glorified. These hymns appear to be simple prayers to the deities. Yet couched in highly symbolic language, they contain great philosophical and metaphysical meaning. All the thoughts of Indian philosophy flow from the profound origin of the Ṛg Veda. The Yajur Veda contains some mantras from the Ṛg Veda and some that are not found there. It focuses on mantras that were used in the performance of rituals, called *yajnas.* The mantras of the Sāma Veda are the same as those found in the Ṛg Veda, but here they are repeated according to rules of prosody and are to be sung in a specific tone during rituals. If these mantras are not sung on a particular pitch, their meanings are distorted. The sound and its profound impact on the human mind was researched thoroughly during the Vedic period. Seven notes, which are used in all the great music of the world, were discovered by the Vedic seers. The Atharva Veda contains mantras that are believed to have great supernatural power. Unlike the mantras of the Ṛg, Yajur, and Sāma Vedas, whose purposes are spiritual, most mantras of the Atharva Veda deal with the mundane world and are for material gains.

All of Vedic literature is divided into four chronological stages—Saṃhitā, Brāhmaṇa, Āraṇyaka, and Upaniṣad—and thus each of the four Vedas has four stages of development. The Saṃhitā portion of Vedic literature is composed of all the various Vedic mantras. The Brāhmaṇa literature takes the first step in interpreting or giving commentary on the meaning of the mantras found in the Saṃhitā portion. It gives a ritualistic interpretation of the Vedic mantras with instructions for their use in the archaic rituals of the bygone cultural, religious, and social systems of ancient Indian civilization. The instructions given in the Brāhmaṇas are designed to be practiced by householders, that is, by those people who live in the customary manner, fulfilling their duties toward family and society.

Each successive stage of Vedic literature represents a development and deepening of both theory and practice. In the Āraṇyakas, methods of training the mind for higher attainment are described. This literature is meant for householders who have learned to calm down their senses and control their minds through a correct understanding of their relationship with the external world. These teachings are meant to be practiced in solitude. Indeed, the word *Āraṇyaka* itself means "designed to be studied in the calm and quiet corners of the forest." The Āraṇyakas establish a link between householders and renunciates.

The Upaniṣads, the fourth and last stage of Vedic literature, represent the culmination of the Vedic approach. There are one hundred and eight prominent Upaniṣads, eleven of which are considered to be preeminent. In these eleven, the wisdom of the Veda reaches its acme. The Upaniṣads are the later part of the Veda, the storehouse of philosophical gems. The word *Veda* means "knowledge," and *Vedānta* means "the end of knowledge"; Vedānta is another name for the Upaniṣads. The word *Upaniṣad* means to "sit close beside" the competent teacher, and many Upaniṣads are written in the form of a dialogue between teachers and students. In these works, truth is revealed in many stages, according to the capacity of the student. As the student's capacity increases, the teacher gradually reveals to him a higher level of truth. The different approaches toward truth in the Upaniṣads do not contradict one another but rather give a systematic progression of theoretical and practical teachings for different levels of students.

Because of the diversities in social, religious, and cultural backgrounds, in *samskāras* (latent tendencies), and in individual attitudes and capacities, it is not possible for everyone to adopt the same lifestyle and spiritual practice. Likewise, the same single reality cannot be revealed in its entirety to all seekers. Thus in the Upaniṣads, the truth is revealed in various stages, degrees, and grades. For example, at one place in the Upaniṣads food is said to be Brahman, while in the next passage, *prāṇa* (vital force) is said to be Brahman—and then finally the Ātman, the pure Self, is said to be Brahman. In the Upaniṣads, one finds examples, such as that of Virocana and Indra, two students who practiced the same *sādhanā* (spiritual discipline) under the same preceptor, but who realized the truth at different levels and thus in different ways. Virocana realized truth only at the physical level, while Indra, dissatisfied with what he had learned, continued his inner journey and gradually realized higher and more subtle states of truth.

The various schools of Indian philosophy likewise represent the same single truth as realized at different levels and from different perspectives. The Upaniṣads are the greatest source of Indian philosophical thought, and all of the systems of Indian philosophy can be found, in their latent but potential form, in these works. The philosophical expositions in the Veda, however, are expressed in the form of aphorisms, which are compact, terse, and abstruse. The theories take on explicit form only in the Upaniṣads. For example, the *Nāsadīya-sūkta* expounds ten kinds of philosophical theories; the *Puruṣa-sūkta* is a source of Vedāntic theory; and the *Rātri-sūkta* and the *Devī-sūkta* are the sources of Śākta philosophy.

The Vedic literature contains all the seeds from which sprouted the various schools of philosophy, each with its own particular emphasis and style. Of the seven major systems discussed here, six acknowledge the authority of the Veda. These six orthodox schools are Nyāya, Vaiśeṣika, Sāṃkhya, Yoga, Mīmāṃsā, and Vedānta. Although the heterodox schools, such as Buddhism, do not acknowledge the authority of the Veda, their teachings can actually be found there. Buddhism claims to stand independently, but its nihilistic theory is one of the ten philosophical theories mentioned in the Nāsadīya-sūkta of the Ṛg Veda. Even among the orthodox schools, however, one can find wide differences of emphasis. For instance, the Mīmāṃsā system states that rituals are the ultimate means to attain the highest goal of life, while Vedānta emphasizes the theory of knowledge and the practice of meditation and contemplation. The different systems of Indian philosophy came into being from the Vedic literature at various times and developed according to the prevailing needs of the society.

The chronology of the Upaniṣads is the source of some confusion. The earliest Upaniṣads date from approximately 1,000 to 400 B.C. They are said to be the culmination of the Veda and a reform movement against the excessively ritualistic life prescribed by the Brāhmaṇas. However, rituals from the Brāhmaṇas continued to be performed during the time of the Upaniṣads.

It is often said that Buddhism, which developed in the sixth century B.C., constituted a revolution against the rituals, sacrifices, and rigid caste system of Brāhmaṇism. But the Upaniṣads—which are full of teachings of knowledge, love, and morality, and which provide an alternative to Brāhmaṇism—already existed at the time of Buddha. At that time, however, the vast majority of society was still entangled in the complicated and misunderstood ritualistic way of life characterized by Brāhmaṇism. The great sages of the Upaniṣads, however—such as Vaśiṣṭha, Yājñavalkya, Gārgya, and others—lived alone in the forests in search of knowledge. Only occasionally did they visit the towns to teach students and to help the kings in the performance of yajnas (rituals and ceremonies). These sages knew the importance of rituals and moral practices in the establishment of peace within the individual and within the community. So they simultaneously practiced the philosophies of Vedānta (*jñāna* yoga, the yoga of knowledge), Mīmāṃsā (rituals) and *karma* yoga (the yoga of action). The Upaniṣads, then, were known only to a few adepts who practiced their teachings faithfully, but who did not spread the teachings widely. Therefore, Buddhism came into existence to reform the major portion of society, which was dominated by Brāhmaṇism.

The Brāhmins, the intellectual class of Indian society, were the original custodians of Vedic knowledge. They were highly disciplined, and through their well-polished intellects they were capable of preserving this great cultural heritage. As long as they remained selfless and devoted to the service of humanity and the search for knowledge, the Brāhmins were universally respected. However, when they became greedy, self-centered, and hypocritical, they lost their time-honored dignified status. Before this falling away, the Brāhmins were called *Bhūsura* or *Bhūdeva*, meaning "celestial beings on earth." Their whole lives were devoted to metaphysics, spirituality, religion, and human welfare, but when they forgot their purpose in life and became attracted to the charms and temptations of the world, they remained Brāhmins in name only.

They gradually lost mastery of the process for internalizing and spiritualizing external objects and began to emphasize only the external ritualistic behaviors rather than their deep symbolic meanings. This was the darkest time of Indian history, during which the caste system became rigid and the religious practices empty and dogmatic. The priests commercialized rituals and sacrifices in the name of *dharma* (virtue) and God, and this became a curse for the community. Just as Christianity suffered from the selling of indulgences in the Middle Ages, and Judaism suffered from the literal pedanticism of the Pharisees in Jesus' time, so wealthy and powerful Indian society suffered during this time. However, there still remained a group of people who were devoted to both the search for knowledge and service to humanity. They experienced the various levels of truth and taught what they had experienced directly. It is through these solitary sages that the traditional knowledge was preserved.

Some say that the four stages of Vedic literature are meant to be practiced in the four corresponding stages of life described in the scriptures. These four *āśrama*, or stages, are *brahmacarya*, the student stage; *gārhasthya*, the householder stage; *vānaprastha*, the stage of retirement from worldly life; and *sanyāsa*, the stage of complete renunciation and perfect detachment. According to this format, the Saṃhitā portion of the Veda would be studied during the student stage; the Brāhmaṇas would provide the householder with guidelines for practice; the Āraṇyakas would be studied in solitude by the retired person; and the wisdom of the Upaniṣads would be practiced in a perfect state of detachment by the renunciate.

Gradual Development of the Systems of Philosophy

All systems of Indian philosophy share a similar process of origination and development. The Veda, as has already been seen, is either the direct or indirect basis for the philosophical schools of India. The philosophical viewpoints of the various schools are mingled in the Veda in the same way as the different colors and limbs of a peacock are mingled in its yolk, and these embryonic perspectives take clear shape in the Upaniṣads. It is from these Upaniṣadic writings that complete systems of philosophy develop. The first stage in this development is the systematization of Upaniṣadic truth by the great sages (*ṛṣis*) who had direct experience of the truth and who then codified their experience in *sūtra* (aphorism) scriptures. Thus sūtra literature is the first step in establishing a particular philosophical school.

Etymologically, *sūtra* means "thread," but in this context it means a mnemonic statement. For a long time, philosophical discussions took place verbally and were handed down by teachers to students through oral traditions. With the gradual passage of time, the teachers felt it necessary to codify their main thoughts so that the students could keep these teachings intact. This initial type of writing is called sūtra literature. It is the most compact, precise, and meaningful of all literature. A sūtra text is a collection of many aphorisms arranged in numerous sections according to various topics. For example, the Mīmāṃsā Sūtra of Jaimini contains aphorisms that sum up the philosophical discussions related to the teachings of specific rituals and their uses in the Veda, Brāhmaṇas, Araṇyakas, and Upaniṣads. They also raise and refute the existent objections to these views. The Mīmāṃsā Sūtra of Jaimini thus represents the earliest systematic treatise on the Mīmāṃsā philosophy. Likewise, the Brahma Sūtras of Bādarāyaṇa describe the philosophy of Vedānta, and the Yoga Sūtras of Patañjali describe the philosophy of Yoga.

The sūtras are very terse, and their meaning is consequently unclear without the proper guidance of a competent teacher. To avoid confusion, various teachers have therefore felt it necessary to write commentaries on the sūtras. The chief commentaries on the sūtras are called *bhāṣyas*, meaning "elaborate interpretations." There are bhāṣyas on all the sūtra works of all the systems of philosophy. Sometimes there are many commentaries on a single set of sūtras, and each interprets the meaning of the sūtras in a different way. Diverse interpretations are possible both because the sūtras are extremely terse, and also because it is quite common in Sanskrit for a single word to have numerous meanings. Therefore, various authors may write a variety of expositions on the same sūtra work, interpreting the sūtra with strong arguments to justify their respective viewpoints. In this way, numerous schools have branched out from the same original philosophy. For example, there are commentaries on the Brahma Sūtra by Śaṅkara, Rāmānuja, Madhva, Ballabha, Nimbārka, and many others. Each interprets the Brahma Sūtra in his own way, using reasoning and logic to elucidate the original meaning, and each believes his explanation of the text to be the original intent of the author. The followers of each interpretation then gradually form sectarian schools within Vedānta and superficially separate themselves from each other.

All the *ācāryas* (teachers) have maintained the practical aspects of their philosophies so their followers could practice them in their daily lives. Philosophical debates have been continuous among the followers of these diverse schools, and these debates have prepared a fertile ground for the development of a vast philosophical literature full of elaborate prior views and subsequent views. The commentaries and independent treatises written by the followers of these individual schools or systems are called *ṭīkas*. Thus, there has been an unbroken flow of philosophical thought that has resulted in the development of a vast philosophical literature. In summary, the systems were first codified into sūtra literature by ṛṣis, who directly experienced the truth; then they were taught by ācāryas, who derived their authority from the ṛṣis; then they were expanded in bhāṣyas (commentaries) and lastly in ṭīkās (subcommentaries).

The Common Characteristics of Indian Philosophy

Although each school of Indian philosophy maintains its own unique flavor, they all hold certain characteristics in common that make them recognizable as members of a single body of knowledge, for they all have their source in the Veda. Among these shared characteristics, the following ones are most important.

Direct experience. All systems of Indian philosophy claim to be derived from the Veda, but the Veda itself is the written record of the direct experiences of great sages who realized the truth within. To solve the questions related to the nature of life, death, birth, and cosmic and individual existence, seekers of truth began their quest with observation and rational inquiries. When they started concentrating on these issues, they found that these methods were insufficient to establish final conclusions regarding the issues in question. After much experimentation, they discovered various methods of meditation that help one to attain the higher levels of consciousness in which one may have direct experience of the truth. Direct experience is therefore the foundation of all the systems of Indian philosophy. Each school originated with an enlightened teacher, a ṛṣi, who described his experiences of the truth and his process for attaining it.

Practicality. All systems of Indian philosophy contain a practical aspect called *sādhanā*. Thus these theoretical systems of philosophy can be applied in a practical way by their adherents to solve their problems in daily life and to attain the highest goal of life. A philosophy that does not come into the realm of practical action is considered to be useless and is not thought by the sages to be a philosophy at all. Self-realization, the direct experience of one's own essential nature, is the goal of all the systems of Indian philosophy. Therefore every system presents a method of practice through which one can overcome pains and miseries and attain the goal of life. Even the lowest of philosophies, Cārvāka (which is materialistic), also prescribes a specific way of life, familiar to modern man, which urges one to "Eat, drink, and be merry," and "Gather ye rosebuds while ye may." The attainment of salvation or perfection is considered to be the greatest responsibility of a human being, and each Indian philosophy prescribes a lifestyle through which one can explore one's true nature and carry out one's responsibilities in life. The means provided to attain this goal include selfless love, service to others, purification, and self-control. Because of their usefulness and practicality, each system of Indian philosophy is as new and fresh today as it was in its initial stages.

Acceptance of authority. Respect for sages and ancient scriptures is a strong tradition in India. When a teacher advocates a new philosophical system, he cites the established scriptures or writings of authorized sages to support his statements. The founders of the different systems of Indian philosophy stress the importance of direct experience, yet they always refer to the Veda to support their theories. This is not because they are skeptical of direct experiential knowledge, but rather because they have a great respect and regard for the ancient sages whose teachings have come through direct experience. In the orthodox schools, the Veda is considered to be the highest authority. Therefore, the orthodox philosophical systems always try to support their theories in accordance with the Veda. Even the nonorthodox schools, which do not accept the authority of the Veda, follow the authority of their own founders and teachers. Buddha, for example, retained many views held in the

Veda, but he did not cite the Veda as the authority for his views. His followers, however, accepted his authority, and so the tendency to rely on the work revealed by the realized teacher is maintained even in Buddhism. Reformers have always made adjustments in presentation and method to suit contemporary society, but they have also respected the ancient concepts.

Openmindedness. Indian philosophy is distinguished by a broad outlook that reflects its unflinching devotion to truth. Each system has sought to cast away narrowmindedness and to remain open to the views of all other systems. Most of the major systems developed together chronologically and geographically. Through an exchange of ideas expressed in philosophical debates (*śāstrātha*), the concepts of one school would be explored and often adopted with modifications by another school. A system of Indian philosophy never comes to a conclusion before considering what others have to say. The established method of philosophical exposition in the Indian tradition involves explaining and critiquing the prior view (*pūrvapakṣa*) of the subject at hand, then refuting this prior view and describing a subsequent view (*uttarpakṣa*), which establishes a higher step that is called a conclusion or final theory (*siddhānta*). Because of this exchange of ideas, the philosophical systems have continually become more sophisticated and complete. In fact, the systems fall into a hierarchy based on complexity and refinement, rather than on chronological development. Cārvāka, for instance, has been established as the lowest system because it has no text and criticizes no philosophies, yet all the systems refute it. Vedānta, on the other hand, the highest system, criticizes every other system of philosophy even though it is quite ancient and is based on the last portion of the Veda. Its proponents have continued to refute less sophisticated philosophies as they have arisen. Always the willingness to listen, the desire to explore and to discover more, and the thirst to understand all the philosophies and go beyond them have provided the various systems of Indian philosophy with a remarkable openmindedness and breadth of vision.

Thoroughness. Because of this broad outlook, there is an extreme thoroughness in Indian systems of philosophy. Indian philosophy is like a river that originates from a mountain in the form of a small stream. Running down to the plains and collecting waters from many different sources, it gets wider and wider, deeper and deeper, until it finally reaches the ocean and merges itself with the vast all-embracing sea. In the same way, Indian philosophy starts from the most obvious levels of human understanding, but it gradually incorporates experiences through the ages and assimilates increasingly complex and refined thoughts from the sages until it finally becomes a vast and thorough ocean of knowledge. Wealth of tradition, respect for the ancient sages, and thirst for knowledge are the main factors that make Indian philosophy so vast and encyclopedic.

Support of logic and reasoning. Direct experience is the foundation of Indian philosophy, but reason and logic are the chief tools that enable the system to grow and develop. The theories are presented in a way that the conscious, rational mind can easily accept. All systems of Indian philosophy apply the methods of logic to argue their points of view and to protect themselves from the criticism of their opponents. These arguments and rational inquiries are the supporting tools that constitute a part of the philosophy, but they are not the central focus of the study of the philosophy. Reason only justifies that which intuition or direct experience has revealed. Sometimes critics make charges against Indian philosophy, saying that it is not based on independent reasoning but on the authority of the founders and scriptures and that, therefore, Indian philosophy is dogmatic rather than critical. This criticism is not really valid. The Mīmāṃsā and Vedānta systems of philosophy do stress the importance of authority, but at the same time their tenets are supported by strong independent arguments; their theories can stand by reasoning alone. Other systems such as Nyāya and Vaiśeṣika are predominantly based on logic, and Navya-Nyāya, a later school of Nyāya, is the acme of intellectual sharpness and argumentation.

Unbroken flow and stability. Indian philosophy has its roots firmly hidden in the depth of time. The tradition, which is thousands of years old, has been scrupulously preserved intact first by an oral tradition and later through writings. Since the teachings of the Veda and Upaniṣads address the fundamental questions and problems of human life, they transcend the limitations of time, place, and culture. For this reason students and teachers have always made great efforts to preserve the traditional knowledge. In Brāhmin families, precise methods for maintaining the integrity of the original Vedic teachings have passed continuously from generation to generation as a precious inheritance. In addition, the Sanskrit language has provided the necessary stability and precision for transmitting this knowledge. For these reasons, the Indian philosophies have maintained their Vedic heritage intact.

Parallel growth and coexistence of many schools. The various systems of Indian philosophy, after their initial periods of origination and flourishing, continued parallel courses of growth throughout many centuries. The main reason for this continued growth is that the practical aspects of the diverse systems attracted students who carried on the traditions, for these systems were not composed of mere metaphysical speculations divorced from practical application. Whenever a message was delivered by an experienced teacher, it was studied, and its teachings were put into practice by a group of people whom it suited. In this way a school of that philosophy formed. The various schools were kept alive because each provided a theoretical and practical philosophy to meet the emotional and intellectual needs of students on different levels of realization. Thus throughout the centuries numerous schools continued to exist in an unbroken chain of successive adherents. Even today one can see the coexistence of many different schools, for example, Shaivism in Kashmir and Kerala, and Vaishnavaism, Shaktism, and Yoga throughout India. The five major schools of Vedānta still exist today, and practitioners of these systems are found throughout India and around the world. These systems continue to coexist and also to grow. There is a continuous process of change and reformation that does not disturb the most basic teachings of the ancient sages or founders.

Harmony among the schools. All systems of Indian philosophy have the unique quality of cooperating with each other. When debates take place, the aim is not to destroy another's philosophy but to help in the process of clarifying one's own and other theories. The proponents criticize others and want to be criticized themselves so that they can identify and discard any rigidly held tenets that are no longer helpful in an ever-changing society. This flexibility is the main reason for the harmony among the different schools. Indian philosophers understand that one specific philosophical or spiritual discipline is not suitable for all individuals. Even in one family, individual members are found to follow different philosophical disciplines while maintaining peace and harmony among themselves. A learned or intellectual member of the family may practice jñāna yoga, while other members practice other disciplines according to their interests and sāmṣkaras (tendencies).

Practice of yoga. As has been stated previously, Indian philosophy tries to solve the ultimate problems of human life, and to do this, it provides techniques for practice. Generally speaking, the practical aspect is called yoga. Here yoga is used as a general term and is not meant to denote that particular school which is based on the system promulgated by the sage Patañjali. Each system of Indian philosophy has its own practical approach based on its own philosophy. Philosophy without practice is not considered to be true philosophy. Each philosophy promises concrete results if one practices its system sincerely and faithfully. Each prescribes some type of practice of meditation, concentration, and mental control, as well as moral and physical disciplines. Each system explains the nature of the internal and external world so that one can establish harmony between them. Coordination of thought, speech, and action is considered to be a necessary prerequisite for the expansion of peace within and without. The schools agree on physical and mental disciplines for the enhancement of personal and universal well-being, and many kinds of meditation are described and taught in each system. However, the emphasis given to any particular type of meditation differs from one school to another. Therefore the yoga practiced by Vedāntins differs from that practiced by, say, Sāṃkhya students.

The law of karma. Each school of Indian philosophy accepts the immutable law of karma, which states that for every effect there is a cause, and for every action there is a reaction. A man performs his actions and receives remuneration for them. If he becomes attached to the results of his actions, then he becomes a victim of his own karmas because it is attachment to the results, or fruits, that then motivates or conditions a person to perform future actions. The fruit has arisen out of the action, and the action out of the fruit. This cycle is referred to as the wheel of karma. To act with the motive of gaining fruits invites bondage, but to relinquish this motivation frees one from all miseries. All schools of Indian philosophy agree that this concept of karma is the only satisfactory explanation for the existence of suffering. The apparent good fortune of nonvirtuous people and bad fortune of virtuous people can be explained only through the law of karma, which explains the reason and purpose for a person's existence in his present life. According to this law, nothing is accidental; whatever happens in one's life is because of karmas performed in this life or in a past life.

There is lengthy discussion of the law of karma in each system, and each system explains the method for performing duties selflessly without being attached to their fruits. Directly or indirectly, each system teaches how to discipline the mind while performing actions and relating to the external objects of the world. With the help of those disciplines, one can understand the nature of both the inner and outer worlds and can live happily without being attached to temporal objects. Slavery to the phenomenal world occurs due to one's selfish karmas, but everyone is free to break that rope of bondage by learning how to perform his actions selflessly. Thus, the law of karma solves the ultimate questions of life and provides ethical and moral laws for the individual and humanity.

Moral and ethical teachings. For external peace and harmony, an orderly and law-abiding society is necessary. There must be some discipline in one's daily life related to family, society, and the nation, for without law and order the external world becomes disorganized and a source of misery. When external tranquility is disturbed, it is hard to maintain tranquility within. Eastern philosophers have always understood the fact that external disturbances reflect inside as well.

Lack of morality and discipline creates misunderstandings in relationships with others. This misunderstanding is the root cause of all emotional problems. Purification and rechanneling of emotions depends on some sort of discipline. Disciplines related to body and mind are generally known as moral and ethical laws, and the practical aspects of all systems of Indian philosophy are based on these disciplines. However, these ethical guidelines are not seen as commandments imposed by an outside source but rather as commitments accepted in order to create the external peace and harmony that is a prerequisite for internal equilibrium and tranquility.

Acknowledgment of suffering. In each system of Indian philosophy, the main cause of suffering is considered to be the misunderstood relationship between the Self and the external world. Most quests for Self-realization start with an analysis of pain and suffering. Sometimes Indian philosophy is criticized because of this apparently pessimistic approach, but Indian philosophy is pessimistic only in the sense that it begins with an inquiry into the cause of pain and suffering. It never considers life as a tragedy. In each system of Indian philosophy, there is a message of hope and an assurance that man's original state of peace and happiness can be regained. The goal of each system is to transcend suffering and to establish oneself in the state of perfection. To take the most famous example: Buddha begins his philosophy with the statement that there is suffering. Next he says that there is a cause of suffering, that there is a state in which suffering ceases, and finally that there is a systematic way to attain the state free from all pains and miseries. These four statements are known as the Four Noble Truths. In the same way, other schools proclaim that a state of pain and misery is not man's essential nature. The experience of pain is due to man's failure to realize his true nature or Self. Thus, in Indian philosophical systems, pessimism is only initial and not final. The initial focus on suffering in Indian philosophy makes one aware of one's false identifications with the external objects of the world and inspires one to attain the goal of life, which is freedom from pain and misery.

Belief in eternity. Each system of Indian philosophy proclaims that there is an eternal center of consciousness in man, and that the realization of this center of consciousness, or Self, is the goal of life. The Self is considered to be omniscient, omnipotent, and omnipresent. All imperfections are the projection of ignorance and exist merely on the surface of the personality. Deeper within lies the perfect state of bliss, beauty, and consciousness. In different schools, this center of consciousness is known variously as Vijñana, Sūnya, Ātman, Puruṣa. Man's physical existence depends on karma and saṃskāras, and his physical and mental conditions are therefore temporary and subject to death and decay. But the center of life itself is eternal and is not subject to experiencing the pairs of opposites (that is, pain and pleasure, heat and cold, death and birth, and so on).

Holistic approach. As previously mentioned, Indian philosophy is actually comprised of many disciplines. It is a systematic combination of metaphysics, ethics, aesthetics, epistemology, sociology, and psychology. All the sciences related to life are included in its scope. It studies man's entire being, including body, prāṇa (energy), mind, and the Self, as well as man's relationships with the external world. It integrates into a single whole all the discoveries that have been made in the physical, psychological, and spiritual realms.

An Overview of the Seven Systems

Dr. R. D. Ranade, a matchless teacher and well-known philosopher of his time, has listed the most basic philosophical questions that all seven systems of Indian philosophy attempt to answer. As Swami Rama* states them, these important questions are

1. Who am I? From where have I come and why have I come? What is my relationship with the manifold universe and other human beings?
2. What is the essential nature of my being, and what is the essential nature of the manifested world and its cause?
3. What is the relationship of the center of consciousness and the objects of the world?
4. What is the nature of the forms and names of the objects of the world and how do they serve the essential nature of man or universal consciousness?
5. What are the guidelines for action as long as we live in the physical body? Do we live after death?
6. What is truth, and how do we arrive at rational conclusions on questions of truth?

In the present survey, the seven systems of Indian philosophy are reviewed in the following order: Buddhism, Nyāya, Vaiśeṣika,

***Living with the Himalayan Masters: Spiritual Experiences of Swami Rama*, ed. Swami Ajaya (Honesdale, Pa.: Himalayan Institute, 1978), pp. 265-6.

Sāṃkhya, Yoga, Mīmāṃsā, and Vedānta. The order of presentation is not chronological. Instead, with the exception of Buddhism, the schools are presented in order of a gradual increase in sophistication and comprehensiveness. The first, Nyāya, is a system of logic that forms the basis for scientific inquiry and rules of debate used in all the other schools. Vaiśeṣika concerns itself chiefly with logic, physics, and chemistry. Sāṃkhya is a dualistic school that sees two primary constituents of the universe—nature and consciousness. Yoga is essentially a system for the practical application of Sāṃkhya theory. Mīmāṃsā emphasizes the use of ritual, worship, and ethical conduct to achieve salvation. Vedānta deals with the concept of consciousness as the reality, or substratum, underlying all forms of manifestation. In this order, there is a gradual progression from concern with the scientific methods for investigation of the material aspects of the universe to concern with the dualities of the universe in terms of matter and consciousness—and finally, in Vedānta, to a concern with the essential nature of consciousness itself.

Indian philosophy is divided into two major categories: the systems of philosophy that accept the authority of the Veda, and those systems that do not accept the authority of the Veda. These are known as the orthodox and the heterodox schools, respectively. The heterodox schools include three major systems of philosophy—Cārvāka, Jainism, and Buddhism—two of which are not included in this survey. These three systems of philosophy, although not relying on the authority of the Veda, nonetheless do believe in the authority of their own spiritual leaders and founders. The founder of the Cārvāka school, which is a materialistic philosophy, is traditionally considered to be Bṛhaspati. This school does not have any independent literature, but all systems refer to it as a part of their prior view. Jainism was founded by Mahāvīra, who was a contemporary of Buddha. Although Mahāvīra was the twenty-fourth in a line of teachers, he was the first to systematize the teachings of this school. Jainism is based on the concept of *ahiṃsā*, nonviolence, and all other doctrines are subsidiary to this one. This school has a rich literature in Sanskrit as well as in the Prākṛta language. Of the three heterodox schools, only Buddhism is discussed here. There follows a brief summary of each of the seven philosophical systems included in this volume.

Buddhism. The founder of this school, Gautama Siddhārtha, the Buddha, was born in Kapilavastu in the northeast part of India around the sixth century B.C. Gautama studied with many teachers, including a teacher named Arāḍa, who was a proponent of the Sāṃkhya system of philosophy. Eventually the Buddha abandoned his study with teachers and spent all his time in solitary contemplation. During this time he discovered the Four Noble Truths, which are the foundation of Buddhism. These are (1) Suffering exists; (2) There is a cause of suffering; (3) Suffering can be eradicated; (4) There is a means for the eradicatioṇ of suffering. Prior to Buddha's lifetime these four noble truths were already present in Sāṃkhya philosophy, and they were later explained fully in the Yoga Sūtras of Patañjali. Buddha placed great emphasis on the doctrine of *Anātma Vāda*—the theory of the nonexistence of self. This theory had been described previously in the Upaniṣads by the concept *neti, neti*—"not this, not this." Buddha refused to engage in metaphysical speculation, which he considered to be useless intellectual sidetracking. His approach was practical—to teach his students the eightfold path to liberation from suffering.

After Buddha's death, his followers modified his original teachings and formed two major schools: Therāvāda (also called Hīnāyana) and Mahāyāna. Therāvāda, "the doctrine of the elders," retained Pāli as the medium for scriptures. This school held more rigidly to the original teachings of Buddha and did not integrate tenets from other schools. Therāvādins believe in the statement, "Be thou a light unto thyself." Therāvāda accepts Buddha as an enlightened teacher and nirvāṇa, the extinguishing of suffering, as the goal of life. The second school, Mahāyāna, interacted with other schools of Indian philosophy and accepted the Sanskrit language for its philosophical discussion and writing. Thus it integrated teachings from other philosophical schools. One of its greatest scholars, Nāgārjuna, described the ultimate state of reality as Śūnya, the void. Another subschool, called Vijñānavāda, describes the Ultimate Reality as Ālayavijñāna, that is, the storehouse of consciousness or cosmic consciousness. The Mahāyāna school adopted many practices from other philosophies and cultures and thus continued to grow and change. Over time its adherents, who came from diverse cultural, religious, and social backgrounds, changed its original form tremendously.

Nyāya. The Nyāya school was founded by the sage Gotama. Sixteen major topics are discussed in this system, the most important of which is *pramāṇa*, the source of valid knowledge. Actually, Nyāya is a school of logic, and all the other systems of Indian philosophy use the Nyāya system of logic, in whole or in part, as a foundation for philosophical reasoning and debate. Navya-Nyāya, or Neologic, a further development of this school, occurred in the sixteenth century in Bengal and Mithilā.

Vaiśeṣika. Kaṇāda was the founder of the Vaiśeṣika school, which is allied with the Nyāya system. This school discusses seven major topics: substance, quality, action, generality, uniqueness, inherence, and nonexistence. This school is called Vaiśeṣika because it considers *viśeṣa*, uniqueness, as an aspect of reality and studies it as a separate category. Under the topic of substance, Vaiśeṣika deals with the physics and chemistry of the body and the universe. The theory of atomic structure was established by this school. Its practical teaching emphasizes dharma, the code of conduct that leads man to worldly welfare and to the highest goal of life.

Sāṃkhya. Kapila is traditionally cited as the founder of this school, although his Sāṃkhya Sūtras have been lost. The *Sāṃkhya-kārikā* of Īśvarakṛṣṇa, the oldest text on this philosophy, cites the names of Kapila, Āsuri, and Pancaśikha as previous teachers of this school. Sāṃkhya is a dualistic philosophy that believes in two coexistent and interdependent realities: conscious *Puruṣa* and unconscious *Prakṛti*. Sāṃkhya is considered to be the oldest of all philosophical systems. Theoretically, it stands like a rock behind the practical system of Yoga philosophy. Puruṣa is ever-pure, ever-wise, and ever-free, but it becomes the subject of pain and pleasure when it forgets its nature and identifies itself with Prakṛti. Prakṛti is the material cause of the universe and is composed of the three *guṇas* (qualities)—*sattva, rajas,* and *tamas*—that correspond to light, activity, and inertia, respectively. The state in which the gunas are in perfect equilibrium is called Prakṛti, but when their equilibrium is disturbed, the same Prakṛti is called *Vikṛti*, or the heterogeneous state. Disturbance of the equilibrium of Prakṛti, or predominance of one of the guṇas, produces the material world, including the mind, which is considered to be the finest form of material energy. The entire universe is derived from the three guṇas, and the process of its manifestation passes through twenty-four successive states in which all external and mental phenomena are manifested. Sāṃkhya philosophy explains the dynamics of the body and the nature of mind. It is also the mother of mathematics as well as *Āyurveda* medical science and is indeed the very basis of Eastern psychology.

Yoga. Yoga and Sāṃkhya are allied systems. Although Yoga philosophy was known even in Vedic and pre-Vedic ages, it was not formally systematized until it was codified by Patañjali in approximately 200 B.C. The Yoga Sutras of Patañjali contain 196 aphorisms which are divided into four sections. Yoga studies all aspects of human personality and teaches one how to control the modifications of the mind through the practice of meditation, detachment, and surrender to higher consciousness. It prescribes a holistic system of practice beginning with the *yamas* and *niyamas* (ethical and behavioral codes) and proceeding through the *āsanas* (physical postures), *prāṇāyāma* (breathing exercises), *pratyāhara* (control of the senses), *dhāraṇā* (concentration), and *dhyāna* (meditation), and culminating in *samādhi* (superconsciousness). In this system, the individual self is the seeker, and pure consciousness is the ultimate reality that he finds within. Practicality is the main characteristic of this system. The underlying theories are essentially the same as those found in Sāṃkhya.

Mīmāṃsā. Jaimini was the founder of this system, which accepts the Veda as the final authority on all questions. Mīmāṃsā provides a comprehensive method for interpreting and understanding the underlying meaning of the Veda. It lays great emphasis on rituals, worship, and ethical conduct, and provides a systematic lifestyle and direction. In this system, the whole of life is considered to be a grand ritual. Mīmāṃsā offerss guidelines for the practical application of Vedāntic theory. This school is foremost in the analysis of the science of sound and mantra.

Eventually this school was divided into two groups: the school founded by Prabhākara, and the school founded by Kumārila Bhatta. According to the Prabhākara school, there are five sources of valid knowledge (*pramāṇas*): perception, inference, comparison, testimony, and postulation. But Kumārila Bhaṭṭa admits an additional source of knowledge—noncognition.

Vedānta. Vedānta is the most comprehensive of these seven systems. It was taught and practiced by the sages of the Veda and Upaniṣads and was handed down through a long line of sages. But Bādarāyaṇa Vyāsa, who codified these teachings in the Brahma Sūtras, is considered its founder. Until the time of Śaṅkarā, Vedānta was mainly transmitted through the oral tradition, but then, sometime between the sixth and eighth centuries A.D., Śaṅkarā reorganized the system of this monistic school of thought. After Śaṅkarā, many other teachers wrote commentaries on the Brahma Sūtras, interpreting it in various ways and thus establishing numerous schools of philosophy within the single system of Vedānta. The major schools of Vedānta are Advaita (nondualistic), Dvaita (dualistic), Dvaitādvaita (both dualistic and nondualistic), Viśiṣtādvaita (qualified nondualism), and Viśuddhādvaita (pure nondualism).

Of the five schools of Vedānta, Śaṅkarā's Advaita and Rāmānujacārya's Viśiṣṭādvaita are the most important. Advaita is the most thorough. Śaṅkara's Advaita Vedānta is like an elephant's large footprint that covers all the little footprints of all the other subsystems within Vedānta. The main teachings of Vedānta are that Self-realization is the goal of life; that the essence of the Self is ever-existent consciousness and bliss; that the Self is free from all qualifications and limitations—it does not come from anywhere nor go anywhere, but it assumes many forms and names; that the individual Self is essentially Brahman, supreme consciousness; and that this Brahman is the absolute, transcendent, attributeless reality, but it eternally embodies within itself the capacity or power called *māyā*, which is the basis of mind and matter.

These seven systems of Indian philosophy represent the cream of the Vedic culture and wisdom. They are described in detail in the following chapters of this book.

chapter 2

Buddhism

Transcendence of Suffering

Buddha was born around 600 B.C. as Siddhārtha Gautama, a prince of the Sākya clan in the northeastern part of India in the foothills of the Himalayas. He entered into this world under a tree in the Lumbinī forest during his mother's journey to her family's home in present-day Nepal. In his early childhood, Gautama had a very peaceful and tranquil philosophical nature, but his ambitious father tried his best to teach him worldly behaviors so that he would mature into a strong ruler.

To curb any inclinations toward renunciation, the young Gautama was isolated within the confines of the luxurious family palace, which lacked any form of restraint, simplicity, and spirituality. He was purposefully surrounded by youth, gaiety, luxury, pleasure, and social refinement. Young Siddhārtha was amply provided with all worldly objects including the finest clothes, entertainment, and surroundings, but he did not have a suitable atmosphere for his sensitive nature. Despite the temptations surrounding him, he did not become distracted but was always striving to understand the reality of both the external and internal worlds. In an attempt to bind him to worldly concerns, his father arranged for his marriage to a beautiful princess, and in due course she gave birth to a baby boy.

But all the cultivated artificiality of palace life could not mold Siddhārtha's inner nature. Most of the time he was absorbed in his thoughts, although his father continued to prod him into the external arena. Finally four major incidents took place that jolted Siddhārtha and awoke the spiritual destiny of the young prince. These were the passing sights of an old person, a sick person, a dead body in a funeral procession, and a renunciate. The first three sights shocked and tormented him, but the fourth one gave him the light of hope. His mind was restless in search of knowledge, and the sight of the renunciate inspired him to quit his regal chambers and leave his wife and their infant son. Siddhārtha ventured out into the world to discover the source of the tranquility that was apparent in the face of the wandering ascetic. Thus he broke caste, shattered his career as a great world ruler, and renounced his position and inheritance. As a wandering mendicant, he sought to understand the cause of suffering to stop its continuous flow. He sought to attain a state of peace and tranquility.

Siddhārtha wandered from teacher to teacher and from monastery to monastery, but nothing he found satisfied his thirst for knowledge. Next he practiced extreme disciplinary austerities and came to the conclusion that neither extreme—complete indulgence nor severe asceticism—is beneficial for spiritual growth. Ultimately he realized the value of the middle path and experienced the Truth within, discovering the cause of suffering and the way to go beyond worldly pain and misery. Out of compassion for the helpless world, he began to impart his experiences to others, teaching the path that avoids the two extremes of worldly indulgence and severe penance. Buddha's philosophy is sometimes known as *madyama-mārga*, "the middle path," because it takes into account the capacity of each human being and the importance of external objects as well as the body and the mind in attaining the goal of life. As a teacher, his emphasis was on meditation and on following the middle path in daily life.

Buddha's message spread far and wide from India to Ceylon, Burma, and Siam in the south, and Tibet, China, Korea, and Japan in the northeast. Like all the great teachers of India, Buddha taught through conversation, and for a long time his teachings were handed down orally from generation to generation. His original teachings were collected chiefly in three major scriptures called *tripiṭakas*, which means "the three baskets of knowledge." These three scriptures are *Vinayapiṭaka*, which deals chiefly with the codes of conduct for the general population; *Sūtrapiṭaka*, which contains the ceremonies and dialogues related to ethics, morality, and spirituality; and *Abhidhammapiṭaka*, which contains an exposition of Buddha's philosophical theories. After Buddha's death, his followers divided into two major schools—Hīnayāna and Mahāyāna. Hīnayāna is the orthodox school of Buddhism, and its students believe in the original teachings as written in the Pāli language. Hīnayāna flourished mostly in the south, and Ceylon, Burma, and Thailand are its present strongholds. Mahāyāna is the protestant school of Buddhism, which flourished mostly in the North and East and whose followers are found in Tibet, China, and Japan. The enormous philosophical literature of this school is in the Sanskrit language, but scriptures were also translated into Chinese and Tibetan. Many valuable Sanskrit works of this school that were lost in India are currently being recovered from those translations and restored to Sanskrit. There are now more than twenty sects of Buddhism, and the teachings are so distorted, especially in the West, that it is sometimes difficult to discern the original teachings of Buddha.

The Ten Unanswered Questions

Buddha realized the Truth within, and he understood the importance of ethical and moral teachings. He was primarily an ethical teacher and a social reformer rather than a metaphysician. His message addressed the problem of how to lead one's life in order to cross the ocean of suffering and misery. Whenever questions pertaining to the soul and its condition after death were asked, Buddha always remained silent because he considered such speculations to be useless. For him, the most urgent imperative in life is to analyze the existence of suffering so as to put it to an end. He felt that a person who indulges in theoretical speculation while suffering with worldly problems is behaving nonsensically; such behavior can be likened to that of a person shot by an arrow who, instead of trying to pull it out immediately, wastes his time on idle speculation regarding the origin, the maker, and the shooter of the arrow.

According to Buddha, there are ten uncertain and ethically useless questions. They are as follows: (1) Is the world eternal? (2) Is the world noneternal? (3) Is the world finite? (4) Is the world infinite? (5) Are the soul and body one and the same? (6) Is the soul different from the body? (7) Does a realized person live after his death? (8) Does a realized person not live after his death? (9) Does a realized person live and not live after his death? (10) Does a realized person neither live nor not live after his death? These ten questions are known in Buddhist literature as the indeterminate questions (*avyaktāni*). After his death, Buddha's followers started interpreting the meaning of his silence on these questions. This speculation gave rise to the different philosophical schools of Buddhism. Buddha's main effort was to solve the fundamental problems of pain and misery in this very life, but his followers did not always adhere to his teachings. They tried to discuss these unanswerable questions, as all speculative philosophers do. But Buddha himself always tried to make people aware of the sorrow inherent in the human condition so that they might thereby understand its origin, its cessation, and the path leading to its cessation.

The Four Noble Truths

The essence of the Buddha's teaching is condensed within the Four Noble Truths (see chart). These truths are that suffering exists; that there is a cause of suffering; that suffering can be stopped; and that there is a method for stopping it.

Suffering Exists

Buddha realized the first Noble Truth, that life is full of suffering, in the beginning of his search for knowledge, when he witnessed the sights that inspired him to embark on his remarkable quest. Buddha dove deeper, however, and came to understand that suffering results not only from old age, disease, and death, but that life itself is suffering. Birth, wishes, despair, frustrations, dejection, emotions, and failures in desired attempts are all sources of suffering. In short, all that is born of attachment is misery; desire for transitory, worldly objects leads to a long chain of suffering. For instance, a man suffers to obtain wealth, and when he obtains it he still suffers, for he must take pains to protect it from thieves or from the ruling authorities. Its transitory nature leads to unending pain and misery. All the sensuous enjoyments that human beings long for and strive to obtain are absolutely ephemeral, and they end in exhaustion and disappointment. Instead of being satisfied after obtaining a worldly object, one finds oneself in the grip of a never-ending chain of dissatisfaction and increasing desire that is the root cause of manifold pain and misery.

There Is a Cause of Suffering

Through keen observance and personal experience, Buddha eventually found the cause of suffering, which he described as a chain with no end and no beginning. Every cause has an effect, which becomes another cause, and thus there is an unbroken flow of effects and causes. This theory of causation is known as *pratītya-samutpāda*. According to this theory, nothing is unconditional; the existence of everything depends upon certain conditions. Therefore,

Buddha's Four Noble Truths

1) Suffering exists

2) There is a cause of suffering

The twelve-linked chain of causation

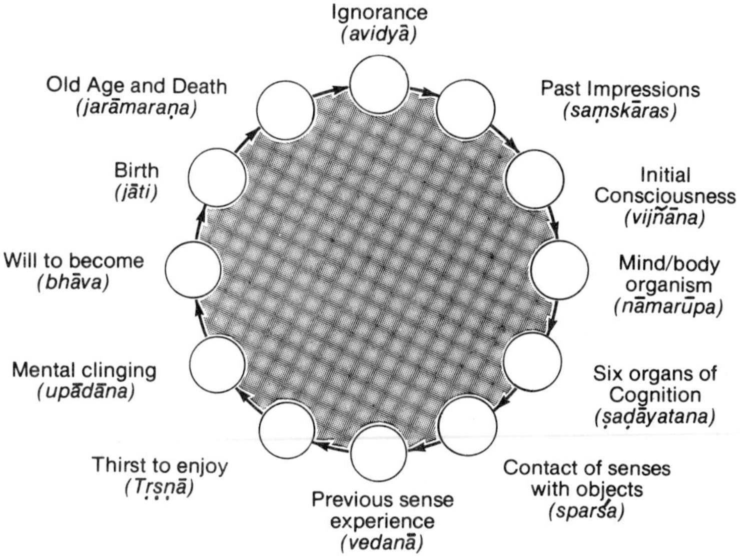

3) There is cessation of suffering

4) There is a means to cease suffering

The Eightfold Path

- Right views (samyagdṛṣṭi)
- Right resolve (samyaksaṃkalpa)
- Right speech (samyagvāk)
- Right conduct (samyakkarmānta)
- Right livelihood (samyagājiva)
- Right effort (samyagvyāyāma)
- Right mindfulness (samyaksmṛti)
- Right meditation (samyaksamādhi)

the existence of suffering and misery also depends upon something. This series of the cause and effect of suffering is described as the twelve-linked chain of causation, called *dvādaśanidāna.* The links in the chain are ignorance (*avidyā*); past impressions (*saṃskāras*); initial consciousness (*vijñāna*); the body / mind organism (*nāmarūpa*); the five cognitive senses and the mind (*ṣaḍāyatana*); contact of the senses with objects (*sparśa*); previous sense experience (*vedanā*); thirst to enjoy (*tṛṣṇā*); mental clinging (*upādāna*); will to become (*bhāva*); birth (*jāti*); old age and death (*jarāmaraṇa*).

To explain the causal relationship among the links in this chain, one can go backwards starting from the point of birth because suffering in life starts for everyone at birth. If one were not born, one would not be subject to the miserable conditions of life. But birth also has its conditions. If there were no will to be born, then there would be no birth. What is the cause of this predisposition to be born? Mental clinging to the objects of the world is the main cause of the desire to be born. Why do people cling to the objects of the world? This is due to the thirst or craving to enjoy worldly objects, namely, sights, sounds, tastes, smells, and touch. But from where does this desire to enjoy worldly objects originate? One cannot have any desire to enjoy worldly objects if one has not already tasted or experienced them. Some previous experience reminds one of a momentary sensuous pleasure, and thus these experiences inspire further desire to achieve worldly objects. What is the cause of that previous sense experience? Sense experience cannot arise if there is no contact of the different senses with their respective objects, so the contact of the senses with their objects is the cause of sensuous experience. But the senses and the mind also depend on the body, so the combined state of body and mind constitutes the perceptible being of man. When a worldly object is experienced by the mind through the senses, then it is also influenced by that experience.

But what is the cause of the mind and body organism? What

is that fine agency that is responsible for the development of the embryo in the mother's womb? That is consciousness. Without the presence of consciousness in the cells, the multiplication of cells is not possible, and if there is no multiplication of cells, there will be no growth in the embryo. So, without this consciousness, the mind cannot join the body. But why does this consciousness descend into the embryo in the mother's womb? Why does it inspire the whole cycle of life, which is full of pain and misery? Consciousness descends and identifies itself with the embryonic body because it is under the influence of past impressions gathered in past lives. The last state of the past life initiates present existence and contains the impressions or effects of all past karmas or actions. The impressions of past karmas are responsible for driving consciousness to move the wheel of life. But what is the cause for these past impressions? Why are they stored, and how are they printed on the screen of consciousness? Ignorance is the main cause of imprinting the impressions on the screen of consciousness. Ignorance means misunderstanding the nature of external objects. According to Buddha, when a person forgets the law of change and the constant flow of consciousness (vijñāna), he grasps things as though they were permanent, and he becomes mentally attached to those external objects. This attachment, born of ignorance, causes all the pain and misery that one experiences, which are known as *jarā-maraṇa* (old age and death).

Thus this twelve-fold cycle of cause and effect is completed and goes on until one learns how to break it. The process of disconnecting these links is explained in detail in Buddha's exposition of the Four Noble Truths. The chain of twelve links encompasses the past, present, and future in the following way: The past consists of ignorance and impressions; the present is composed of consciousness, the mind/body organism, the mind and the five cognitive senses, sense contact, sense experience, thirst, clinging, and will to become; the future is made up of rebirth and old age/death.

There Is Cessation of Suffering

Buddha's second Noble Truth clarifies that life is not accidental but conditional, and his third Truth affirms that suffering in life can be voluntarily brought under one's control. All suffering is because of the twelve links of the causal chain, and their effective power results from one's own involvement in them. If one keeps oneself away from the conditions that invite suffering, then there will not be suffering anymore. The state that is free from conditions is called *nirvāṇa*. In the very beginning of the twelve-linked cycle, there is desire and attachment, which are ultimately derived from ignorance. If one can parch the seed of desire, the flow of suffering stops then and there.

The method of parching the seed of desire is the subject matter of Buddha's fourth Noble Truth. Perfect control of the passions and constant contemplation of the Truth leads a person gradually to the state of perfection and wisdom where the sway of worldly attachment ceases. That is the state of *Buddhatva* (Buddhahood) or nirvāṇa, and one who has broken all the bondages is called a liberated one. The state free from suffering is attainable in this very lifetime if certain conditions are fulfilled, and one who attains this state here and now is called *arhat*, a venerable person.

The state of nirvāṇa should not be confused with a state of nonaction, for after attaining nirvāṇa an enlightened person lives in the world and discharges his duties. He does this, however, without any intention of attaining fruits from his actions. He lives in the world and uses external objects as the instruments for the continuation of his journey of life. For the attainment of perfect wisdom, one has to withdraw his mind and senses from external objects and establish himself within. But once wisdom is permanently established within, once one is no longer influenced by the charms and temptations of the world, then he is free from the rope of karma (actions). Buddha himself demonstrated this fact as he traveled, preached, and lit the candle of universal brotherhood during the forty-five years that he lived after enlightenment.

Buddha emphasized meditation in action, and he differentiated between two kinds of actions. One is performed under the influence of passion and attachment (such as hatred, infatuation and so on), and the other is done for the sake of duty itself or in the service of humanity. The first is a fertile seed of the cycle of death and birth, while the second is like a roasted seed that no longer has the power to germinate. An enlightened heart living in the world begins to beat with compassion and sympathy for the countless beings who are still living in the darkness of ignorance and writhing in the turmoil of the pain and misery of the world. An enlightened person's actions are performed, directed, and guided by love and righteousness, which is the intrinsic nature of perfect wisdom, while an ordinary person's actions are driven by ignorance and are aimed at false gratification.

The attainment of nirvāṇa does not mean the extinction of all existence (otherwise, Buddha could not be said to have been liberated before his death). Also, it does not necessarily mean that after death the liberated being does not continue in any form. Etymologically, the word *nirvāṇa* means "blown out," and metaphorically it means the state in which the cause of sufferings is completely extinguished, and man is established in his essential nature of peace. Although Buddha did not state whether a person who attains nirvāṇa ceases to exist altogether or not, his silence on the question does not imply the complete cessation of existence after the attainment of nirvāṇa or after death. His silence simply means that liberation cannot be described in terms of ordinary experience.

There Is a Means to Cease Suffering

Buddha gave a complete and systematic guide for attaining the state of nirvāṇa, and his way of *sādhanā* (path to liberation) consists of eight different stages. That Noble Eightfold Path leading to liberation or final cessation of suffering is called *aṣṭāṅgamārga.*

Its eight stages are: right views (*samyagdṛṣṭi*), right resolve (*samyak-saṃkalpa*), right speech (*samyagvāk*), right conduct (*samyak-karmānta*), right livelihood (*samyagājīva*), right effort (*samyagvyā-yāma*), right mindfulness (*samyaksmṛti*), and right meditation (*samyaksamādhi*).

Right views. Among the twelve links in the chain of causation that results in suffering, *avidyā* (ignorance) is the beginning point in the flow of consequences. In daily life, ignorance can be termed as misunderstanding or wrong views (*mithyādṛṣṭi*) regarding one's relationship with the objects of the world. False identification with worldly things or persons and preoccupation with expectations of them are the main cause of all misery and pain. Therefore Buddha first of all prescribes the way to have right views of external objects and of their relationship with the individual. Here especially the term *right view* is used in the sense of correct knowledge about the Four Noble Truths. Knowledge here does not imply any theoretical speculation regarding the nature of the Self, but rather refers to an awareness of the imperfection and impermanence of the world and of a person's relationship with it.

Right resolve. Mere knowledge or understanding is not sufficient to free one from the conflagration of suffering; knowledge needs to be put into practice. A theoretical understanding that is not assimilated by the personality for practical application is useless. Theoretical truth should be firmly established in the mind through constant awareness. Right resolve means firm determination to reform one's life in the light of truth, so in practicing this second rung of the eightfold path to liberation a student has to renounce all attachments to the world, give up ill feelings toward others, and desist from doing harm to anyone. This mental reformation calms down the mind's fluctuations and makes the mind turn inward.

Right speech. Right resolve or firm determination that remains as a mere pious wish is not sufficient for the attainment of the goal. It must also be coordinated with speech, which of all human behaviors is the highest vehicle of communication. Right resolve coordinated with right speech prevents a person from engaging in lies, slander, unkind words, and frivolous talk. Through speech, a person can make someone happy or sad, a person can help someone or cheat him. Thus, right resolve followed by right speech is a systematic way to practice nonviolence and truthfulness.

Right conduct. Right resolve coupled with right speech naturally leads one to the next stage; the truth resolved in the mind and spoken by the tongue should be issued forth into action.* Right conduct includes five vows (*Pañcaśīla*): nonviolence, truthfulness, nonstealing, nonsensuality (celibacy), and nonpossessiveness (or according to some scriptures, nonintoxication). These five vows are to be practiced with right resolve, right speech, and right action. These three limbs of the eightfold path to liberation are the foundation of the moral and ethical teaching of Buddha. Practicing spirituality while living in the world is difficult without incorporating the moral and ethical laws concerning daily life. By removing external barriers, these moral and ethical guidelines promote increased harmony in one's inner world.

Right livelihood. Anyone who has a body cannot get rid of his bodily needs. If these are not provided for properly, they create a great barrier in one's external and internal growth. One must therefore earn a living to meet those needs, but essential livelihood earned by improper means makes a person the victim of guilt feelings, which deteriorate inner strength and invite suicidal tendencies. Therefore Buddha emphasizes right (honest) livelihood that does not harm or interfere with others' lives and does not disturb social harmony.

Right effort. While a person is trying to live a reformed life

*The holistic approach of rāja yoga, which emphasizes perfect coordination of thought, speech, and action, is commonly accepted by Buddhism as having great importance.

through right views, right resolve, right speech, right conduct, and right livelihood, he still has to deal with his deeply rooted saṃskāras that produce negative thoughts. A person must be very careful to maintain equilibrium while practicing the first five steps of the eightfold path to liberation. Constant effort to uproot old, negative thoughts and to prevent new ones from forming is very important in the path of spirituality. The mind cannot be kept empty, but it should not be filled with garbage. First one has to clean it out and then immediately fill it with positive thoughts. This process is called right effort, or constant endeavor to maintain moral as well as spiritual progress by banishing negative thoughts and assimilating positive ones.

Right mindfulness. It becomes apparent from reviewing the first six steps that one must constantly remember each of these with full-mindedness. The mind becomes scattered by doubt, confusion, and passion, but if it is free from these problems and is always led by right determination, then it has no chance to wander here and there. It remains focused single-mindedly on one thought pattern. According to Buddha, right mindfulness means a constant remembrance of the perishable nature of things. This is essential for keeping one's mind away from attachments to worldly things and their charms. With right mindfulness, the mind is not attracted by these things and thus remains in a tranquil and harmonious state. These seven steps prepare a concrete foundation for concentration, which requires a strong and one-pointed mind. An untrained mind that does not know how to observe an object with full endeavor cannot concentrate on the object of concentration and cannot go beyond its habituated limits. All practical disciplines put an emphasis on mindfulness for higher attainment in worldly as well as eternal life, and this mindfulness should be practiced in the light of right knowledge.

Right meditation. One who lives his life in the light of the first seven steps and thereby gradually frees himself from all passions and misunderstandings gains emotional maturity. He has prepared himself step-by-step for the inward journey by trying to understand and bring into operation in his own life the moral and ethical laws that teach one how to live in the world and yet remain above it. These seven steps protect a student from the charms and temptations of the world and give him inner strength to explore the finer avenues of life. These inner explorations of consciousness constitute the final step of the Eightfold Path.

According to Buddha, there are four stages of meditation. In the first stage, the student concentrates his pure and unruffled mind on reasoning and investigation regarding truth. Here the student enjoys the pure thinking born of detachment. In the second stage, all doubts and confusions are completely dispelled, and the student's mind is perfectly established in the Four Noble Truths. In this stage joy, peace, and internal tranquility born of meditation are considered to be objects of meditation. This is a state of duality in which the student is the enjoyer and peace is the object of his enjoyment. In the third stage, by intense and deep meditation, the student transcends even the joy of concentration and tranquility, and there is an indifference even to such joy. However, the student does not yet lose the feeling of his physical existence. Ultimately, though, there does come a state of mind in which the feeling of bodily existence and the joy of equanimity also cease. This is the fourth state of meditation, in which there is perfect equanimity and indifference. This is called nirvāṇa—the state of perfect wisdom.

Thus the first seven steps of the Eightfold Path to liberation are prerequisites for meditation, which finally leads to nirvāṇa. According to Buddha, perfect knowledge and wisdom are impossible without morality, for virtue and knowledge purify each other, and the two are inseparable from each other. The beginning seven steps furnish a continuous discipline for resolving the conflicts within and without by reforming one's old saṃskāras and charging the battery of the human mind with right and positive thoughts.

Such a purified mind leads the student to the state of enlightenment. Buddhism states that there are four progressive levels of enlightened beings. At the lowest level is the *śrotāpanna*—one who has entered the stream of the Eightfold Path to liberation. At the second level is the *sakṛdāgāmin*—one who will return only once more to this world. The third level is that of an *anāgāmin*—one who will not return to this world. And the fourth is that of an *arhat*—one who is liberated in this very life.

Other Major Theories of Buddha

Besides the Four Noble Truths, there are some other philosophical and ethical points that were explicitly stated by Buddha himself. These are the theory of dependent origination, the theory of universal change, the theory of the nonexistence of the soul, and the theory of karma. A discussion of each of these follows.

The Theory of Dependent Origination

According to the theory of dependent origination (*pratītyasamutpāda*), all of existence is conditional; every event is dependent on a cause. There is a continuous flow of cause and effect, in which nothing happens accidentally or by chance. This theory therefore dismisses the view of accidental origination, while implying the purposeful origin and existence of the universe and of life. Nothing exists without a cause, nor does anything perish without leaving some effect.

This theory is the foundation for many other Buddhist theories, such as the theory of universal change, the theory of the nonexistence of the soul, and the theory of karma. It is this theory on which Buddha based his Four Noble Truths. With this theory, Buddha traced back the cause of suffering and found the way to attain that state which is beyond miseries and pains, that transcendent and unconditional state which is the goal of life. This theory is so important in Buddhist philosophy and practice that

Buddha regarded it as indispensable to understanding his teachings. He called it *dharma*, which means "eternal law." According to him, one who sees the truth of dharma sees the truth of dependent origination, and one who sees dependent origination sees dharma, because both are one and the same. One who fails to grasp this principle of conditional origination and who is not capable of building his philosophy of life based on it has no option but to flow helplessly with the painful current of life. But one who understands and practices this principle goes back to the original cause of suffering and gets rid of it.

The Theory of Universal Change

The theory of dependent origination also yields the theory of universal change, which states that whatever exists is derived from some condition and is therefore transitory. Everything originates from a definite condition, and it disappears when the condition ceases to exist. Whatever has a beginning also has an end. All things are, therefore, absolutely impermanent. In Buddha's own words, "That which seems to be durable will perish; that which is high will be laid low; where there is meeting, separation will be there; where there is birth, death will be there." Another name of the theory of universal change is the theory of impermanence or transitoriness. The original aim of this theory was to warn against having attachments to and expectations of transitory things and to brighten the light of renunciation for those who were striving for permanent peace and happiness.

Later, this theory was developed into the doctrine of momentariness (*kṣaṇikavāda*), according to which a thing is not only transitory or impermanent, but it exists for a moment that is so minute it cannot be divided again. The theory of momentariness was strongly upheld by later Buddhist philosophers and has been supported with elaborate arguments. For example, an opponent might argue that if a thing exists for a moment only, then how can it be perceived for a long time, as is commonly the case in daily life? The Buddhist reply would be that a thing exists for a single moment only, but it produces a thing like itself before it perishes. This process of change and conversion is going on at every moment, but the span of time is so short and the process of change is so fast that our senses are not able to perceive the time span between the momentary cause and effect. A thing produces a similar thing in one single causal moment; thus the flow of similar cause and effect is maintained. For example, a thing in the second moment is not the same as it was in the first moment, but because of the similarity of cause and effect and its unbroken flow, it seems to be one and the same. This constant flow of momentary cause and effect can be depicted in the following way: A, A^1, A^2, A^3, A^4, A^5. . . . The metaphors of a stream or a flame are often used to describe this process of constant change.

The Theory of the Nonexistence of the Soul

Neither living nor nonliving beings are exempt from the laws of conditional origination and universal change. Generally, people believe that there is some permanent changeless substance that persists through all changes and that exists before birth and after death. Such a changeless but immaterial substance is called the soul. Based on his doctrine of universal change, Buddha does not accept the existence of the soul. But he does not deny the continuity of the stream of successive states that composes physical existence for a certain period of time, that is, birth, childhood, youth, maturity, and old age. According to Buddha, however, this consciousness is not permanent and changeless; it is, rather, an ever-changing flow, and it has to follow the rules of conditional origination and universal change. Life is a flow of consciousness that is prolonged or lit by saṃskāras, just as the flame of a lamp keeps glimmering because of the presence of oil. When the oil of saṃskāras is depleted, then the lamp of life is extinguished. Buddhism holds that it is ignorance to be attached to the concept of the soul and to consider the soul to be permanent. The desire to make the soul happy by attaining salvation could be likened to falling in love with a beautiful woman who does not actually exist, or to building a staircase in space to reach a palace that has never been seen.

Buddhism views a human being as a combination of five kinds of changing states, called the *pañcaskandhas*. These five *skandhas*, or skeins, are form (*rūpa*)—the material body; feeling (*vedanā*)—the experiences of pain, pleasure, and indifference; perception (*sanjñā*)—the comprehension and naming of things; past impressions (*saṃskāras*)—latent memories and tendencies; and consciousness (*vijñāna*). The existence of man depends on the combination of these five different constituents, and this existence ceases when the combination dissolves or breaks down.

Buddha's Outlook

The aim of Buddha's teaching is to make one aware of his self-created suffering. Buddha does not talk about the soul or God; he is very practical and discusses only suffering and the way to overcome it. When he talks about the impermanent and ever-changing nature of consciousness, he takes pains to avoid entangling himself in a metaphysical discussion. He simply warns human beings not to be attached to the charms and temptations of the external world and not to have any expectations of anything or anyone either here or hereafter. He emphasizes being here and now and living this present life happily instead of brooding on the past or worrying about the future. His theory of the nonexistence of the soul is not intended to make one stop exploring the finer avenues of life and consciousness, but to provide a firm ground for detachment and renunciation. These theories are efficient inner tools for clearing out the clouds of misunderstanding and false expectations that cause pain and misery in daily life. Buddha gives great importance to the discussion and practice of dharma (*pratīt-yasamutpāda*—the conditional origination of things) and the Four Noble Truths. When implemented in one's life, these provide a practical approach for solving the problems of all human beings. His formula of the Eightfold Path to liberation serves individuals as well as the whole of humanity in the various aspects of life: socially, morally, ethically, physically, mentally, and spiritually.

The Four Main Schools of Buddhist Philosophy

It has been stated that Buddha always avoided discussing metaphysical topics such as God, the soul, the condition of man after death, and the origin or manifestation of the universe. He clearly termed these problems as *avyaktāni* (indescribable) and emphasized only the Four Noble Truths. His teachings contained the seeds of empiricism, phenomenalism, positivism, and nihilism. But indirect references to metaphysics and especially his silence on the questions of unknown phenomena led his faithful followers to formulate a variety of explanations from his implicit sayings after his passing away.

Buddha's silence on the ten metaphysical questions was interpreted in various ways. According to one school of Buddhism, his silence should be taken to mean that the senses are not capable of understanding the ultimate state of reality. Others say that Buddha's silence means that this phenomenal world as well as the mental world are subject to dependent origination and the law of universal change and that, therefore, ultimately nothing is real. Another group interprets his silence neither as a denial of reality nor as the acceptance of it, but rather as an implication that transcendental experience and reality cannot be described. To justify their various interpretations, the upholders of these differing viewpoints have applied well-polished techniques of reasoning that have given birth to many philosophically rich schools. Although there are about thirty schools of later Buddhism, only four among them are prominent. They are Śūnyavāda, or Mādhyamika; Vijñānavāda, or

Yogācāra; Sautrāntika; and Vaibhāṣika.

The fourfold classification of Buddhist philosophy, that is the four schools, is based on two major philosophical problems. The first is the metaphysical question: Is there any reality, mental or nonmental? One school replies that reality is neither mental nor nonmental, that all is *Śūnya*, void. This school is therefore known as Śūnyavāda. According to another school, reality is only mental; this school is known as subjective idealism (Vijñānavāda). Another group believes that reality is both mental and nonmental. This third school is further divided into two groups, based on the epistemological question, How is this external world known? One group, known as Sautrāntika, asserts that external objects are not perceived, but are known by inference. The other group, called Vaibhāṣika, believes that the external world is perceived directly. These four schools of Buddhism are the most important ones, and the viewpoints of each are strongly supported by logic and reasoning.

Śūnyavāda

The founder of the Śūnyavāda school is said to be Nāgārjuna, a south Indian Brahmin who lived during the first century A.D. Aśvaghoṣa, who was the contemporary of King Kaniṣka (fl. c. 70 A.D.) is another pioneer of this school. According to the Śūnyavāda school, all that is perceived within or without is unreal, like the objects of a dream. There is nothing mental or nonmental that is real; the entire universe is unreal. Sometimes the word *Śūnya* is misunderstood to mean void, empty, or absent of reality, but this nihilistic interpretation is not its real meaning, for Śūnyavāda denies only the phenomenal world and not all of reality. The state beyond this phenomenal world, the state from which the mental and the nonmental illusory world arises, is termed Śūnya. The Śūnyavāvadin viewpoint is not really nihilistic because it does not deny all of reality; it denies only the existence of the apparent phenomenal world. Behind this phenomenal world, there is believed to be a reality that cannot be described by any mental or nonmental analysis or examples.

The ultimate state or reality is called Śūnya by this particular school because it is devoid of phenomenal characteristics. This is a negative method of describing the nature of ultimate Reality; thus *Śūnya* means the indescribable nature of reality. In this sense, reality is neither real nor unreal; nor is it both real and unreal; nor is it accompanied by both the real and the unreal. That which is real must be independent for its existence and origination; but everything that is known depends on some condition, and therefore all this cannot be real. But again, it cannot be said to be unreal, because it exists, and something that is unreal cannot come into existence. It also cannot be said that it is both real and unreal or that it is neither real nor unreal because then it would be unintelligible and self-contradictory. The word *Śūnyatā* is used to indicate this indescribable nature of things.

Actually, Śūnya has two meanings, related to two kinds of truth, namely empirical or phenomenal (*saṃvṛti satya* or *vyavahārika satya*) and transcendental or absolute (*paramārtha satya*). Buddha's teaching regarding dependent origination, universal change, and so on, is applied only to the phenomenal world commonly experienced in daily life. Śūnyatā refers to the character of ordinary experiences and external objects that follow the law of dependent origination (*pratītyasamutpāda*). Dharma (the character of things) is always dependent on something else for its existence and origin, and this dependency is Śūnya. Thus Śūnya means the conditional character of things and their changeability, indeterminability, indescribability and transitoriness. It is the intrinsic character (*svabhāva*) of things to be dependent on something else for their origin, and this intrinsic character of the thing is called *Śūnyatā*.

The second meaning of Śūnya is transcendental. When

nirvāṇa is attained and the sequential conditions of phenomenal objects and their experiences are controlled, then there is a higher experience free from change, conditionality, and all other phenomenal character. That is called Absolute Truth (*paramārtha satya*), and Śūnyatā is another name for this Absolute Truth. This Śūnyatā is beyond the grasp of the senses and mind, and therefore even Buddha himself was helpless to describe this state. Ordinarily Śūnya may be considered to be a void, emptiness, or nothingness. But those who have attained nirvāṇa and established themselves in perfect wisdom describe this void or nothingness as the potential for everything—whatever exists or does not exist. Thus, the theory of Śūnyavāda is completely different than the theory of nihilism. Many scholars have mistakenly translated the term Śūnyavāda to be synonymous with nihilism. This has led to fundamental misunderstandings of this school of Buddhism.

According to Nāgārjuna, those who do not know the distinction between these two sets of truth (empirical and absolute) cannot understand the profound mystery of Buddha's teachings. For those who stop the search for truth at the stage of dependent origination, Śūnya means "the fact of dependent origination." But those who continue their inward journey realize the higher levels of truth, and for them the meaning of Śūnya changes. Then, there is no longer any void or nothingness in the state of Śūnya , but there is an absolute that contains the potential of all. The truth of the lower order is only a stepping-stone to attaining the higher one. This higher experience cannot be described but can only be suggested negatively.

The twofold concept of truth and the denial of the phenomenal world described by Śūnyavādins is very close to the description in the Upaniṣads, but a comparative study of the theories held by Nāgārjuna and Śaṅkarā on the theory of Śūnyavāda and Brahmavāda requires extensive treatment and is not within the scope of this survey.

Vijñānavāda—Subjective Idealism

Asaṅga, Vasubandhu, Diṅnaga, and Dharmakīrti are the great pioneers of the Vijñānavāda school of subjective idealism. This school is also known as Yogācāra because it incorporates the practice of yoga, through which one can realize the vast unconscious mind (*ālaya-vijñāna*) and dispel belief in the existence of the external world. Another reason this school is called Yogācāra is that it combines both yogic disciplines and good conduct (*ācāra*). According to this school, external objects are unreal, but the mind in itself cannot be accepted as unreal. If the mind were unreal, then all reasoning and arguments would be false, and one could not himself be sure whether his own arguments were correct or incorrect. But the mind also follows the rule of dependent origination and changeability. The mind is a stream of many different ideas, and things that appear to be outside the mind—including the body and other worldly objects—are merely ideas of the mind. Just as the things of dreams are perceived, though they do not actually exist, so external objects that appear to exist during the waking state are actually only ideas in the mind. Whenever a thing is known, it is because of a sense experience or a feeling. This feeling of mind is called consciousness. The existence of any external object cannot be proved because it cannot be known separately from the feeling of the object. The color blue and the consciousness (feeling) of the color blue are identical because they are never perceived to exist separately.

Refuting the existence of external objects, the scholars of this school argue that if an external object exists, then it must be either partless (atomic) or composite (composed of many parts). If an external object is atomic, then it cannot be perceived because atoms are too small to be perceived. Likewise, if it is composite, then it cannot be perceived because it is impossible to perceive all of its parts simultaneously. Thus the existence of external objects cannot be explained through perception. But if one holds that external objects are nothing but consciousness, then the question of perceiving the parts or the whole of an object does not arise. Thus, this school contends that there is only one single reality, which is consciousness or mental feeling, and all the objects that seem to be material or external to consciousness are really only different states of consciousness. An external object is not different from the internal perceiver, the mind.

The question arises that if all objects exist within the mind and if there are different states of consciousness within the mind, then why can the mind not create anything at any time according to its will? Why do the objects not change, appear, or disappear at the will of the perceiver (mind)? The scholars of this school reply that the ideas of objects are latent in the mind. The mind is the continuous flow of the stream of momentarily conscious states, and within that stream, past saṃskāras (the impressions of all experiences) are buried. These saṃskāras are the conditions that cause a particular idea to become conscious and vivid at a particular moment. When a latent impression becomes mature, it rises to the surface of consciousness and develops into immediate consciousness or perception. In this way an object comes to be perceived at a particular specific time, not all the time and not at the will of the mind.

The potential mind, in which all impressions are stored, is called *ālaya-vijñāna*, and according to other philosophies this is the same as the soul or the Self. This is not an unchanging and permanent substance, as is believed by many other systems of philosophy, but is rather the stream of continuously changing states. This mind, *ālaya-vijñāna*, is the only reality; it makes heaven out of hell and hell out of heaven. Through properly training and culturing the mind, one can gradually stop undesirable mental states from arising.

Sautrāntika—Representationalism

The Sautrāntika school of Buddhism is so called because it

bases its validity on the authority of the *Sūtrapiṭaka*, the original Pali text. According to this school, both mental and external objects are real. Thus it differs sharply from the Vijñānavāda school just discussed, which holds that external objects are simply past impressions coming to the surface of the mind from its internal storehouse (*ālaya-vijñāna*) and that these impressions are mistakenly experienced as external objects. But the Sautrāntikas ask: From where did these impressions come and how were they stored in the mind? Is it possible to have an impression without an external object related to it? Is it possible to make the second step without taking the first one? Thus, according to the Sautrāntika school, the existence of external objects cannot be denied.

Whenever an object is perceived, it is felt to be external, and its consciousness or feeling is felt to be internal (mental). So when they are perceived, objects are completely different from their consciousness in the mind. If the external objects and one's consciousness of them were identical, then one would feel those objects to be an inseparable part of his own being, because in that case anything and everything would be simply one continuous flow of feelings. For example, if a plant were perceived as being identical with one's consciousness, one would say, "I am the plant" instead of saying, "There is a plant." But this never happens; no sane person experiences a plant as being identical with his own being. Hence, the existence of external objects outside of consciousness has to be accepted. Thus the view of Vijñānavāda is refuted.

The perception of an object according to this school depends on four factors: object, mind, sense, and contributing conditions. All these combined together bring about the perception of the object, but the existence of the object is not perceived or known directly. External objects give particular forms to the different states of consciousness, and the existence of objects outside the mind is inferred based on these pictures of the objects in the mind. Thus, the ideas of objects are not the objects themselves, but only mental pictures of the external objects. External objects can therefore be inferred from mental pictures or ideas, but they cannot be perceived directly. What the mind perceives is a representation or copy of the object. From this sensory replication the mind infers the object to be the primary cause without which the copy would not arise. Therefore, this theory is sometimes called the theory of the inferability of external objects (*bāhyānumeyavāda*).

Vaibhāṣika—Direct Realism

The school of Vaibhāṣika (direct realism) bases itself on the authority of the Vibhāṣā's (commentary) on the *Abhidharma jñāna-prasthāna*. It is therefore called *Vaibhāṣika*—"that which is related to Vibhāṣā." This school developed from criticism of the Sautrāntika school, which believes that both mental and nonmental things are real. Vaibhāṣikas agree with the Sautrāntika theory of the reality of both the mind and external objects, but they do not agree with the theory of the inferability of external objects. According to the followers of this school, external objects are known directly by perception; they are not inferred. If external objects were never perceived, they ask, then how would it be possible to infer them simply from their mental forms? Thus Vaibhāṣikas hold to the theory of direct realism (*bāhyapratyakṣavāda*)—that external objects are directly known.

Summary and Conclusion

Buddha's original emphasis was to overcome suffering. He did not involve himself in mere philosophical or metaphysical discussions but rather emphasized only practical discussions. He taught that practicing the Four Noble Truths and adopting the Middle Path would lead one to a state free from suffering. Buddha's central teaching is that one should guide his life by the Four Noble Truths in order to eliminate self-created pain and misery. Buddha gave more importance to the laws of karma and dharma than he did to God. Every individual on this platform of existence obtains mind, body, and other instruments according to his past karmas. In the beginning, Buddhism was a philosophy of self-analysis, self-control, and self-enlightenment. As Buddha says, "Be a light unto thyself. . . . Work out your salvation with diligence."

In the course of time, Buddhism spread throughout India and abroad. It embraced within its folds not only the few prepared and deserving persons who were fit to follow this path, but the multitudes as well. There were already many religious beliefs and philosophical theories and practices in existence before Buddha's theory emerged, and his teachings attracted a multitude of half-convinced nominal converts. The people who accepted Buddhism came from many different religious, cultural, and national backgrounds and brought many beliefs, habits, and traditions with them that soon became a part of Buddhism. It was not unusual for the common crowd either to misunderstand the path or to lack the necessary moral strength to follow it.

Buddhism gradually came to be divided into two major groups. The first group tried to maintain the original teachings of Buddha. This group is called *Hīnayāna*, meaning "small vehicle." But the other group was like an open platform made available for everybody at the cost of the purity of the Buddha's original ideals. This second group made itself flexible in order to adjust to all varieties of people, whatever their tastes and cultures, and so people flocked to it. Thus it was termed *Mahāyāna*, meaning "great vehicle." Sautrāntika and Vaibhāśika are branches of the Hīnayāna school, while Śūnyavāda and Vijñānavāda are branches of the Mahāyāna school. Hīnayāna gradually spread to South India, Ceylon, Indonesia, Burma, and Thailand, while Mahāyāna spread northeast through Tibet, Mongolia, Asia Minor, China, and Japan.

In the earlier stages of Buddhist philosophy and religion, great emphasis was placed on self-enlightenment or self-salvation. But the threefold views of the early Buddhists—"I take refuge in

Buddha, I take refuge in dharma, and I take refuge in *saṅgha* (the organization)"—prepared strong ground for the development of diverse theories and practices. The Hīnayānists tried to keep the teachings of Buddha intact. Because of their orthodoxy, while their teachings flourished, they attracted a more limited following than the Mahāyāna school. The Mahāyānists twisted and diluted the teachings, making them simple so as to appeal to one and all. The popular success of the Mahāyāna organizations was in large part due to the great emphasis they placed on Buddha's concern for the salvation of his fellow beings. They taught that it was selfish to seek one's own liberation instead of helping others attain liberation. In the course of time, both schools became extreme. Hīnayāna emphasized self-help and self-enlightenment while ignoring one's fellow beings, and Mahāyāna stressed the virtue of doing good deeds without giving any importance to the realization of the truth within. In the darkest age of Buddhism, both schools degraded their dignity with useless metaphysical debates and thus lost the practicality of their philosophy.

In its earlier stages, Buddhism did not teach the existence of any permanent soul or God. Buddha himself refused to engage in discussions on this topic, considering them unprofitable in comparison to problems related to the suffering of all beings. But Buddha's silence could not resolve the emotional problems of his followers because it is human nature to lean on someone, especially when one finds himself helpless and incapable of solving his problems by himself. Therefore, the concept of God or an all-loving Supreme Being and almighty supporter was gradually developed among his devotees, with Buddha himself identified as an incarnation of transcendental Reality. Thus in Buddhist literature, Buddha is conceptualized as a Supreme Being who is completely above this phenomenal world. This aspect of Buddha is called *dharmakāya*—the dharma body of Buddha. On another level, he is considered to be God presiding over the entire universe. This aspect of Buddha is called *sambhogakāya*—that which controls this phenomenal world and lets the world continue as it follows the rules of dependent origination and universal change. Finally, on a third level, he is the historical Buddha—the incarnation of his own *sambhogakāya*. This is the state of *nirmāṇakāya*—comprised of the five skeins (*pañcaskandhas*). On this level, the Buddha is said to incarnate himself in the form of different spiritual teachers and to help all beings follow the path of liberation. Thus Buddha as *dharmakāya* is comparable to Brahman, the transcendent Reality as described in the Upaniṣads; as *sambhogakāya* he is Īśvara, the theistic God on whom devotees can focus and rechannel their thoughts and emotions; and as *nirmāṇakāya*, he is the guru or incarnated soul (*avatāra*) who shows the path to liberation.

Buddhism absorbed various thoughts and beliefs from many diverse cultures, religions, and philosophies. Therefore a variety of spiritual practices and mythologies arose on the wide horizon of Buddhism between the first century B.C. and the sixth century A.D. For example, some Buddhists adopted the tantric sādhanās (spiritual practices) and distorted them for the sake of comfort and enjoyment. But the highly advanced philosophy of tantric sādhanā is difficult to understand without the proper guidance of a competent teacher. This undigested knowledge of tantra—including the use of wine, meat, fish, gestures, and physical union—led these Buddhist followers to their complete downfall. In addition, physical practices became the emphasis in the Vijñānavāda school. People then misunderstood these physical practices to be a complete path of spiritual unfoldment. These distortions of Buddhism produced a variety of schools of sādhanā, chief among which were Kāpālika, Kṣapaṇaka, Siddha, and Nātha. These were not pure Buddhist schools, however, because they each contained non-Buddhist practices.

The growth of Buddhism historically follows this sequence: Hīnayāna, Mahāyāna, Vajrayāna, Siddhayāna, and Sahajayāna.

The last three schools developed between the fifth and tenth centuries A.D. in northeastern India and spread to Nepal, Sikkim, Bhutan, and Tibet. The founders of these subschools were primarily great yogis who synthesized different practices, but later those teachings and practices were misused by unworthy followers. As a result, the great philosophy of Buddhism, which originally was full of love and compassion and was a boon for humanity, became a burden to society. For anyone who had difficulty earning a living became a monk. As a result, society had the responsibility of supporting an ever-burgeoning population of monks. And so eventually it came to pass that Kumārila Bhaṭṭa and Śaṅkara reformed society and uprooted Buddhism from its motherland, India. After that Buddhism flourished only outside of India, although without maintaining many of its original values.

chapter

3

Nyāya

Valid Knowledge Through Logical Criticism

The founder of the Nyāya system of philosophy was the sage Gotama. As he was also known as Akṣapāda, this system is also sometimes referred to as the Akṣapāda system. Nyāya philosophy is primarily concerned with the conditions of correct knowledge and the means of receiving this knowledge. Nyāya is predominantly based on reasoning and logic and therefore is also known as Nyāya Vidyā or Tarka Śāstra—"the science of logic and reasoning." Because this system analyzes the nature and source of knowledge and its validity and nonvalidity, it is also referred to as Ānvīkṣikī, which means "the science of critical study." Using systematic reasoning, this school of philosophy develops and uses a concrete method of discriminating valid knowledge from invalid knowledge.

This philosophy asserts that obtaining valid knowledge of the external world and its relationship with the mind and self is the only way to attain liberation. If one masters the logical techniques of reasoning and assiduously applies these in his daily life, he will rid himself of all suffering. Thus, the methods and conditions of determining true knowledge are not the final goal of Nyāya philosophy; logical criticism is viewed only as an instrument that enables one to discriminate valid from invalid knowledge. The ultimate goal of Nyāya philosophy, like that of the other systems of Indian philosophy, is liberation—the absolute cessation of pain and suffering. Nyāya is a philosophy of life, even though it is mainly concerned with the study of logic and epistemology.

The common aims of all six orthodox schools of Indian philosophy are to describe the nature of the external world and its relationship to the individual, to discuss the metaphysical aspects of ultimate Reality, and to state the goal of life and the means for attaining this goal. In this attempt, all the systems of Indian philosophy divide their course of study into two major categories: the study of unmanifested reality, and the study of manifest reality. In Nyāya philosophy, both aspects of reality are studied under sixteen major divisions, called *padārthas* (see chart on next page). These sixteen philosophical divisions are: *pramāṇa*, the sources of knowledge; *prameya*, the object of knowledge; *saṃśaya*, doubt or the state of uncertainty; *prayojana*, the aim; *dṛṣtānta*, example; *siddhānta*, doctrine; *avayava*, the constituents of inference; *tarka*, hypothetical argument; *nirṇaya*, conclusion; *bādha*, discussion; *jalpa*, wrangling; *vitaṇḍā*, irrational argument; *hetvābhāsa*, specious reasoning; *chala*, unfair reply; *jāti*, generality based on a false analogy; and *nigrahasthāna*, the grounds for defeat. The subjects discussed under pramāṇa, the source of knowledge, are the most important and the most thoroughly and profoundly expounded of all the divisions. For this reason, pramāṇa will be explained in detail after the other fifteen divisions of studying reality have been described (see p. 77).

Prameya—The Object of Knowledge

Prameya may be translated as "that which is knowable," or "the object of true knowledge." The word *prameya* is derived from the Sanskrit word *pramā* meaning "buddhi" or "cognition." That

Nyāya's Sixteen Divisions (Padārthas) of Studying Reality

Pramāna, four sources of valid knowledge (pramā):
- Perception (pratyakṣa)
  - Ordinary (laukika)
  - Indeterminate (nirvikalpa)
  - Extraordinary (alaukika)
    - Classes (sāmānyalakṣaṇa)
    - Association (jñānalakṣaṇa)
    - Intuition (yogaja)
- Inference (anumāna)
  - Statements (pratijñā)
  - Reason (hetu)
  - Example (udāharaṇa)
  - Universal proposition (upanaya)
  - Conclusion (nigamana)
- Comparison (upamāna)
- Testimony (śabda)

Prameya, twelve objects of knowledge:

Ātman, the body, the five senses, the objects of the senses, cognition, mind, activity, mental defects (attachment, hatred, and infatuation), rebirth, results, suffering, freedom from suffering.

Doubt (saṃśaya)
Aim (prayojana)
Example (dṛṣṭānta)
Doctrine (siddhānta)
Constituents of inference (five avayavas)
Hypothetical argument (tarka)
Conclusion (nirṇaya)
Discussion (bādha)
Wrangling (jalpa)
Irrational reasoning (vitaṇḍā)
Specious reasoning (hetvābhāsa)
Unfair reply (chala)
Generality based on a false analogy (jāti)
Grounds for defeat (nigrahasthāna)

which is the object of cognition is prameya, and whatever is comprehended or cognized by buddhi is categorized into the twelve objects of cognition known as the prameyas. These twelve divisions are: *Ātman*, the Self; *śarīra*, the body—the abode of the experience of pain and pleasure that is the seat of all organic activities; *indriyas*, the five senses—smell, taste, sight, touch, and hearing—which contact external objects and transmit the experience to the mind; *artha*, the objects of the senses; *buddhi*, cognition; *manas*, the mind—the internal sense that is concerned with the perception of pleasure, pain, and all other internal experiences and that, according to Nyāya, limits cognition to time and space. The mind is compared to an atom (not the atom of modern physics; see page 106) because it is minute, everlasting, individual, and all-pervading; *pravṛti*, activity—vocal, mental, and physical; *doṣa*, mental defects that include attachment (*rāga*), hatred (*dveṣa*), and infatuation or delusion (*moha*); *pretyabhāva*, rebirth or life after death; *phala*, the fruits or results of actions experienced as pain or pleasure; *dukha*, suffering—the bitter or undesired experiences of mind; and *apavarga*, liberation or complete cessation of all suffering without any possibility of its reappearance.

According to Nyāya philosophy the goal of life is to understand these twelve aspects of reality, the *prameyas*, as they actually are. Bondage is born of the misunderstanding of these twelve knowable objects, and one obtains freedom from bondage when he attains the correct knowledge of these twelve aspects of reality. Most of the time, however, this knowledge remains incomplete, and the means for attaining an integral comprehension of reality is not learned, so defective or invalid knowledge is maintained. In order to cast off this invalid knowledge, Nyāya provides a profound method for determining valid knowledge. This is studied under the category of *pramāṇa*, which will be discussed following brief descriptions of the other fourteen components in the Nyāya process for attaining valid knowledge.

Doubt. *Saṃśaya* means "doubt." It is the state in which the mind wavers between conflicting views regarding a single object. In a state of doubt, there are at least two alternative views, neither of which can be determined to lead to a state of certainty. Saṃśaya is not certain knowledge; neither is it a mere reflection of knowledge; nor is it invalid knowledge. It is a positive state of cognition, but the cognition is split in two and does not provide any definite conclusion. For example, in the dark of the night a person may be looking at a plant, but because he cannot see clearly he does not recognize the plant for what it is and falsely perceives it as a man. However, if it would be logically impossible for a man to be present at that place, then the mind does not accept that the figure is a man. The mind becomes confused at that moment, questions whether it is a man or a plant, and cannot come to a decision about what it actually is. Thus, doubt is a product of a confused state of mind that is not able to perceive with clarity.

Aim. The word *prayojana* means "aim." Without an aim or a target, no one can perform any action. It does not matter whether that aim is fully understood or just presumed. One acts either to achieve desirable objects or to get rid of undesirable ones; these desirable and undesirable objects that motivate one's activities are known as prayojana.

Example. *Dṛṣṭānta* is the use of an example to illustrate a common fact and establish an argument. This is a very important aspect of reasoning, for frequently a useful example can be accepted by both parties involved in a discussion without any disputation or difference of opinion. For instance, when one argues that there must be fire because there is smoke, he may use the example of smoke in the kitchen to confirm the permanent relationship between fire and smoke. The relationship between fire and smoke in the kitchen is a common occurrence and may be readily accepted by both parties. Therefore, the example of the kitchen for confirming the existence of fire inferred from the presence of smoke is potentially very helpful.

Doctrine. *Siddhānta* means "doctrine." It is an axiomatic postulate that is accepted as the undisputed truth and that serves as the foundation for the entire theory of a particular system of philosophy. This accepted truth might be derived either from direct experience or from reasoning and logic. For example, it is the doctrine of Nyāya philosophy that there is a God (*Nimitta Kāraṇa*) who is the efficient cause of the universe and who organizes and regulates the atoms.

Constituents of inference. The term *avayava* literally means "constituents" or "parts," and in this context it refers to the constituents of inference. This is an important topic in Nyāya philosophy because Nyāya strongly emphasizes describing the minute complexities of the *pramāṇas*, the sources or methods of receiving correct knowledge. Among these methods, inference is the most important source of correct knowledge, and Nyāya therefore provides a technical method to test the validity of inference. If an inference contains five necessary constituents, then it can give correct knowledge. These five requisite components of inference are *pratijñā* (statements); *hetu* (reason); *udāharaṇa* (example); *upanaya* (universal proposition); and *nigamana* (conclusion). These are discussed later in this chapter in the section on inference (see page 82).

Hypothetical argument. *Tarka* may be translated as "hypothetical argument." All the systems of Indian philosophy agree that it is simply the mind's jabbering that creates confusion and misunderstanding within and without. Because the mind is clouded by its own modifications, it is very important to wash out these confusions before attempting to understand something solely through the mind. For this purpose, Nyāya philosophy discusses the possible problems of the mind and clarifies its confusions, using such processes as tarka. Tarka is the process of questioning and cross-questioning that leads to a particular conclusion. It is a form of supposition that can be used as an aid to the attainment of valid knowledge. Tarka can become a great instrument for analyzing a common statement and for discriminating valid knowledge from invalid knowledge.

Conclusion. *Nirṇaya*, conclusion, is certain knowledge that is attained by using legitimate means. If the mind has doubts concerning the correctness or validity of a conclusion it has drawn, then employing the process of tarka (hypothetical argument) can help to resolve those doubts. But it is not always necessary for a conclusion to pass through a doubtful state. It may be indubitably perceived, either through direct perception, inference, testimony, or intuition. Nirṇaya is this ascertainment of assured truth about something that is attained by means of recognized and legitimate sources of knowledge.

Discussion. *Bādha*, discussion, is a kind of debate between two parties—the exponent and the opponent—on a particular subject. Each party tries to establish its own position and to refute that of the other, arguing against any theory propounded by the other. Both, however, are trying to arrive at the truth by applying the methods of reasoning and logic. This is an effective and efficient way to reach valid knowledge if both parties are honest and free from prejudices.

Wrangling. *Jalpa*, or wrangling, is the process by which the exponent and opponent both try to attain victory over the other without making an honest attempt to come to the truth; there is an involvement of ego instead of a search for knowledge. Jalpa contains all the characteristics of a valid debate except that of aiming to discover truth. It is that type of discussion in which each party has a prejudice for his own view and thus tries to gather all possible arguments in his own favor. Lawyers sometimes apply this method to win their cases in court.

Irrational reasoning. *Vitaṇḍā* is irrational reasoning. Specifically, it is argumentation that is aimed exclusively at refuting or destroying an antagonist's position and that is not at all concerned with establishing or defending one's own position. It is mere destructive criticism of the views of one's opponent. Whereas in wrangling both the exponent and opponent try to establish their own position, in irrational reasoning either or both tries to refute the other's position instead of establishing his own. This usually occurs when one or both parties realize that his own case is weak and that he cannot defend his point of view. Consequently, he irrationally attacks the other's case with destructive intent.

Specious reasoning. *Hetvābhāsa* means "irrational argument." It is reasoning that appears to be valid but is really unfounded. This specious reasoning is a fallacy of inference, and it is therefore discussed later in this chapter in the section on inference (see p. 82).

Unfair reply. *Chala* means "unfair reply." Here it is used to designate a statement that is meant to cheat or to fool someone. In unfair reply one takes a word or phrase that has been used in a particular sense, pretends to understand it in a sense other than that which was intended, and then denies the truth of this deliberate misinterpretation of the original speaker's words. For example, suppose someone's name is Bizarre, and in referring to this person, someone says, "He is Bizarre." If the listener knowingly misconstrues this statement and replies, "He is not bizarre; he is just a common ordinary man," then that person is using chala.

Generality based on a false analogy. *Jāti* means generality, but as used here, it is a technical term used to describe a debate in which an unfair reply or conclusion is based on a false analogy. Suppose, for example, that someone is arguing that sound is noneternal because it is an effect of a certain cause, just as a pot is produced from clay. But another argues that sound must be eternal because it is nonmaterial, like the sky. This counterargument of trying to prove the eternity of sound by comparing it with the nonmaterial sky is fallacious, because there is not necessarily a universal relationship between the nonmaterial and the eternal. (In the Nyāya system itself, sound is considered to be a noneternal quality because it is produced and can be destroyed. Some other systems, however, do not agree with this view).

Grounds for defeat. *Nigrahasthāna* may be translated as "the grounds on which a person is defeated in his argument." When a proponent misunderstands his own or his opponent's premises and their implications, then he becomes helpless and must eventually admit his defeat in the debate. The point at which he accepts his defeat is called *nigrahasthāna.*

Pramāṇa—The Sources of Valid Knowledge

Pramāṇa is that through which or by which the *pramā* (valid knowledge) is received. It is the last of Nyāya's philosophical divisions to be discussed. There are four distinct fountains of correct knowledge. These four pramāṇas are: perception (*pratyakṣa*); inference (*anumāna*); comparison (*upamāna*); and testimony (*śabda*). Before discussing these sources of knowledge, the nature or definition of knowledge should first be examined and the method for distinguishing correct knowledge from false knowledge should be determined.

In Nyāya philosophy, knowledge is divided into two major categories; *anubhava* (experiential knowledge) and *smṛti* (memory). Experiential knowledge is received through the four pramāṇas mentioned above—perception, inference, comparison, and testimony. The second type of knowledge, that which is based on memory, is derived from the storehouse of one's own mind, but ultimately these memories also depend on experiential knowledge because no one can remember something that he has not experienced. During the process of remembering, a memory is called up from its storehouse and is then received as knowledge of an object. These two major categories of knowledge can be divided into two parts: valid and invalid. In the language of Nyāya philosophy, valid experiential knowledge is called *pramā*, and nonvalid experiential knowledge is called *apramā*. Pramā can be received through perception, inference, comparison, and testimony; therefore there are four types of valid knowledge based on these four means. Apramā is divided into doubt (*saṃśaya*), faulty cognition (*bhrama* or *viparyaya*), and hypothetical argument (*tarka*). Certain and unerring cognition (such as the visual perception of a chair) is valid knowledge because the knowledge is presented directly to the senses as it really is. Memory is not original knowledge because it is not experiential; it is a mere reproduction of experiential knowledge. Knowledge based on memory may be either valid or invalid, depending on the correctness of the recollection of the experiential knowledge that occurred in the past. A doubtful cognition cannot be called valid (pramā) because it is not definite knowledge. Faulty cognition likewise cannot be pramā because it is not true to the nature of its object. Tarka (hypothetical argument) cannot be called pramā because in itself it is not knowledge. Although it may help in drawing some conclusions about a fact, it is only a means of attaining knowledge.

According to Nyāya philosophy, true knowledge is that which corresponds to the nature of its object; otherwise the knowledge is false. To perceive a thing in its true nature is true knowledge. For example, the knowledge of a red rose is true if the rose is really red, but the knowledge of a red rose as white is not true because the rose is not white. How can one know if the rose is truly red and not white? How is it possible to prove the validity or falsity of knowledge? Nyāya philosophy says that the validity or invalidity of knowledge depends on its correspondence or noncorrespondence to the facts. For example, if one wants to have correct knowledge of sugar, one tastes it. If there is some powdery white crystal in the kitchen and one puts a pinch of it in his mouth thinking that it is sugar, he will be surprised and disappointed if he finds that it is salty and not sweet. But he will have certain knowledge that what he had thought to be sugar is instead salt. True knowledge leads a person to successful practical activity, while false knowledge makes one helpless and leads to failure and disappointment.

Perception

As mentioned earlier, according to Nyāya there are four sources of valid experiential knowledge or pramā—perception, inference, comparison, and testimony—among which perception is foremost. Most people believe that whatever is experienced through perception must be true, and they do not further test the data that are received via the senses. Nyāya philosophy, however, is very critical in this respect and makes a thorough examination of perception.

Perception is knowledge produced by the contact of the senses with the objects of the world. For example, one has perceptual knowledge of a table when a table comes in contact with the eyes. To be considered valid, the contact of the senses with their objects must be clear and doubtless. The perception of something a long distance away as being either a bush or a bear is a doubtful and indefinite cognition and is, therefore, not true perception. Mistakenly perceiving a rope as a snake may be neither doubtful nor indefinite, but it is a false and therefore invalid perception.

Nyāya philosophy has several different systems of classification of perception. According to the first kind of classification, there are two types of perceptions: *laukika* (ordinary) and *alaukika* (extraordinary). When a perception is derived from direct contact with a sense object, that is ordinary perception. When the object is not directly present to the senses but is conveyed to the senses through unusual modes, then that perception is called alaukika—extraordinary. Modes of perception are either external (*bāhya*) or internal (*mānasa*). In external perception, any or all of the faculties of sight, hearing, touch, taste, and smell are involved in bringing the object to the mind. Thus, there are five kinds of external perceptions (bāhya): visual, auditory, tactile, gustatory, and olfactory. The five senses of hearing, touching, seeing, tasting, and smelling are all gross senses, while mind is the subtle sixth sense. Mind is the internal faculty that perceives the qualities of soul such as desire, aversion, pleasure, pain, and cognition.

In Nyāya philosophy, ordinary perception (laukika) is either indeterminate (*nirvikalpa*) or determinate (*savikalpa*). Indeterminate perception is the primary cognition of a thing before judgment is used to specify diverse characteristics. For example, in the first glance at a table, one perceives the mere existence of the table without comprehending its color, shape, and other specific characteristics; one perceives only a general appearance without details. Only upon further inspection does one recognize that it is, say, a round wooden table with a drop leaf. This determinate perception is the cognition of an object that registers some definite characteristics about it. Determinate perception is always preceded by indeterminate perception, and determinate perception is always valid knowledge because it is definite and explicit.

Nyāya claims that there are three kinds of extraordinary (alaukika) perceptions: perception of classes (*sāmānya lakṣaṇa*); perception based on association (*jñāna lakṣaṇa*); and intuitive perception (*yogaja*). The realization that all people are mortal is an instance of the external perception of classes (*sāmānya lakṣaṇa*). How does one know that all people are mortal? One cannot come to this realization by ordinary perception because the mortality of all people in all times cannot be physically perceived by the senses. But because a person is never perceived without his personhood—that is, the class essence or universality all human beings share—then a conclusion can be made based on that essence. A person is known as a person because of the presence of personhood in him. This direct perception of personhood is the medium through which all people, or the class of people, are perceived. To perceive personhood means to perceive all people as individuals in which this characteristic resides. The perception of all people is due to the perception of the universality of humanity in all people. Therefore, this type of knowledge is called the extraordinary perception of classes.

A different type of extraordinary perception—jñāna lakṣaṇa (association)—is involved when one says that something looks delicious, or that a block of ice looks cold, or that a stone looks hard. These assertions imply that the taste of food, the coldness of ice, and the hardness of stone can be perceived by the eyes. But how can the eyes perceive the qualities of taste and touch? Nyāya says that the past experience of touch and taste are so closely associated with the visual appearance of the causative agents of those experiences that whenever these sources come in contact with the eyes they bring about the perception of taste and touch simultaneously with that of their color. This present perception of taste and touch due to the revived past knowledge of the color of the food, ice, or stone is called jñāna lakṣaṇa—perception based on association. This type of knowledge is extraordinary because it is conveyed by a sense organ that ordinarily is not capable of perceiving that type of knowledge. Because the mind incorporates previously associated experiences, it is able to perceive such knowledge.

The third kind of extraordinary perception is called yogaja, the knowledge born of yoga practices. It is intuitive knowledge that never depends on sense-object contact and is never false; it is perceived after the mind is cleansed through yogic practices. This knowledge from within is divided into two categories, depending on the degree of perfection of yogic attainments. Those who have completed their inward journey and have attained spiritual perfection, who perceive intuitive knowledge of all objects constantly and spontaneously, are called *yukta yogins*. Those who are still on the path of the spiritual journey, for whom concentration and other auxiliary conditions are required to attain an intuitive knowledge, are called *yuñjān yogins*.

Inference

Nyāya philosophy provides a detailed and systematic description of inference. Inference is the process of knowing something not by means of contact between the senses and the objects of the world and not by observation but rather through the medium of a sign, or *liṅga*, that is invariably related to it. Inference involves the process of analyzing memories, correlations, and uncontaminated arguments. There is a systematic method for testing the validity of inferential knowledge, for there are always some inseparable constituents to an inference, and if any of these parts are missing or if there is any defect in the parts, then the knowledge inferred is invalid.

The Sanskrit word for inference is *anumāna*, and may be defined as "the cognition or knowledge that follows from some other knowledge." Two examples are: "The hill is on fire because there is smoke on the hill, and where there is smoke there is fire," and "John is mortal because he is a man, and all men are mortal." In the first example, we perceive smoke on the hill and arrive at the knowledge of the existence of fire on the hill on the basis of our previous knowledge of the universal relationship between smoke and fire. In the second example, we begin with the perception of a man, John, which inspires the knowledge of the mortality of John based on our previous knowledge of the universal relationship between men and mortality. Thus, it is apparent that inference is a process of reasoning in which one passes through certain necessary stages to reach a conclusion, which is called inferential knowledge. The necessary stages are the conditions for a valid inference. In the process of inference, one reaches a conclusion regarding a particular fact through the knowledge of a sign and of the sign's universal relationship to the conclusion.

In the example of the inference of fire on a hill, one ascertains the presence of the unperceived fire on the hill through the perception of the smoke on the hill, because one already has the knowledge of the universal relationship between smoke and fire. A primary condition of this inference is the knowledge of smoke on the hill; this part of the inferential process is called *liṅga*, or sign. Next arises the awareness of the universal relationship between smoke and fire based on past observations; this is known as *vyāpti*. As a result of this, knowledge of the existence of the unperceived fire on the hill arises. This stage is called *nirṇaya* or conclusion. In the terminology of logic, the hill is the minor term (*pakṣa*) in this inference because the hill is the subject under consideration. Fire is the major term (*sādhya*) because this is what we want to prove in relation to the hill. The presence of smoke on the hill is the middle term (*liṅga*) because it is the sign that indicates the presence of fire. This middle term is also called *hetu* or *sādhana* meaning "the reason or grounds for inference."

Three parts of inference. Thus, an inference contains three parts: the minor term (pakṣa), the major term (sādhya), and the middle term (hetu or liṅga). In the process of inference, the first step is the apprehension of smoke (hetu) on the hill (pakṣa); the second step is the recollection of the universal relationship between smoke and fire (hetu and sādhya); and the third step is the cognition of fire (sādhya). When used as a formal statement or verbal expression designed to convince others, however, the structure of inference is changed. In stating an inferential verbal expression for others, the first step will be the predication of the major term in relation to the minor term: "There is fire on the hill." The second step will be the formation of the middle term in relation to the minor term:"There is visible smoke on the hill." The third step will be the formation of the middle term in its universal or invariable relationship with the major term: "Where there's smoke, there's fire." In this last step it is sometimes helpful to use a specific example to confirm the relationship between the middle term and major term. For instance, "Where there's smoke there's fire, as in the kitchen."

Thus, inference may be said to be a syllogism consisting of at least three categorical premises. But when one is analyzing the whole process of an inference, and especially when one is using inference to prove or demonstrate something, then it is necessary to state the inference in a systematic and comprehensive chain of arguments. One must then state a syllogism in the form of five premises. These five premises (*avayavas*) that constitute a valid inference are *pratijñā* (fact); *hetu* (reason); *udāharaṇa* (example); *upanaya* (application); and *nigamana* (conclusion). Here is an example: (1) John is mortal (fact); (2) Because he is a man (reason); (3) All men are mortal—for example, Napoleon, Lincoln, Socrates, and so on (example); (4) John is a man (application); (5) Therefore John is mortal (conclusion). The first premise states a positive fact. The second premise states the reason for this assertion. The third premise then confirms the relationship between the reason for the assertion and the asserted fact itself as supported by a well-known example. The fourth constituent of the syllogism represents the application of the universal proposition to the present case. The fifth part, or conclusion, is drawn from the preceding four parts.

To gain a proper understanding of the workings of logic, it is necessary to examine more closely how a systematic syllogism functions. For this purpose, the following example may be reanalyzed. "There is fire on the hill because there is smoke, and where there is smoke, there is fire." As was previously discussed, fire is the major term, hill is the minor term, and smoke is the middle term. The middle term (smoke) is so-called because, on the one hand, it is connected to the minor term (hill), and, on the other hand, it is universally related to the major term (fire). This middle term is also called reason or grounds since it is because of its perception that the major term is inferred. Thus, an inference has two conditions: the knowledge of the middle term must exist in the minor term; and a relationship must exist between the middle and the major terms. It is not possible to realize the existence of fire on the hill as a conclusion based on inferential reasoning if the invariable concomitance between the middle and major terms is not established. This invariable concomitance between these two terms of an inference is called *vyāpti*, the logical ground for inference. Concomitance guarantees the validity of the conclusion; the validity or invalidity of an inference depends on the validity or invalidity of vyāpti. Therefore, Nyāya philosophy goes into great detail concerning the nature of concomitance and the fallacies related to it.

Logical ground for inference. Vyāpti, meaning "the state of pervasiveness," implies both that which pervades and that which is pervaded. For example, in the inference of fire and smoke, smoke is the pervaded and fire is the pervader. Here smoke is always accompanied by fire—wherever there is smoke, there will also be fire. The reverse, however, is not necessarily true: it is possible to have fire without smoke—for example, a Bunsen burner. But there are examples in which both the pervader and the pervaded coexist permanently—for example, fire and heat. There are, therefore, two kinds of concomitance: equivalent and nonequivalent. Nonequivalent concomitance (*asamavyāpti*) is an invariable concomitance between two unequal entities (such as smoke and fire). It has already been shown that in this type of concomitance, one entity may be inferred from the other, but not vice versa. Equivalent vyāpti (*samavyāpti*) is an invariable concomitance between two coexistent terms, either of which can be inferred from the other. For example, a chair is a nameable thing because a chair is knowable, and whatever is knowable, is nameable. Here nameable and knowable can both be inferred from each other.

Concomitance denotes a relationship of coexistence (*sāhacarya*). But not every instance of coexistence is an example of concomitance. Fire, for example, often coexists with smoke, yet it may exist without smoke. The coexistent relationship of fire and smoke depends on certain conditions—temperature and wetness, for instance. The condition on which the relation of coexistence depends is called *upādhi*, and for an inference to be valid, the relation between the middle and major terms of a syllogism must be independent of any and all conditions. In other words, a valid concomitance represents an invariable and unconditional concomitant relation (*nitya anaupādhika saṃbandha*) between the middle and major terms of a syllogism.

But how does one know that a relation is invariable and unconditional? Vedāntins reply that concomitance is established by the uncontradicted experiences of the relationship between two things. But according to Nyāya, concomitance is established through the perception of classes (*sāmānya lakṣaṇa* perception), which has been discussed earlier in this chapter in the section on extraordinary perceptions (see p. 80). Actually, the Nyāya method of inference uses inductive reasoning; that is, it draws a particular conclusion on the grounds of a general and universally known truth. The universal truth is considered to fall within the range of vyāpti. In Nyāya, there are three types of inductive analysis, or generalization. The first is *anvaya*, or uniform agreement in presence. This type of inductive process arises from observing a relationship in which if one constituent is present, then in every instance the other constituent is also present—for example, wherever there is smoke there is fire. The second type of inductive analysis is the obverse of the first, and is called uniform agreement in absence (*vyatireka*). In this method, a negative universal relationship or invariable concomitance is observed—for example, wherever there is no fire, there is no smoke. The third kind of inductive process is a combination of the first and second methods. In this method, known as uniform agreement in both presence and absence (*anvaya-vyatireka* or *vyabhicāragraha*), both constituents of a relationship are always found together; neither is ever present without the other. From this, it is induced that there must exist a natural relationship of invariable concomitance between them.

These three methods of generalization demonstrate a systematic technique for inductive reasoning. The most crucial concern, however, in any systematic inference is how to make certain that concomitance, the logical basis for the inference, is valid—that is, free from limiting conditions (upādhis). This process of insuring that vyāptis are free from all vitiating conditions is called *upādhinirāsa*. One way of insuring this is by the repeated observation of both constituents of a relationship under all possible circumstances to make certain that the relationship is in fact invariable. Another way is to employ hypothetical critical argumentation or *tarka*. But nyāya places the greatest emphasis on *sāmānya lakṣaṇa*—the perception of classes—as the major means for insuring the validity of vyaptis.

Classifications of inference. Nyāya provides three general classification systems for inference. The first classification system is based on psychological grounds; the second is based on the nature of vyāpti or the universal relationship between the middle and major terms; and the third is based on the logical construction of the inference.

According to the first system of classification, there are two kinds of inference: *svārtha*, meaning "for oneself," and *parārtha*, meaning "for others." In svārtha,the purpose of the inference is for one to gain correct knowledge by oneself and for himself. In this kind of inference, the whole process of reasoning is internal—one employs systematic logical reasoning to protect oneself from confusion and doubt and to arrive at correct inferential knowledge. In parārtha, on the other hand, the inference is meant for others. Here someone is trying to prove the truth of his view. For instance, a man who is convinced of the existence of fire on a hill would use parārtha when attempting to convince others of the fire's existence.

The second classification system divides inferences into three categories: *pūrvavat*, *śeṣavat*, and *sāmānyatodṛṣṭa*. Both pūrvavat and śeṣavat inferences display causal uniformity between the middle and major terms, while sāmānyatodṛṣṭa inferences exhibit non-causal uniformity of the middle and major terms. Here the term *cause* refers to an invariable and unconditional antecedent of an effect, and *effect* refers to an invariable and unconditional consequence of a cause. When an unperceived effect is inferred from a perceived cause, that inference is deemed a pūrvavat inference. For example: "It will rain because there are dark heavy clouds in the sky, and whenever there are dark heavy clouds, it rains." Here the future rain (effect) is inferred from the appearance of dark heavy clouds (cause). Śeṣavat is the reverse type of reasoning, in which an unperceived cause is inferred from a perceived effect. For instance: "It has rained recently because there is a swift muddy current in the river, and whenever there is a swift muddy current in the river, it has recently rained." Here we infer the cause (the past rain) from the effect (the swift muddy current). And finally, in sāmānyatodṛṣṭa, the third type of inference in this system of classification, the invariable concomitance between the middle term and the major term does not depend on a causal uniformity. One term is not inferred from the other because they are uniformly related. In this kind of reasoning, conclusions are based on direct experience and on generally known truths. An example of this sort of inference is the movement of the moon which is inferred on the basis of its changing position in the sky, although the movement of the moon is not perceived directly by the senses.

The last general classification system is based on the nature of induction, by which one obtains the knowledge of the invariable concomitance between the middle and the major terms of an inference. This system distinguishes among three types of inference. In the first, *kevalānvayī*, the middle term is only positively related to the major term. For example: "All knowable objects are nameable." In the second, *kevalavyatireka*, the middle term is only negatively related to the major term. For example: "Whoever is dead has no pulse; this person has a pulse; therefore, he is not dead." In the last category, *anvayavyatirekī*, the middle term is both positively and negatively related to the major term. This is the joint method of both anvaya and vyatireka. For example: "All smoky objects are on fire;

the hill is smoky; therefore, the hill is on fire. No nonfiery object is smoky; the hill is smoky; therefore the hill is on fire."

The fallacies of inference. In the Nyāya system, fallacies of inference are called *hetvābhāsa.* This term literally means "a reason (hetu) that appears to be valid but is not really so." There are five kinds of fallacies, called *sabyabhicāra, viruddha, satpratipakṣa, asiddha,* and *bādhita.* The first, sabyabhicāra, means "irregular middle." In a correct inference, the middle term is uniformly and without exception related to the major term. An irregular middle term is destructive to an inference because it can lead to a wrong conclusion. For example: "All Himalayan beings are saints; tigers are Himalayan beings; therefore, tigers are saints." The conclusion of this inference cannot be said to be correct, because the middle term, Himalayan beings, is not invariably related to the major term, saints. Himalayan beings come in many different varieties. Instead of leading to one single valid conclusion, such an irregular middle term leads to varied opposite conclusions.

Viruddha, the second kind of fallacy, means "contradictory middle." A contradictory middle is one that dismisses the very proposition it is meant to prove. For example: "Sound is eternal, because it is caused." Whatever has a cause is noneternal, and so here the middle term, caused, does not prove the eternity of sound but rather confirms its noneternity. The distinction between an irregular middle and a contradictory middle is that while the irregular middle fails to prove its conclusion, the contradictory middle proves the opposite of what is intended.

The third type, satpratipakṣa, means "inferentially contradictory middle." This type of fallacy arises when the middle term of an inference is contradicted by the middle term of another inference that proves a completely opposite fact about the major term. For example, the argument "Sound is eternal because it is audible" is contradicted by the inference "Sound is noneternal because it is produced, as a pot is produced." The distinction between a contradictory middle and an inferentially contradictory middle is that in the former, the middle term itself proves the contradiction of its conclusion, while in the latter, the contradiction of the conclusion is proved by another inference.

The fourth type of fallacy is asiddha, an unproved middle. In this type of fallacy, the middle term is not an established fact but is an unproved assumption. For example: "The sky-lotus is fragrant because it has lotusness like a natural lotus." Here the middle term, lotusness, does not have any substantial existence because such a thing as a sky-lotus actually does not exist.

The fifth is bādhita, a noninferentially contradicted middle. Here the middle term is contradicted by some other source of knowledge. Examples are: "Fire is cold because it is a substance," and "Sugar is sour because it produces acidity." Here "cold" and "sour" are the major terms and "substance" and "acidity" are the middle terms. The existence of heat in the fire and sweetness in sugar is directly perceived by the senses, so one has to consider substance and acidity as contradictory middle terms. Therefore, the inference is fallacious.

Comparison

According to Nyāya, comparison is the third valid source of experiential knowledge. This kind of knowledge comes when one perceives the similarity between the description of an unfamiliar object and its actual appearance before one's senses. For example, suppose that a trustworthy person has told you that there is such a thing as a crabapple that looks like a regular red apple but is smaller and has a longer stem. One day in the woods you come upon a tree bearing fruit that you've never seen before but that reminds you of apples. You then remember your friend's description of crabapples, and you come to the conclusion that this must be a crabapple tree.

This source of knowledge, *upamāna*, is not recognized as valid in many of the other systems of Indian philosophy. The

Cārvāka system of philosophy, for instance, does not accept this as a source of knowledge, because this system maintains that perception is the sole source of valid knowledge. The Buddhist system of philosophy recognizes upamāna as a valid source of knowledge but regards it as a mere compound of perception and testimony. The Vaiśeṣika and Sāṃkhya systems explain upamāna as simply a form of inference, and the Jaina system maintains that it is merely a kind of recognition. The Mīmāṃsā and Vedānta systems agree with Nyāya in considering upamāna as an independent source of knowledge, but they explain it in a different way, which will be discussed in the chapter on Mīmāṃsā.

Testimony

Śabda or testimony literally means "words"; it is the knowledge of objects derived from words or sentences, and is, according to Nyāya, the fourth and final source of valid experiential knowledge. Not all verbal knowledge, however, is valid. In Nyāya philosophy, śabda is defined as the statement of an *āpta*, a person who speaks and acts the way he thinks. Such a person's mind, action, and speech are in perfect harmony, and he is therefore accepted as an authority. Thus his verbal or written statement is considered to be a valid source of knowledge. The Veda is considered to be the expression of certain venerable āptas, great sages who realized the truth within and who transmitted their experiences into words. The validity of the Veda is derived from the authority of these āptas.

The validity of verbal knowledge depends upon two conditions: first, the meaning of the statement must be perfectly understood, and, second, the statement must be the expression of a trustworthy person, that is, an āpta. There are two main ways of classifying śabda, or testimony. The first method of classification divides testimonial knowledge into two categories based on the nature of the object of the knowledge. The first category consists of the trustworthy assertions of ordinary persons, saints, sages, and scriptures on matters related to the perceptible objects of the world. Examples are the evidence given by expert witnesses in court, the statements of reliable physicians about physiology, and scriptural declarations concerning the performance of certain rites. The second type of testimony consists of the trustworthy assertions of persons, saints, sages, and scriptures on matters concerning the supersensible realities. Examples are a physicist's assertions about atoms, a nutritionist's statements regarding vitamins, a prophet's instructions on virtue, and scriptural statements about God and immortality. The second way of classifying śabda is based on the nature of the source of the knowledge. This method categorizes all testimony as being either scriptural or secular. Here the word *scriptural* refers only to the sacred writings related to the Veda and to the Veda itself. The words of scriptural testimony are considered to be perfect and infallible. Secular śabda is the testimony of fallible human beings and therefore may be either true or false; secular testimony that comes from a trustworthy person is valid, but the rest is not.

The Nyāya system gives a detailed description of the nature of śabda because testimony is considered to be a valid source of knowledge and should therefore be analyzed thoroughly. In a scripture or a testimony, words and sentences are used—but what is a sentence, what is a word, and what is the nature of their construction? Here, a sentence may be viewed as a group of words arranged in a certain manner, and a word as a group of letters or phonemes arranged in a specific order. The essential nature of any word lies in its meaning, and there must be specific rules governing the arrangement of words in the formation of sentences. Without such rules, the words spoken even by a trustworthy person—an āpta—could be reordered to convey a different meaning from the one intended or could mislead a common person because of their lack of clarity of meaning.

The potency of words. The Nyāya system states that all words are significant symbols and that all words have the capacity to designate their respective objects. This capacity of words is called *śakti*, potency, and in the Nyāya system, potency is said to be the will of God. The words used in a sentence have certain meanings because of the potencies within them, and that is why they express certain meanings in a particular context. So the ordering of words in a sentence is very important. In addition, Nyāya maintains that there are four other factors that are essential in the proper functioning of sentences, and without the fulfillment of these four conditions a sentence cannot express the intended meaning. These conditions are: *ākāṃkṣā* (expectancy), *yogyatā* (fitness), *sannidhi* (proximity), and *tātparya* (intention).

Ākāṃkṣā, the first condition, means "expectancy." Ākāṃkṣā is the quality by which all the words of a sentence imply or expect one another; it is the need that each word has for the other words in that sentence. According to the Nyāya system, a word is not in itself capable of conveying a complete meaning; it must be brought into relationship with other words in order to express the full meaning intended. For example, when someone hears the word "bring," he asks or he thinks about what to bring. It could be a jar, a book, a pencil, a doughnut, or anything else. Thus, expectancy is the interdependence of the words in a sentence for expressing a complete meaning.

Yogyatā, the second condition, means "fitness." It refers to the appropriateness of the words in a sentence, to the absence of contradiction in its terms. For example, sentences like "Moisten with fire," or "He is frustrated because of his inner peace," make no sense because there is a contradiction between fire and moistening, between frustration and peace. Fire has no ability to moisten anything, and inner peace cannot engender frustration. Therefore, although these sentences may be grammatically correct, they do not express valid knowledge.

Sannidhi, the third condition, means "proximity." It is very important for words to be used within the limits of an appropriate time and space. If the duration of their use is prolonged, then words no longer have the capacity to give the desired meaning. For example, if someone who desires to make a statement speaks one word today, another word tomorrow, and a third the day after, his efforts at effective communication are certain to fail. The same holds true for the written word. If someone writes one word on page one, another on page three, one more on page five, and another on page ten, then his meaning will not be communicated effectively. Continuity of time and space is therefore essential for a sentence to convey meaning.

Tātparya, the fourth condition, means "intention," and it refers to the meaning one intends a sentence to convey. A word may have various meanings depending on its context, so one has to be careful to determine the real intention of the person who uses the word. This is also the case with scriptural testimony—even the greatest scholars have disagreements concerning some passages because they do not understand the original intention of those sentences. A very simple illustration is this: Suppose someone tells you to bring him a bat; you have no way of knowing whether you are being asked to provide a particular type of flying mammal or a wooden club. To understand the real intention of a sentence, one has to comprehend accurately the context in which the words are used. Because of the unique nature of the Sanskrit language and its symbolic usages, the Veda and related ancient religio-philosophical scriptures are full of this kind of complexity and indeterminability of intention. In order to clarify this and understand the Vedic testimony properly, Nyāya recommends that one study the Mīmāṃsā philosophy because it provides systematized rules and interpretations for understanding the real meaning of the Veda.

The Nature of the Physical World

As mentioned previously, the Nyāya system groups all the objects of the world into twelve major categories: soul, body, senses, objects of the senses, cognition (buddhi), mind (manas), activity, mental modifications, rebirth, feelings, suffering, and absolute freedom from all sufferings. Not all these objects of knowledge are found in the physical world because the physical world is composed only of the four gross elements—earth, water, fire, and air. Although the soul and the mind are involved in the physical world, they are not physical elements. Likewise, time and space are completely nonmaterial, but they nonetheless belong to the physical world. *Ākāśa* (space or ether) is considered to be a physical substance, but it is not considered to be a productive cause of anything. In fact, the ultimate constituents of earth, air, fire, and water are eternal and unchanging atoms. Ether and time and space are also eternal and infinite substances, each being one single whole. All in all, the Nyāya theory of the physical world is very similar to that of the Vaiśeṣika school, and a more detailed discussion of this world view will be provided in the next chapter.

The Concept of the Individual Soul

There are many apparently different concepts of the soul among the various schools of Indian philosophy. The Cārvāka system states that the soul consists of the living physical body and its attributes. According to Buddhist philosophy, there is no soul. Buddhism teaches that the stream of ever-changing thoughts and feelings is the ultimate reality. This may be termed *soul*, but it is not considered to be a permanent entity, as is maintained by other philosophies.

According to the concept of soul held by the Nyāya and Vaiśeṣika systems, the soul is a unique substance, of which all desires, aversions, pleasures, pains, and cognitions are qualities. There are different souls in different bodies. The soul is indestructible and eternal, and its attribute is consciousness. Because it is not limited by time and space, the soul is also seen as infinite or all-pervading. There are many souls, because one person's experiences do not overlap those of another person; one's experience is completely distinct from any other's.

Nyāya gives numerous arguments to prove the existence of the soul. It first argues that the body is not the soul because immaterial consciousness cannot be said to be an attribute of the material body, which in itself is unconscious and unintelligent. Neither can the functioning of the senses explain the process of imagination, memory, and ideation—none of these functions depends on any external sense. The mind can also not be the soul because the mind is considered to be an imperceptible substance. Nor can the soul, as the Buddhists maintain, be identified as the ever-changing series of cognitions. The soul cannot be said to be an eternal and self-effulgent consciousness because consciousness cannot subsist without a certain locus. At the same time, the soul is not mere consciousness or knowledge but is the knower of knowledge and the enjoyer of objects. In sum, the soul is not consciousness but is a substance having consciousness as its attribute.

The soul experiences the external world through the mind and senses. All the cognitions and conscious states arise in the soul when the soul is related to the mind, the mind to the senses, and the senses to external objects. It is because of this sequential contact or relationship that the whole process actuates; otherwise there would be no consciousness in the soul. In its disembodied or disintegrated state, the soul has no knowledge or consciousness. How then can one know whether there is such a thing as an individual soul? The Nyāya system answers that the soul is not known by sensory perception but rather by inference or testimony. The existence of the soul is inferred from the functions of desire, aversion, and volition, from the sensations of pain and pleasure, and from memories of these. These memories cannot be explained unless one admits a permanent soul that has experienced pain and pleasure in relation to certain objects in the past. The process of knowledge based on memory requires the existence of a permanent self that desires to know something and then desires to attain certain knowledge about it. Desire, volition, pain, and pleasure cannot be explained by the body, senses, or mind. Just as the experiences of one person cannot be remembered by another person, the present states of the body or the senses or the mind cannot remember their past states. The phenomenon of memory must depend upon a permanent entity—the soul. One's own soul can be known through mental perception, but someone else's soul in another body can only be inferred.

The Concept of Liberation

Like all the other systems of Indian philosophy, the Nyāya system maintains that the ultimate goal of human life is to attain liberation. By liberation is meant absolute freedom from all pain and misery. This implies a state in which the soul is completely released from all bondage and from its connection with the body. It is impossible for the soul to attain the state of complete freedom from pain and misery unless the soul is totally disconnected from the body and senses. In liberation, the soul is unconditionally and absolutely freed from all shackles forever.

To attain the state of liberation, one has to acquire true knowledge of the soul and of all the objects of experience. This knowledge is called *tattvajñāna*, which means "to know reality as completely distinct from unreality." Nyāya philosophy prescribes a three-stage path for reaching the goal of liberating knowledge. The first step is *śravaṇa*, the study of the scriptures. One has to study the spiritual scriptures and listen to authoritative persons and saints. Following this, one must use his own reasoning powers to ponder over what he has learned. This process of rumination is called *manana*. Finally, one must contemplate on the soul, confirm his knowledge, and practice that truth in his life. This is called *nididhyāsana*. Through the practice of śravaṇa, manana, and nididhyāsana, a person realizes the true nature of the soul as being totally distinct from the body, mind, senses, and all other objects of the world. The truth realized within dispels the darkness of self-identification and misunderstanding (*mithyājñāna*) concerning "I-ness and Thy-ness." When this happens, a person ceases to be moved by his passions and impulses and begins to perform his duties selflessly without having any desire to reap the fruits of these actions. The fire of true knowledge roasts one's past karmas like seeds, thereby making them unable to germinate. Thus, true knowledge leads a person to the state where there is no cycle of birth and death. This state is called liberation.

The Concept of God

According to Nyāya, God is considered to be the efficient cause of creation, maintenance, and destruction of the universe. God does not create the world out of nothing or out of himself but rather out of the eternal atoms of space, time, mind, and soul. The creation of the universe refers to the ordering of these eternal entities, which are in coexistence with God, into a mortal world. Thus God, as the first efficient cause of the universal forces, is the creator of the world. And God is also the preserver, as he causes the atoms to hold together and continue their existence in a particular order that maintains the physical universe. God is also called the destroyer of the universe, because he lets loose the forces of destruction when the energies of the mortal world require it. God is one, infinite, and eternal, and the universe of space and time, of mind and soul, does not limit him. God is said to possess six perfections: infinite glory, absolute sovereignty, unqualified virtue, supreme beauty, perfect knowledge, and complete detachment.

Nyāya provides a few arguments to establish the theory of God. The first is the causal argument. According to this line of reasoning, the entire universe is formed by the combination of atoms. Mountains, fields, rivers, and so on must have a cause, for they are made up of parts, possess limited dimensions, and are not intelligent. This being so, they cannot be the cause of themselves; they require the guidance of an intelligent cause. That intelligent cause must have direct knowledge of all matter and of the atoms that underlie all matter. He must be omnipresent and omniscient. This intelligent entity cannot be the individual soul because the knowledge of the soul is limited—a soul, for instance, does not have the knowledge of other souls. Therefore, there must be an ultimate intelligent entity, which is termed God.

The second argument is based on *adṛṣṭa*, which means "the unseen" or "the unknown," and may be translated as *providence* or *fate*. The philosophers of the Nyāya system inquire as to why some people are happy and others are not, why some are wise and others ignorant. One cannot say that there is no cause, because every event has a cause. The causes of pain and pleasure must therefore be one's own actions in this life or in previous lives. People enjoy or suffer according to the merits or demerits produced by their past good or bad actions. This law of karma, which governs the life of every individual soul, requires that every human being must reap the fruits of his own actions.

There is often a long interval of time between an action and its effect, however, and many pleasures and sorrows cannot be traced to any action performed in this life. Likewise, many actions performed in this life do not produce fruits immediately. The subtle impressions of all one's actions persist long after the actions themselves and are collected in the soul in the form of credits or merits (*puṇya*) and deficiencies or demerits (*pāpa*). The sum total of all merits and demerits that are accrued from good or bad actions is called *adṛṣṭa*, fate, and this produces present pain and pleasure. Adṛṣṭa is not an intelligent principle, however, and it cannot inspire its own fructification. It must therefore be guided or directed by some intelligent agent to produce the proper consequences. The individual soul cannot be said to be the director or controller of adṛṣṭa because souls do not know anything about their adṛṣṭa. Thus, the almighty intelligent agent who guides or directs adṛṣṭa through the proper channels to produce the proper consequences is the eternal, omnipotent, and omnipresent supreme being termed God.

A third Nyāya argument for the existence of God is based on scriptural testimony. According to this reasoning, the Veda, Upaniṣads, and all other authoritative scriptures state the existence of God. These scriptures were not written by common people but were formulated by those great sages who experienced truth from within. Thus, the authority of testimony depends on direct experience, which is the only source of knowledge about any and all facts. The fact of the existence of God is experienced directly by individual souls, and some of these individuals have expressed their God-realizations. The Veda is the expressions of such direct experiences of God. Therefore, God exists.

chapter 4

Vaiśeṣika

Analysis of the Aspects of Reality

The founder of Vaiśeṣika philosophy is the sage Kaṇāda, who was also known as Ulūka, so this system is sometimes called Aulūkya. Kaṇāda wrote the first systematic work of this philosophy, *Vaiśeṣika Sūtra*. This work is divided into ten cantos, each canto containing two sections. Praśastapāda wrote a great commentary on this Sūtra entitled *Svārtha Dharma Saṃgraha* that is so profound and famous that it is called *Bhāṣya*, which means simply "commentary." In Indian philosophical discourse, whenever the word *Bhāṣya* is used by itself without further specification, it is understood to refer to this commentary. Two well-known and excellent explications of Praśastapāda's work are Udayana's *Kiraṇāvalī* and Śridhara's *Nyāyakandalī*. The most remarkable concept of this system is the introduction of a special category of reality called uniqueness (*viśeṣa*). Thus, this system is known as Vaiśeṣika.

Vaiśeṣika is allied to the Nyāya system of philosophy. Both systems accept the liberation of the individual self as the end goal; both view ignorance as the root cause of all pain and misery; and both believe that liberation is attained only through right knowledge of reality. There are, however, two major differences between Nyāya and Vaiśeṣika . First, Nyāya philosophy accepts four independent sources of knowledge—perception, inference, comparison, and testimony—but Vaiśeṣika accepts only two—perception and inference. Second, Nyāya maintains that all of reality is comprehended by sixteen categories (*padārthas*), whereas Vaiśeṣika recognizes only seven categories of reality (see chart). These are: *dravya* (substance), *guṇa* (quality), *karma* (action), *sāmānya* (generality), *viśeṣa* (uniqueness), *samavāya* (inherence), and *abhāva* (nonexistence). The term *padārtha* means "the object denoted by a word," and according to Vaiśeṣika philosophy all objects denoted by words can be broadly divided into two main classes—that which exists, and that which does not exist. Six of the seven padārthas are in the first class, that which exists. In the second class, that which does not exist, there is only one padārtha, *abhāva*, which stands for all negative facts such as the nonexistence of things. The first two categories of reality—substance and quality—are treated in greater detail in the following discussion than are the remaining five.

The Category of Substance—Nine Dravyas

Dravya, substance, is that in which a quality or an action can exist but which in itself is different from both quality and action. Without substance, there cannot be a quality or an action because substance is the substratum of quality and action, and it is also the material cause of the composite things produced from it. A cloth, for example, is formed by the combination of a number of threads of certain colors. The threads are the material or constitutive causes of the cloth because it is made of the threads that subsist in the cloth.

There are nine kinds of substances: earth, water, fire, air, ether, time, direction, soul, and mind. The first five of these are called physical elements because each of them possesses a specific

Vaiśeṣika's Seven Categories (Padārthas) of Reality

Substance (nine dravyas)
Earth, water, fire, air, space or ether, time, direction, soul, and mind.

Quality (twenty-four guṇas)
Color, taste, smell, touch, sound, number, magnitude, distinctness, union, separation, remoteness, nearness, cognition, pleasure, pain, desire, aversion, effort, heaviness, fluidity, viscidity, tendency, virtue, and nonvirtue.

Action (karma)

Generality (sāmānya)

Uniqueness (viśeṣa)

Inherence (samavāya)

Nonexistence (abhāva)

quality that can be perceived by an external sense faculty. Each of the senses is composed of elements, whose distinguishing qualities are registered by specific sensory receptors. For example, smell is the particular property of the earth, and it is apprehended by the nostrils. Taste is the particular property of water, which is perceived by the tongue. Color is the particular property of fire or light, and it is discerned by the eyes. Touch is the particular property of air, which is experienced by the skin. And sound is the particular property of *ākāśa* (ether), which is received by the ears.

Paramāṇu—the smallest particle of earth, water, fire, and air. In Vaiśeṣika the smallest indivisible part of matter is called *paramāṇu*, or atom. This is not to be confused with the modern scientific term *atom* because an atom as described in nuclear physics is itself composed of many parts. The Vaiśeṣika usage of the word is different. It simply refers to the most minute indivisible state of matter. The atoms of earth, water, fire, and air are eternal because an atom is partless and cannot be produced or destroyed. The common elements of earth, water, fire, and air, however, are noneternal because they are produced by combinations of atoms and therefore can disintegrate or change. The existence of atoms is proved by inference—not by perception—in the following way. All the composite objects of the world are made up of parts. In separating the parts of a composite object, one passes from the larger to the smaller, and then from the smaller to the smallest part. But when one comes to the smallest part that cannot be further divided in any way, then the process of separation has to stop. That indivisible and minutest part in Vaiśeṣika is called the atom. If one does not accept the concept of indivisibility, then he will commit the fallacy of infinite regression. Because it has no parts, the atom cannot be said to be produced, and it cannot be destroyed because destruction means to break a thing down into its parts, and in an atom there are no parts. Atoms, therefore, can be neither produced nor destroyed; they are eternal.

Ākāśa—ether. There are four kinds of atoms—atoms of earth, atoms of water, atoms of fire, and atoms of air—each having its own peculiar qualities. Ākāśa (ether), the fifth substance, is the substratum of the quality of sound; it is not made up of atoms. Ākāśa is also translated as space. Sound can be perceived, but ākāśa cannot be perceived because it lacks two conditions necessary for the perception of an object: perceptible dimension and manifest color. Ākāśa is unlimited, so it does not have a perceptible dimension, and it is formless, so does not have any color. Therefore, ākāśa cannot be perceived, but it can be inferred from the perception of the quality of sound which it contains. It cannot be said that sound is the quality of time, direction, soul, or mind because these exist even when there is no sound to qualify them. Therefore, there must be some other substance that has the quality of sound in it; that substance is called ākāśa. Ākāśa is one and eternal because it is not made up of parts and does not depend on any other substance for its existence. It is all-pervading in the sense that it has an unlimited dimension and that its quality (sound) is perceived everywhere.

Direction and time. Direction and time are also imperceptible substances, and they are likewise single, eternal, and all-pervading. Direction is inferred on the basis of such concepts as here, there, near, far, on this side, by that way, and so on. Time is inferred from the concepts now, today, tomorrow, past, present, future, older, younger, and so forth. Although space, direction, and time are singular and all-pervading, indivisible and partless, they are spoken of as many because of certain limiting conditions, known as *upādhis*. For example, when the all-pervading, indivisible space is limited by the walls of a jar, that space is known as the space of the jar (*ghaṭākaśa*). In the same way, direction and time are also thought of as multiple because of the notions of variety and specificity expressed as east, west, one hour, two hours, and so on.

Soul. The eighth kind of substance, the soul or Ātman, is also considered to be eternal and all-pervading and is the substratum of the phenomenon of consciousness. According to Vaiśeṣika philosophy, there are two kinds of souls: individual and supreme. Individual souls are known as *jīvātman*, and the Supreme Soul is known as *Paramātman*, or *Īśvara*. The Supreme Soul is inferred to be the creator of the world in the same manner as has been explained in the discussion of Nyāya philosophy. In contrast to the Supreme Soul, the individual soul is perceived as possessing mental qualities, such as "I'm happy, I'm sorry," and so forth. Individual souls do not perceive other individual souls, but they do infer their existence in the manner described in the Nyāya section.

Mind. The mind is considered to be the ninth kind of substance. It is the eternal sense faculty of the individual soul and the soul's qualities, such as pleasure and pain. Like the soul, the mind is atomic and indivisible—there is one in each body. The existence of the mind is not perceived but is inferred from the following propositions. First, it is apparent that external sense faculties are necessary for the perception of external objects of the world. Likewise, an internal sense faculty is required for the perception of internal objects, such as soul, cognition, feeling, pleasure, pain, and so on. The mind is this internal sense faculty. Second, it is apparent that the five external senses may all be in contact with their respective objects simultaneously, but not all of these perceptions are received at the same time. This demonstrates that there must be some other agent besides the external senses that both limits the number of received perceptions to one perception at a time and that orders the perceptions in sequential succession. In other words, although two or more external senses may be simultaneously receiving data, only that which is being attended to is actually perceived. Attention therefore represents the coordination of the mind with the senses, and every perception requires the contact of the mind with an object by means of the senses. We must, therefore, admit the existence of mind as an internal sense faculty. Additionally, if the mind were not a partless entity, then there would be simultaneous contact of many parts of the mind with many senses, and many perceptions would subsequently appear at one time. The fact that this never happens proves that the mind is a partless, atomic, and internal sense faculty of perception.

The Category of Quality—Twenty-four Guṇas

Guṇa, quality, the second of the seven categories of reality, cannot exist by itself but exists only in a substance.* It cannot, therefore, be the constituent or material cause of anything's existence. It may be considered a nonmaterial cause of things, however, because it determines the nature of a thing. It differs from both substance and action in that it is an unmoving property. There are twenty-four kinds of qualities: *rūpa* (color), *rasa* (taste), *gandha* (smell), *sparaśa* (touch), *śabda* (sound), *sāṃkhya* (number), *parimāṇa* (magnitude), *pṛthaktva* (distinctness), *saṃyoga* (conjunction or union), *bibhāga* (separation), *paratva* (remoteness), *aparatva* (nearness), *buddhi* (cognition), *sukha* (pleasure), *dukha* (pain), *icchā* (desire), *dveṣa* (aversion), *prayatna* (effort), *gurutva* (heaviness), *dravatva* (fluidity), *sneha* (viscidity), *saṃskāra* (tendency), *dharma* (merit or virtue), and *adharma* (demerit or nonvirtue). A brief description of these follows.

According to Vaiśeṣika there are six colors—white, black, red, blue, yellow, and green—and there are also six tastes—sweet, sour, bitter, pungent, astringent, and salty. Smell is divided into two categories—good and bad—and touch is divided into three—hot, cold, and neither hot nor cold. There are two kinds of sound: *dhvani* (inarticulated) and *varṇa* (articulated). Number is that quality by virtue of which a thing can be counted. Many numbers starting from one and stretching out beyond the imagination are used, but actually there is only one number which is used as many. Magnitude

*In Vaiśesika "guna" refers to quality, whereas in Sāmkhya this term is used to denote an essential nature of Prakṛti, the material cause of the universe.

is the quality by which things are distinguished as big or small. There are four orders of magnitude: extremely small (the atom), extremely big, small, and large.

Distinctness is the quality by which one knows that one thing is different from another. Conjunction, or union, is the quality by which one knows the existence of two or more things at one place or in one time, such as a book being on a table at noon. Disjunction, or disunion, is that quality by which a substance is perceived as being either remote or near in time or space. Older, younger, before, and after are temporal examples; far, near, here, and there are spatial examples.

Buddhi, a quality of the self, means "knowledge" or "cognition" in Vaiśeṣika and should not be confused with the concept of buddhi that is explained in Sāṃkhya philosophy as "intellect." Pleasure is a favorable experience of mind, and pain is an unfavorable experience of mind. Effort is the quality by virtue of which a substance is capable of changing its position. There are three kinds of effort: striving toward something (*pravṛtti*); striving against something (*nivṛtti*); and vital functioning (*jīvanayoni*). Heaviness is that quality by virtue of which a substance is capable of falling, while fluidity is the quality by virtue of which it flows. Viscidity is the quality—belonging exclusively to the element of water—by which different particles of matter can be absorbed and formed into particular shapes.

Saṃskāras are innate tendencies; they can be of anything, not just the mind. There are three kinds of saṃskāras in a substance: activity, which keeps a thing in motion (*vega*); elasticity, which makes a thing tend toward equilibrium when it is disturbed (*sthitisthāpakatva*); and mental impressions, which enable one to remember and recognize a thing (*bhāvanā*). This last category is exclusive to the mind. Dharma and adharma mean, respectively, that which is in accordance with conscience, and that which is not in accordance with conscience. Dharma leads to happiness, and adharma leads to pain and misery. The remaining five categories of reality are only briefly described.

The Category of Action—Karma

Karma, action, is viewed in the Vaiśeṣika school as being physical movement, but the term *physical* here refers to more than just bodily movements because in Vaiśeṣika mind is also considered to be a kind of substance. Just like quality, the second category of reality, action also exists only in a substance and cannot exist by itself. It is, however, completely different from both quality and substance. The substance of a thing supports both quality and action. Quality is the static character of things, and action is their dynamic character, which is regarded as the independent cause of their union and disunion. Action or movement is always dependent on substances—earth, water, fire, air, and mind. It is impossible to find action in the intangible substances—space, time, direction, and soul—because each is an all-pervading substance, whose position cannot be changed. There are five kinds of action: upward, downward, inward, outward, and linear. The action of perceptible substances like earth, water, fire, and air can be perceived by the five senses, but not all of the actions of tangible substances can be perceived. The movement of the Earth, for example, cannot be perceived; it can only be inferred.

The Category of Generality—Sāmānya

Generality, Sāmānya, refers to an abstract characteristic that is singular and eternal (*nitya*) and yet pervades many. For example, leadership is a single characteristic, but it resides in many individuals. Leadership is also eternal because it was already in existence before the first leader emerged, and it will continue to exist even if there are no more leaders. All the things of a certain class—such as men, or cows, or puppies, or horses—share a common name because of the common nature they possess. Sāmānya, generality, is the essence of the common characteristic that unites different entities into one class. Hence, modern scholars sometimes translate sāmānya as "universality."

Vaiśeṣika recognizes three levels of generality or universality: highest, lowest, and intermediate. The highest kind of generality is existence itself (*sattā*). Beingness or the state of being is the highest generality because all other universals are subsumed under it; it is all-pervading, and nothing is excluded from it. The lowest kind of generality has the most limited referents (such as American-ness, Indian-ness, pot-ness, and chair-ness, which are the generalities present in all Americans, Indians, pots, and chairs, respectively). Concepts such as substantiality (having the nature of substance) represent the intermediate level of generality because they do not include many other categories of reality like quality, action, and so on.

The Category of Uniqueness—Viśeṣa

Viśeṣa, or uniqueness, is that characteristic of a thing by virtue of which it is distinguished from all other things. Like the imperceptible substances of space, time, direction, soul, and mind, viśeṣa is abstract and is therefore eternal. Everything in the world, regardless of whether it is existent or nonexistent, is accompanied by uniqueness. Generality (sāmānya) and uniqueness (viśeṣa) are opposite concepts.

The Category of Inherence—Samavāya

There are two kinds of relationships between things: conjunction (*saṃyoga*), and inherence (*samavāya*). Conjunction is one of the twenty-four qualities (guṇas) of Vaiśeṣika, but inherence is one of the seven categories of reality described in this system. Conjunction is a temporary, noneternal relationship between two things that may be separated at any time. In this kind of relationship, two or more things exist together, but each remains essentially unaffected by the other(s). For example, when a chair and a table are conjoined together, this does not change the existence of the chair or table. Thus, conjunction is an external relationship existing as an accidental quality of the substances related to it. Inherence, on the other hand, is a permanent relation between two entities, one of which inheres in the other, as for example in the relation of the whole in its parts, a quality in its substance, or the universal in the individual. A conjunctional relation is temporary and is produced by the action of either or both of the things related to it. For example, the relation between a man and a chair on which he is sitting is temporary.

An inherent relation, in contrast, is not temporary and is not produced. The relation that exists between a whole and its parts, for instance, is not produced because the whole is always related to its parts. As long as the whole is not broken up, it must exist in the parts. Thus inherence is an eternal or permanent relation between two entities, one of which depends for its existence upon the other (the whole cannot exist separate from its parts). Two terms within an inherent relationship cannot be reversed, as can those that are related by conjunction. For example, in order for there to be a conjunctional relation of hand and pen, pen and hand must both be in some kind of contact with each other, but in an inherent relation this is not necessary. A quality or action is in a substance, but the substance is not in the quality or action; there is color in cloth, but no cloth in color; there is action in a fan but no fan in the action.

The Category of Nonexistence—Abhāva

Abhāva, nonexistence, the seventh and last category of reality is negative in contrast to the first six categories, which are positive. Nonexistence is not found in any of the six positive categories, and yet according to Vaiśeṣika philosophy nonexistence exists, just as, for instance, space and direction do. To illustrate: How does one know that there is no chair in a room? Looking into the room, one can feel as sure of the nonexistence of the chair as of the existence of the carpet or of the people. Therefore, nonexistence also exists as such.

There are two kinds of nonexistence: the absence of something in something else (*saṃsargābhāva*), and mutual nonexistence (*anyonyābhāva*). The absence of something in something else is of three kinds: antecedent nonexistence (*prāgbhāva*), the nonexistence of a thing after its destruction (*pradhvaṃsābhāva*), and absolute nonexistence (*atyantābhāva*). Antecedent nonexistence refers to the nonexistence of a thing prior to its creation. For example, in the sentence, "A book will be written using this paper," the book is nonexistent in the paper. This type of nonexistence does not have a beginning, but it does have an end. The book never existed before it was written; therefore, there is a beginningless nonexistence of the book. But when it does come to be written, its previous nonexistence will come to an end. In direct contrast to antecedent nonexistence, the nonexistence of a thing after its destruction has a beginning but does not have an end. For instance, when a jar is broken into pieces, then there is nonexistence of that jar. The nonexistence of the jar begins with its destruction, but this nonexistence cannot be ended in any way, because the same jar cannot be brought back into existence.

The type of nonexistence that does not belong to a particular time and space but is in all times is called absolute nonexistence. This type of nonexistence is neither subject to origin nor to end—it is both beginningless and endless. Examples are the nonexistence of the son of a barren couple or the nonexistence of color in the air.

Mutual nonexistence (anyonyābhāva), the second of the two major divisions of nonexistence, is the difference of one thing from another. When one thing is different from another, they mutually exclude each other, and there is the nonexistence of either as the other. For example, a pen is different from a book, so there is nonexistence of the book in the pen and of the pen in the book.

The Concept of the Creation and Annihilation of the World

Vaiśeṣika holds to the atomic theory of existence, according to which the entire universe is composed of eternal atoms. But at the same time, Vaiśeṣika does not ignore the moral and spiritual laws that govern the process of union and separation of atoms. In this way, the atomic theory of Vaiśeṣika is different from the atomic theory of modern science. Modern science's theory proposes a materialistic philosophy; it explains the laws of the universe as mechanical, as being the result of the motions of atoms in infinite time, space, and direction. According to this view, the operation of the atoms is governed by mechanical laws, but according to Vaiśeṣika the functioning of atoms is guided or directed by the creative or destructive will of the Supreme Being. The will of the Supreme Being directs the operation of atoms according to the past saṃskāras of individual beings.

Vaiśeṣika states that the universe has two aspects, one eternal and one noneternal. The eternal constituents of the universe are the four kinds of atoms (earth, water, fire, and air) and the five substances (space, time, direction, mind, and self). These are not subject to change, and they can be neither created nor destroyed. Another part of the universe is noneternal, that is, subject to creation and destruction in a particular time and space. In the beginning of creation two atoms are united into a dyad, which is noneternal because it can be divided again into two. The dyads and atoms cannot be perceived but are known through inference. The combination of three dyads is called a triad (*tryaṇuka*), which is the smallest perceptible object. It is from these triads that other larger compounds develop. Thus the common elements comprised of eternal atoms are noneternal because they can be broken down into smaller units.

The entire universe is a systematic arrangement of physical things and living beings that interact with one another in time, space, and direction. Living beings are the souls of the selves who enjoy or suffer in this world, depending on their meritorious or nonmeritorious past impressions. Thus, according to Vaiśeṣika philosophy, the world is a moral stage on which the life and destiny of all individual beings is governed, not only by the physical laws of time and space but also by the moral law of karma. In the performance of present karma, an individual is free and is thus the creator of his own destiny, but the starting and ending point of the universe depends on the creative or destructive will of the Supreme Being, God. The universal law (adṛṣṭa) of the process of creation and annihilation influences the individual selves to function or to be active in the direction of the creative will. Directed by this unknown force of adṛṣṭa, the soul makes contact with an atom of air; thus, the primeval motion comes into being. That primeval activity in air atoms creates dyads, triads, and all the rest of the gross physical manifestations of air elements (*mahābhūtas*). In a similar manner, there arises motion in the atoms of fire, water, and earth, which then compose the gross elements of fire, water, and earth. In this way the vast expansion of the physical world comes into existence.

The Supreme Lord is endowed with perfect wisdom, detachment, and excellence (*jñāna, vairāgya, and aiśvarya*). He releases the adṛṣṭa related to individual beings, which guides the individuals in their flow through the currents of life. At the end of life, the process of dissolution and annihilation also depends on the will of God. He inspires the adṛṣṭa corresponding to the individuals or to the universe, and then a destructive motion in the atoms of the body and senses or in the cosmos starts vibrating. On account of this destructive motion, there arises the process of disjunction and disintegration of the body and senses or of the universe. Compound things break down into simpler and simpler components, finally devolving into the state of triads and dyads and ultimately into atoms. In this manner the physical elements of earth, water, fire, and air, and the related sense organs, are disintegrated. After the dissolution of the manifest universe, there remain the four kinds of atoms of earth, water, fire, and air as well as the eternal substances of space, time, direction, mind, and soul, with their attendant meritorious and nonmeritorious saṃskāras.

Thus, according to the Vaiśeṣika system of philosophy, there is no creation or annihilation but rather an orderly and morally systematized composition and decomposition of compounds. An individual self or soul is involved in the universe because of adṛṣṭa. The karma of each soul is its own earnings, deposited in the safe of the Supreme Being, which come back to the self with interest. The Vaiśeṣika concepts of God, of the liberation of the soul, and of the path to liberation are all basically the same as the Nyāya concepts, which have already been discussed in the preceding chapter.

chapter

5

Sāṃkhya

A Dualistic Theory

Sāṃkhya philosophy, considered to be the most ancient of all the philosophical schools, was systematized by the great sage Kapila. All of Indian literature has been influenced by this philosophy. The first work of Sāṃkhya, the *Sāṃkhya Sūtra*, is traditionally attributed to Kapila, but in its present form it is not his original work. So the *Sāṃkhya-kārikā* of Īśvarakṛṣṇa is actually the earliest available Sāṃkhya text. Among its more well-known commentaries are Gauḍapāda's *Bhāṣya*, Vācaspati Miśra's *Tattva-kaumudī*, Vijñānabhikṣu's *Sāṃkhya Pravacanbhāṣya*, and Maṭhara's *Māṭharavṛtti*. Topics traditionally emphasized by Kapila, Īśvarakṛṣṇa, and other Sāṃkhya commentators are the theory of causation, the concept of *Prakṛti* (the unconscious principle) and *Puruṣa* (the conscious principle), the evolution of the world, the concept of liberation, and the theory of knowledge. The uniqueness of this system lies in its summing up of all of the categories of reality as described in Nyāya and Vaiśeṣika into two categories—Puruṣa and Prakṛti—and thereby introducing a dualistic philosophy.

The Theory of Cause and Effect

All Indian philosophies base their explanation of the evolution or manifestation of the universe on two fundamental theories of cause and effect: *satkāryavāda* and *asatkāryavāda*. According to *satkāryavāda*, the effect exists in its cause prior to its production or manifestation, but the *asatkāryavāda* theory maintains that the effect does not exist in its cause prior to manifestation. This latter theory is also called *ārambhavāda*, which means "the theory of the origin of the effect." All other theories related to cause and effect are based on one or the other of these two fundamental theories. Sāṃkhya philosophy accepts the *satkāryavāda* theory of causation, but there are actually two schools of thought concerning this theory. One, *vivartavāda*, is the view accepted by Advaita Vedāntins. It holds that the change of a cause into an effect is merely apparent. For example, when one sees a snake in a rope, it is not true that the rope is really transformed into a snake; it simply appears to be that way. This theory serves as the basis for this school's explanation of God, of the universe, and of the individual's place in the scheme of existence. Sāṃkhya philosophy does not accept this view but rather holds the view of *pariṇāmavāda*, according to which there is a real transformation of the cause into the effect, as in wood being transformed into a chair, or milk into yogurt.

Sāṃkhya philosophy developed elaborate explanations to establish the pariṇāmavāda theory of satkāryavāda that maintains that the cause changes into the effect. This explanation was established because all of the other Sāṃkhya concepts are based on the premise that the effect exists in its material cause even before the effect is produced. Sāṃkhya provides five proofs of this premise. The first proof, *asadakāraṇāt*, states that the effect exists in its material cause before its production because no one can produce an effect from a material cause in which that effect does not exist. For example, no one can turn the color blue into the color yellow, nor can anyone produce milk from a chair, because yellow does not exist in blue and a chair does not exist in milk. The second proof, *upādānagrahaṇāt*, states that because there is an invariable relationship between cause and effect, material cause can produce only that effect with which it is causally related. Only milk can produce a yogurt because milk alone is materially related to yogurt. If an effect does not exist in any way before its production, then it is impossible for an effect to be related to its cause. Therefore, an effect must already exist in its cause before it is produced. The third proof, *sarvasambhavābhāvāt*, states that there is a fixed rule for the production or manifestation of things. A certain thing can be produced only by a certain other thing; it cannot be produced from just anything or anywhere. This impossibility proves that all the effects exist within their particular causes. The fourth proof, *śaktasya-śakya-kāraṇāt*, states that an effect exists in its cause in an unmanifested form before it is produced. This is the case because only a potent cause can produce a desired effect, and the effect must therefore be potentially contained in the cause. The potentiality of cause cannot, however, be related to an effect if the effect does not exist in that particular cause in some form. The fifth proof, *kāraṇabhāvāt*, states that if the effect does not exist in the cause, then that which was non-existent would be coming into existence out of nothing. This is as absurd as saying that the son of a barren woman once built an empire, or that people decorate their homes with flowers of the sky. Such statements have no logical correspondence to reality.

By means of these arguments, the Sāṃkhya philosophers established the theory of *pariṇāmavāda* or manifestation, according to which an effect is already existent in unmanifested form in its cause. The process of producing an effect from the cause or the process of manifestation and annihilation can be clarified with the analogy of the tortoise, which extends its limbs from its shell. The tortoise does not create its limbs; it merely brings that which was hidden into view. Sāṃkhya philosophers hold that, similarly, no one can convert nonexistence into existence; nor can that which exists be entirely destroyed. A tortoise is not different from its limbs, which are subject to appearance or disappearance, just as golden ornaments such as rings and earrings are not different from the gold used to make them. The theory of manifestation is essential to Sāṃkhya philosophy and indeed serves as the basic foundation upon which all its other theories are constructed.

Prakṛti—The Unconscious Principle

The Sāṃkhya system holds that the entire world—including the body, mind, and senses—is dependent upon, limited by, and produced by the combination of certain effects. Various other schools of philosophy—such as Cārvāka, Buddhism, Jainism, Nyāya, and Vaiśeṣika—maintain that atoms of earth, water, fire, and air are the material causes of the world, but according to the Sāṃkhya system, material atoms cannot produce the subtler products of nature, such as mind, intellect, and ego. Therefore, one has to seek elsewhere for that cause from which gross objects and their subtler aspects are derived. If one examines nature, it becomes obvious that a cause is subtler than its associated effect and that a cause pervades its effect. For example, when a seed develops into a tree, whatever latent quality the seed contains will be found in the tree. The ultimate cause of the world must also be a latent principle of potential, and it must be uncaused, eternal, and all-pervading. It must be more subtle than the mind and intellect, and at the same time it must contain all the characteristics of the external objects as well as of the senses, mind, and intellect.

In Sāṃkhya philosophy this ultimate cause is called *Prakṛti.* To prove its existence, Sāṃkhya offers the following five arguments. First, it is accepted that all the objects of the world are limited and dependent on something else, so there must be an unlimited and independent cause for their existence. That cause is Prakṛti. Second, all the objects of the world possess a common characteristic: they are capable of producing pleasure, pain, or indifference. Therefore, something must exist as the cause of the universe that possesses the characteristics of pleasure, pain, and indifference. That is Prakṛti. Third, all the objects of the world have a potential to produce something else or to convert themselves into something else. Therefore, their cause must also have the same potential, which implicitly contains the entire universe. That is Prakṛti. Fourth, in the process of evolution an effect arises from its cause, and in dissolution it is reabsorbed or dissolved into its origin. The particular objects of experience must therefore arise from a certain cause, which must in turn have arisen from a certain cause, and so on until one reaches the primal cause of the creative process itself. A similar process takes place in involution or annihilation. Here, physical elements are broken down into atoms, atoms are dissolved into gross energies, and gross energies into finer ones until all of these dissolve into the unmanifested One. That unmanifested One is called Prakṛti—the primordial nature. Fifth, if one attempts to go further and imagine the cause of this ultimate cause, he will land himself in the fallacy of infinite regression. Ultimately one has to stop somewhere and identify a cause as the first cause of the universe. In Sāṃkhya philosophy that supreme root cause of the world is called Prakrti.

The Guṇas

Prakṛti is neither atomic substance nor consciousness, but it possesses the three *guṇas* of *sattva*, *rajas*, and *tamas*. Sometimes the *guṇas* are translated as "the qualities or attributes of Prakṛti," but this is not quite the case. They are, rather, the intrinsic nature of Prakṛti. The balanced combination of sattva, rajas, and tamas is Prakṛti, and thus they cannot be Prakṛti's attributes or qualities. They are called *guṇas* (that is, "ropes") because they are intertwined like three strands of a rope that bind the soul to the world. One can say that a rope is the name for three intertwined strands, but if one analyzes the strands separately, he does not see the rope. In a similar way, if he analyzes the guṇas separately, one will not apprehend Prakṛti, since it is a balanced state of the three guṇas. This analogy should be used discriminately, however, because the rope and its strands are grossly manifested material objects, while the guṇas and Prakṛti are completely unmanifested and beyond the grasp of perception.

According to Sāṃkhya philosophy, sattva, rajas, and tamas are the root causes from which the entire universe is derived. These guṇas cannot be perceived but can only be inferred. All objects of the world—external and internal, both the physical elements and the mind—are found to possess the capability of producing pleasure, pain, or indifference. The same object may be pleasurable to some person, painful to another, and of no concern to a third. For example, the same beautiful girl is very pleasant to her boyfriend (sattva guṇa), painful to her girlfriend who also has a crush on the same boy (rajas guṇa), and of no concern to many others not involved (a balanced state of the guṇas). From this example, one can see that the cause of all phenomena, Prakṛti, contains all the characteristics found in worldly objects.

Sāṃkhya philosophy posits that the whole universe is evolved from the guṇas. The state in which they are in their natural equilibrium is called *Prakṛti*, and when their balance is disturbed, they are said to be in *Vikṛti*, the heterogeneous state. These three guṇas are said to be the ultimate cause of all creation. Sattva is weightlessness and light (*laghu*); rajas is motion or activity (*calam*); and tamas is heaviness, darkness, inertia, or concealment (*guru* and *āvaraṇa*). The guṇas are formless and omnipresent when in a state of equilibrium, having completely given up their specific characteristics when thus submerged in each other. In a state of imbalance, however, rajas is said to be in the center of sattva and tamas, and this results in creation because manifestation in itself is an action. Action depends on motion, the force of activity that is the very nature of rajas, and so sattva and tamas are dependent on rajas to manifest themselves and thus produce pairs of opposites. Rajas also depends on sattva and tamas, however, because activity cannot be accomplished without the object or medium through which it becomes activated. In the state of manifestation, one guṇa dominates the other two, but they are never completely apart from each other or completely absent because they are continually reacting with one another. By the force of rajas, sattvic energy evolves with great speed, and its unitary energy becomes divided into numerous parts. At a certain stage, however, their velocity decreases, and they start to come closer and closer together. With this contraction in sattvic energy, tamas is naturally manifested, but at the same time another push of the active force (rajas) occurs also on tamas, and within the contraction a quick expansion occurs. Thus do the guṇas constantly change their predominance over one another. The predomination of sattva over tamas and of tamas over sattva is always simultaneously in process; the conversion of each of them into one another is taking place at every moment. However, this transformation is felt only when it reaches its extreme by becoming manifest in a gross visible state.

Sattva and tamas have the appearance of being in opposition to each other because one is light and weightless and the other is dark and heavy. But these pairs actually cooperate in the process of manifestation and dissolution as things move from subtle to gross and from gross to subtle. The expansion of power stores up energy in some relatively subtle form, from which it manifests to form a new equilibrium. These points of relative equilibrium constitute certain stages in the evolutionary process. It might at first seem that there is constant conflict among the guṇas, but this is not the case. They are in perfect cooperation during the process of manifestation because it is through their constant interaction that the flow of cosmic and individual life continues. They are essentially different from but interrelated with one another. Just as the oil, wick, and flame of a lamp work together to produce light, so the different guṇas cooperate to produce the objects of the world. The guṇas play the same role in one's body and mind as they do in the universe as a whole. An individual's physical appearance is simply a manifestation of the guṇas that has been brought about by consciousness. This intention of consciousness to cause Prakṛti to manifest disturbs the state of equilibrium in Prakṛti, thus causing the guṇas to interact and manifest the universe.

In individual life, rajas can be used to convert tamas into sattva or it can be used to convert sattva into tamas. In this way one has the capacity to generate more sattva in one's life, and with the help of sattva one can attain the state of meditation. One can also use rajas to generate more tamas and thereby enter into the downward flow of inertia. Rajas can also be thought of as a destructive force because it creates overactivity and leads the body to restlessness and the mind to fluctuations that take it away from peace. One should therefore try not to be overpowered by rajas. But, on the other hand, the diminution of rajas can also adversely weaken the functions of sattva and tamas or create imbalance among them. Rajas is very powerful and would ideally be present in each person in the proper balance to provide the required life force, but if one has altered one's life unnaturally through drugs, mental worries, and so on, then rajas becomes unbalanced. To bring rajas into balance, Sāṃkhya recommends emphasizing sattvic actions and thoughts. Sāṃkhya philosophy never advises one to fight with or destroy any of the guṇas, but instead encourages a lifestyle by which one can verify that the nature of sattvic energy is lightness, happiness, knowledge, and peace—even though real peace, happiness, and knowledge have no permanent existence in sattva. It is because of its purity and lightness that sattva is able to reflect peace and happiness from pure consciousness. Thus peace and happiness are perceived in the sattva-predominated state of mind, and the mind experiences peace and happiness as its object.

The most intrinsic quality of the guṇas is their constant changeability; they are always changing or transforming into one another. This occurs in two ways: *virūpapariṇāma*, "change into a heterogeneous state," and *svarūpapariṇāma*, "change into a homogeneous state." Virūpapariṇāma, the first kind of transformation, takes place when one of the guṇas dominates the other two and begins the process of manifestation of a particular object. This type of transformation or interaction of the guṇas with each other is responsible for the manifestation of the world. Svarūpapariṇāma, the other kind of transformation of the guṇas, refers to that state in which the guṇas change internally without disturbing each other. In this state, the guṇas cannot produce anything because they neither oppose nor cooperate with one another. This type of change occurs in the balanced state of Prakṛti. In describing the process of involution, Sāṃkhya states that all gross elements dissolve into subtle elements and finally they all dissolve into their origin—sattva, rajas and tamas. Ultimately these three guṇas also come to a state of perfect balance called Prakṛti. Then there remains no weight of tamas, no weightlessness of sattva, and no activity of rajas because the guṇas no longer have a separate existence in the sense of predominance of any single attribute. This state—Prakṛti—cannot be perceived by one's ordinary perception; it can only be inferred. One can only imagine a state in which all of nature is balanced and there is no levity, no motion, no heaviness; no light, no darkness, no opposing forces; in which the imagination itself, being a product of the mind, is dissolved. Sāṃkhya philosophers describe this state as uncaused, unmanifested, eternal, all-pervading, devoid of effect-producing actions, without a second, independent, and partless.

Puruṣa—Consciousness

As was previously stated, Sāṃkhya is a dualistic philosophy that acknowledges two aspects of reality: the unconscious principle (Prakṛti) and consciousness (Puruṣa or the Self). Each body contains a Self, but the Self is different from the body, senses, mind, and intellect. It is a conscious spirit, at once both the subject of knowledge and the object of knowledge. It is not merely a substance with the attribute of consciousness, but it is rather pure consciousness itself—a self-illumined, unchanging, uncaused, all-pervading, eternal reality. Whatever is produced or is subject to change, death, and decay belongs to Prakṛti or its evolutes, not to the Self. It is ignorance to think of the Self as body, senses, mind, or intellect, and it is through such ignorance that Puruṣa confuses itself with the objects of the world. Then it becomes caught up in the everflowing stream of changes and feels itself to be subject to pain and pleasure.

Sāṃkhya offers five arguments to prove the existence of Puruṣa. First, all the objects of the world are meant to be utilized by and for someone other than themselves. All things that exist serve simply as the means for the ends of other beings. (A chair is not made for the chair itself, nor is a house made for the house itself.) Therefore, there must be something quite different and distinct from such objects. Objects cannot enjoy their own existence, nor can one material object be utilized and enjoyed by another material object; therefore, there must be some other enjoyer of the objects. That enjoyer who utilizes the objects of the world is consciousness, Puruṣa.

Second, it cannot be said that all objects are meant for Prakṛti because Prakṛti is unconscious and is the material cause of all objects. It is the balance of the guṇas, of which all the objects of the world are composed. Prakṛti is thus the potential or essence of all pain, pleasure, and neutral states and cannot therefore be the enjoyer of itself, just as even the smartest of men cannot sit on his own shoulders. The proprietor or utilizer of all worldly objects must consequently be a conscious being who does not possess the three guṇas and who is completely different from them in both their balanced and heterogeneous states. That transcendent Reality is Puruṣa.

Third, all the objects of the external world—including the mind, senses, and intellect—are in themselves unconscious. They cannot function without guidance from some intelligent principle, and they must be controlled and directed by it in order to achieve anything or realize any end. That conscious Self who guides the operation of Prakṛti and its manifestations is Puruṣa. Fourth, nonintelligent Prakṛti and all its evolutes, which are by nature pleasurable, painful, or neutral, have no meaning if they are not experienced by some intelligent force. That experiencer is Puruṣa.

Fifth, every human being wants to attain liberation and be free from pain and misery, but whatever is derived from Prakṛti brings pain and misery. If there is nothing different from Prakṛti and its evolutes, then how is liberation attainable? If there were only Prakṛti, then the concept of liberation and the will to liberate or to be liberated, which is found in all human beings, in the sayings of sages, and in the scriptures, would be meaningless. Therefore, there must be some conscious principle that strives for liberation. That principle is the Self, Puruṣa.

Proof of the Existence of Many Selves

According to Sāṃkhya, there are many selves or conscious principles—one in each living being. If there were only one self related to all bodies, then when one individual died, all individuals would simultaneously die, but this is not the case. The birth or death of one individual does not cause all other individuals to be born or to die; blindness or deafness in one man does not imply the same for all men. If there were only one self pervading all beings, then if one person were active, all the selves would be active; if one were sleeping, then all would sleep. But this does not happen, and there is therefore not one self but many selves. Secondly, human beings are different from God and from animal and vegetable life as well. But this distinction could not be true if God, human beings, animals, birds, insects, and plants all possessed the same self. Therefore there must be a plurality of selves that are eternal and intelligent. Thus it becomes clear that there are two realities: Prakṛti, the one all-pervading (unconscious) material cause of the universe, and Puruṣa, the many pure conscious intelligent entities who are not subject to change. It is from the interaction of these two principles that evolution occurs.

The Process of the Evolution of the Universe

According to Sāṃkhya, the entire world evolves from the interaction of Prakṛti with Puruṣa. This interaction does not refer to any kind of orderly conjunction, as in the contact of two finite male and female material substances. It is rather a sort of effective relationship through which Prakṛti is influenced by the mere presence of Puruṣa, just as sometimes one's body is influenced or moved by the presence of a thought. Evolution cannot occur by the Self (Puruṣa) alone because the Self is inactive; nor can it be initiated only by Prakṛti because Prakṛti is not conscious. The activity of Prakṛti must be guided by the intelligence of Puruṣa; this cooperation between them is essential to the evolution of the universe.

Given this, two questions yet arise: how can two such different and opposing principles cooperate, and what is the interest that inspires them to interact with one another? Sāṃkhya replies that just as a blind man and a lame man can cooperate with each other in order to get out of a forest—by the lame man's guiding while the blind man carries him—so do nonintelligent Prakṛti and inactive Puruṣa combine with each other and cooperate to serve their purpose. What is their purpose? Prakṛti requires the presence of Puruṣa in order to be known or appreciated, and Puruṣa requires the help of Prakṛti in order to distinguish itself from Prakṛti and thereby realize liberation. Thus, according to Sāṃkhya philosophy, the goal of the manifestation of the universe is to attain liberation. Through the interaction of Puruṣa and Prakṛti, a great disturbance arises in the equilibrium in which the guṇas are held prior to manifestation. In this process, rajas, the active force, first becomes irritated, and through this, the two other guṇas begin to vibrate. This primeval vibration releases a tremendous energy within Prakṛti, and the "dance" of these three energies becomes more and more dense, thus manifesting the universe in various grades and degrees. The process of manifestation originates from the unmanifested unity and completes its cycle in twenty-four stages.

The process of manifestation begins with the infusion of Puruṣa (consciousness) into Prakṛti (the material cause of the universe). Metaphorically it is said that Prakṛti is the mother principle, and Puruṣa is the father principle. The mother is fertilized by the father; Prakṛti is the soil in which consciousness can take root. Thus Prakṛti, the material cause of all existence, embodies consciousness.

Mahat or Buddhi

The first evolute of Prakṛti is *mahat* or *buddhi*, the intellect. This is the great seed of the vast universe—therefore the name, *mahat*, which means "great one." This is the state of union of Puruṣa and Prakṛti. Though Prakṛti is unconscious material substance, it seems to be conscious and realizes itself as conscious because of the presence of the conscious Self. Mahat is the state in which Prakṛti receives light from Puruṣa, the fountain of light, and sees itself; and this process of seeing is the beginning of the manifestation of the universe. The individual counterpart of this cosmic state, mahat, is called *buddhi*, the intellect, the finest aspect of a human being that has the capacity to know the entire personality in its full purity. Buddhi is the immediate effect of Prakṛti resulting from the guidance of Puruṣa; therefore buddhi is the evolute closest to Puruṣa. Buddhi is manifested from the sattvic aspect of Prakṛti because the nature of sattva—weightlessness, clarity, and light—is affected sooner by the active force of manifestation than would be the heavy and unclear nature of tamas. Because of the sattvic quality of buddhi, the light of the Self reflects in the intellect similarly to the way an external object reflects in the clear surface of a mirror. The Self, seeing its reflection in the mirror of buddhi, identifies itself with the reflected image and forgets its true nature. Thus the feeling of "I-ness" is transmitted to buddhi. In this way the unconscious buddhi starts functioning as a conscious principle.

According to the Sāṃkhya system, buddhi possesses the following eight qualities: virtue (*dharma*); knowledge (*jñāna*); detachment (*vairāgya*); excellence (*aiśvarya*); nonvirtue (*adharma*); ignorance (*ajñāna*); attachment (*avairāgya*); and imperfection or incompetency (*anaiśvarya*). The first four are sattvic forms of buddhi, while the last four are overpowered by inertia (tamas). All of its attributes except knowledge bind Prakṛti and involve the Self in buddhi, thereby entangling it in worldly concerns and miseries. The pure Self falsely identifies with buddhi and thereby thinks it is experiencing what buddhi is experiencing. But through the use of the buddhi's eighth attribute, knowledge, it reflects pure and well-filtered knowledge onto Puruṣa from its mirror, and Puruṣa comes to realize its false identification with buddhi's objects and to recognize its transcendent nature in all its purity. Thus buddhi, the discriminating or decision-making function, stands nearest to the Self and functions directly for the Self, enabling it to discriminate between itself and Prakṛti and thereby achieve realization of its liberated nature.

Ahaṅkāra: The Sense of "I"

Ahaṅkāra is a derivative of mahat or buddhi; it is the property of individuation that generates a boundary of "I-ness." It is often translated as "ego," but this is very confusing because "ego" is used in a variety of ways in modern psychology and colloquial language. Generally it is associated with concepts, such as "ego trip" and "egotistical", that refer to an exaggerated sense of self-importance. Ahaṅkāra is a broader concept than this; it refers to the sense of "I" that separates one's own self from all others and creates an individual entity. This wall that separates "I" from "not I" leads a person to think, "I am; this is mine, and this is for me." There are three categories of ahaṅkāra—*sāttvika*, *rājasa* and *tāmasa*—determined by which of the three guṇas is predominant in ahaṅkāra. Eleven senses arise from the sāttvika ahaṅkāra: the five senses of perception (hearing, touching, seeing, tasting, and smelling), the five senses of action (verbalization, apprehension, locomotion, excretion, and procreation), and the mind (*manas*). The five *tanmātras* or subtle elements (sound, touch, color, taste, and smell) are derived from the tāmasa ahaṅkāra. The function of the rājasa ahaṅkāra is to motivate the other two guṇas, and thus it is the cause of both aspects of creation: the eleven senses and the five tanmātras.

This explanation of the manifestation of ahaṅkāra is based on the *Sāṃkhya-kārikā*, the major text of Sāṃkhya philosophy (see chart on page 138). The commentators of this text hold various views. Some state that the mind is the only sense derived from the sāttvika ahaṅkāra, that the other ten senses are derived from the rājasa ahaṅkāra, and that the five subtle elements are derived from the tāmasa ahaṅkāra. Irrespective of the origin of the senses, all the scholars view the nostrils, tongue, eyes, skin, and ears as the physical organs that are the sheaths of the cognitive senses. Likewise, the mouth, arms, legs, and the organs of excretion and reproduction correspond to the five senses of action—verbalization, apprehension, locomotion, excretion, and procreation. These physical organs are not the senses; rather, they are given power by the senses. Thus the senses cannot be perceived but can only be inferred from the actions of the physical organs powered by them. The mind, the ego, and the intellect are called the internal senses, while the five cognitive senses and five senses of action are called external. The mind is master of all the external senses, and without its direction and guidance, they could not function. The mind is a very subtle sense indeed, but it also has many aspects, and it therefore comes into contact with several senses at the same time. According to Sāṃkhya philosophy, the mind is neither atomic nor eternal, but it is rather a product of Prakṛti and is therefore subject to origin and dissolution. The cognitive senses contact their objects and supply their experiences to the mind, which then interprets the data into determinate perceptions. Ahaṅkāra then claims the objects of the world, identifying itself with the desirable ones while disidentifying with the undesirable ones, and finally the intellect decides whether to pursue or to avoid those external objects.

The five *tanmātras* of sound, touch, color, taste, and smell are the subtle counterparts to the gross elements; they can be inferred but not perceived. They evolve after the ten senses have come into being and they are the cause of the five gross elements, which are derived in a gradual step-by-step process. First to evolve is the tanmātra that is the essence of sound (*śabda*), from which in turn ether (*ākāśa*), the space element, is derived. Therefore, the space element contains the quality of sound, which is perceived by the ear. The air element is the derivation of the essence of touch (*sparśa* tanmātra), which combines with that of sound. Therefore, the air element contains the attributes of sound and touch, although touch is the special quality of air and is sensed by the skin. The fire element is derived from the essence of color (*rūpa* tanmātra). It combines the qualities of sound, touch, and color, and its special property is sight, which is sensed by the eyes. The water element is derived from the essence of taste (*rasa* tanmātra). All three preceding qualities—sound, touch, and color—are found in it, as well as its special quality, taste, which is sensed by the tongue. The essence of smell (*gandha* tanmātra) produces the earth element, whose special property is odor, which is sensed by the nostrils. This grossest element contains all of the four previous qualities.

Thus the course of evolution takes place in twenty-four stages (see chart on page 138). It starts from the root cause, Prakṛti, and it ends with the earth element, the grossest manifestation. This process is broken down into two major categories: the development of Prakṛti as buddhi, ahaṅkāra, and the eleven senses, and the evolution of the five subtle elements and five gross elements.

The first category is divided again into two parts: the internal senses (*antaḥkaraṇa*) and the external senses (*bāhyakaraṇa*), which are the five cognitive and five active senses, respectively. The second category is also divided into two main parts: nonspecific qualities (*aviśeṣa*) and specific qualities (*viśeṣa*). The five tanmātras, or subtle elements, are said to be nonspecific because they cannot be perceived and enjoyed by ordinary beings. But the five gross elements are said to be specific because they possess specific characteristics of being pleasurable, painful, or stupefying. These specific manifestations can be categorized into two major parts: the external gross elements, and the three bodies—physical, subtle, and causal.

The Sources of Valid Knowledge

Sāṃkhya philosophy accepts only three independent sources of valid knowledge: perception, inference, and testimony. Included within these three are other sources of knowledge such as comparison, postulation, and noncognition, which are therefore not recognized as separate sources of knowledge. According to Sāṃkhya, there are three factors present in all valid knowledge: *pramātā*, the subject; *prameya*, the object; and *pramāṇa*, the medium. Pramātā is a conscious principle that receives and recognizes knowledge. It is none other than the Self, pure Consciousness. Prameya is the object of knowledge that is presented to the Self. Pramāṇa is the modification of the intellect through which the Self comes to know an object; thus it is the source or the medium of knowledge. Valid knowledge is therefore the reflection of the Self in the intellect, which is modified into the form of an object.

Sāṃkhya's Twenty-three Evolutes of Prakṛti

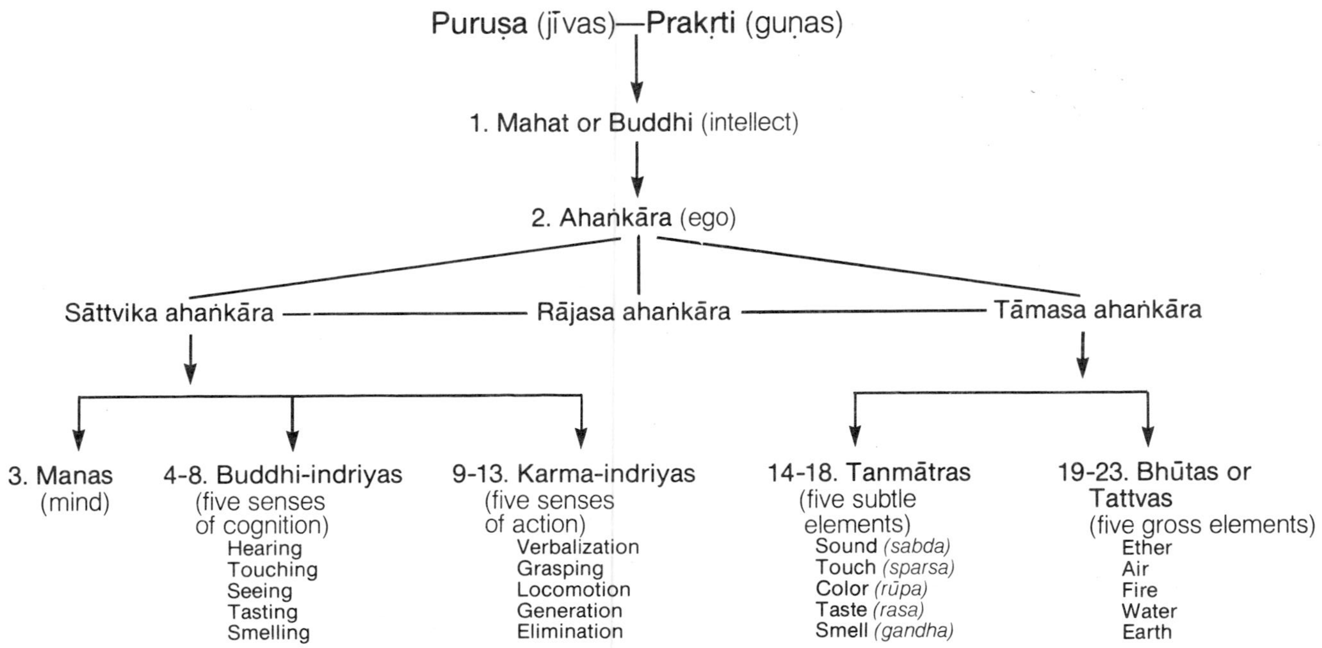
Puruṣa (jīvas)—Prakṛti (guṇas)
1. Mahat or Buddhi (intellect)
2. Ahaṅkāra (ego)
Sāttvika ahaṅkāra
Rājasa ahaṅkāra
Tāmasa ahaṅkāra
3. Manas (mind)
4-8. Buddhi-indriyas (five senses of cognition)
Hearing
Touching
Seeing
Tasting
Smelling
9-13. Karma-indriyas (five senses of action)
Verbalization
Grasping
Locomotion
Generation
Elimination
14-18. Tanmātras (five subtle elements)
Sound (sabda)
Touch (sparsa)
Color (rūpa)
Taste (rasa)
Smell (gandha)
19-23. Bhūtas or Tattvas (five gross elements)
Ether
Air
Fire
Water
Earth

Perception

The Sāṃkhya concept of perception (*pratyakṣa*) as a source of valid knowledge is different from those posited by other systems of Indian philosophy. In Sāṃkhya, valid knowledge means a definite and unerring cognition that is illuminated or made known by the Self through its reflected light in buddhi. The mind, intellect, and senses are unconscious material entities and therefore cannot perceive or experience any object. For perception or experience, consciousness is needed, and consciousness belongs only to the Self. But the Self cannot directly apprehend the objects of the world because the Self is *niṣkriya*, meaning "motionless" or "actionless," and without motion or activity, apprehension is not possible. If consciousness alone could apprehend the objects of the world, then, because the Self is infinite and ever-present, one would know all the objects of the world. But this is not the case. The Self knows objects only through the mind, intellect, and senses. True knowledge of an external object is attained when the impression of the object is perceived through the senses and recorded in the intellect, which then reflects the light of consciousness onto those objects.

Perception is the direct cognition of an object through the contact of the senses. When an object, such as a chair, comes within the range of vision, there is contact between the chair and the eyes. The impression of the chair is produced in the eyes, and that impression is then analyzed and synthesized by the mind. Through the activity of the mind, the intellect then becomes modified and transformed into the form of the chair. The predominance of sattva in the intellect enables it to reflect the modification of the chair in the Self. It is then reflected back to the intellect. Thus the unconscious intellect, which is modified by the object chair, becomes illumined into a conscious state in which perception is possible. Just as a mirror reflects the light of a lamp and therefore illuminates other objects, so the intellect, an unconscious principle, reflects the consciousness of the Self and recognizes objects.

Two major proponents of the Sāṃkhya theory of reflectionism—Vijñānabhikṣu and Vācaspati Miśra—hold differing views. According to Vijñānabhikṣu, the knowledge of an object takes place when there is a reciprocal reflection of the Self in the intellect (the intellect having been modified into the form of the object) and of the intellect in the Self. The senses contact the object and supply the impression of it to the mind, which transmits this impression to the intellect. The intellect then becomes modified by the object, but because the intellect is unconscious substance, it cannot analyze the experience of the object by itself. Its predominance by sattva guṇa, however, enables the intellect to be reflected in the Self, and the Self is in turn also reflected in the mirror of the intellect, which contains the modification of the object. In this way, the intellect then experiences the object. This theory of reflectionism is also accepted by Vyāsa in his commentary on the Yoga Sūtras.

According to the second view, held by Vācaspati Miśra, perception is a process of one-sided reflection: There is a reflection of the Self in the intellect, but there is no reflection of the intellect back into the Self. He maintains that an object comes into contact with the senses, that its impression reaches the mind, that it is transmitted to the intellect, and that the intellect then becomes modified into the form of that object. It is at this stage that the ever-radiating light of the Self illuminates the clean sattvic mirror of the intellect, which reflects the same light onto the object. The intellect then experiences the object as if the intellect were a conscious being. The intellect is just like a mirror that reflects the light of a lamp and itself becomes capable of illuminating other objects as well. This means that the intellect, but not the Self, experiences the pain, pleasure, or neutrality of worldly objects, while according to Vijñānabhikṣu, the pleasure, pain, and indifference are experienced by the Self because the Self and the intellect are reflecting each other.

Both of these views are possible within the major theory of reflectionism because the Self's experience of external objects, or pain and pleasure, depends on the intensity of its identification with the intellect. One-sided reflection and reciprocal reflection are both valid views because whatever comes to the intellect is experienced by the Self. A self-created state of oneness between the Self and the intellect exists, but if the identification is loosened a bit, then the consciousness radiating from the Self allows the intellect to appear as though it were conscious, and thus the intellect experiences the external object. The more the identification is loosened, the more the intellect experiences, and the more the Self watches the experiencing intellect as a witness.

Sāṃkhya recognizes two kinds of perception: indeterminate and determinate. The first is called *ālocana*, which means "merely seeing the object." It arises at the moment of contact between the senses and the object and is antecedent to all mental analyses and syntheses of sensory data. In this state there is recognition of the object as a mere "something" without any recognition of it as a specific object. Determinate perception, in contrast, is the result of the analysis, synthesis, and interpretation of sensory data by the mind. This type of perception is called *vivecana*, meaning "interpretation of the object," because it is the determinate cognition of an object as a particular identifiable thing.

Inference

Knowledge derived through the universal or invariable relationship between two things is called *anumāna* (inference). The Sāṃkhya concept of inference is slightly different from that held by Nyāya philosophy. In Sāṃkhya, inference is of two kinds: *vīta* and *avīta*. Vīta is based on a universal affirmative proposition and avīta is based on a universal negative proposition. Vīta, positive inference, is of two types: *pūrvavat* and *sāmānyatodṛṣṭa*. Pūrvavat inference is based on previously observed uniform concomitance between two things. For example, one can infer the existence of fire from the existence of smoke because one has already observed that smoke is always accompanied by fire. *Sāmānyatodṛṣṭa* inference is not based on any previously observed concomitance between the middle and major terms (see pages 83 ff. in the Nyāya chapter for an explanation of the terms of inference). This type of inference does, however, require facts that are uniformly related to the middle and major terms. For example, how can we know that we have senses? One cannot perceive his senses because they are beyond their own reach, so one must accept the existence of the senses by inference. Their existence can be inferred in the following way: for all action, some kind of instrument is needed; seeing, hearing, smelling, tasting, and touching are actions that must have their corresponding instruments; the senses are these instruments.

Negative inference, avīta, is explained in the Nyāya system (see page 88) as *śeṣavat*, in which an inference results by the elimination of all other possible alternatives. For example, a certain whole number is inferred to be two because it has been determined that it is not three or more, nor is it one or less. Yet it is a certain positive integer; therefore, it is two.

Testimony

Testimony (*śabda*) is the third source of valid knowledge. Sāṃkhya holds the same view of śabda as Nyāya, and so the reader is referred to the discussion of this subject in the chapter on Nyāya (see page 91).

The Concept of Liberation

According to Sāṃkhya philosophy, the universe is full of pain and misery, and even what is thought of as pleasure is mingled with sorrow because all pleasures ultimately end in disappointment, which is the basis of misery. It is the natural inclination of all living beings to rid themselves of pain and misery, but Sāṃkhya states that this can be achieved only through the correct discriminative knowledge of reality.

The entire external world and all internal phenomena belong to Prakṛti, but pure consciousness, Puruṣa, is free from the limitations of space, time, and causation. All activity, change, thought, feeling, pain, and pleasure belong to the body/mind organism, not to the Self. The Self is pure ever-illumined consciousness that transcends the entire phenomenal world, including the body/mind complex. The Self has a body, but the body is not the Self. In the same way, the Self has a mind, ego, and intellect, but it is quite distinct from all of these. Pleasure and pain, virtue and vice, merit and demerit do not color the pure Self; they color the intellect as it becomes involved with its surroundings. All the experiences of the phenomenal world are received by Puruṣa because of its false identification with the mind, intellect, and ego. The intellect is responsible for all experiences, but whenever Puruṣa ignorantly identifies itself with the intellect, it thinks it experiences as the intellect does, even though Puruṣa is actually always and forever beyond the evolutes of Prakṛti.

The manifestation of the universe into the twenty-three evolutes of Prakṛti is not meant to create bondage for Puruṣa but rather to help Puruṣa realize that it is free and distinct from Prakṛti. Although it may seem that external objects are meant for physical, mental, or internal enjoyment, that is not really the case because the mind, ego, and intellect do not function for themselves; they exist to provide experiences to Puruṣa. Feelings of pain and misery are experienced because Puruṣa falsely identifies with rajas and tamas and forgets its capacity to see through its false identification. Thus, also, Puruṣa fails to use Prakṛti's sattvic manifestations as efficient instruments for discriminating the Self from the non-Self. The predominance of rajas and tamas in the mind, ego, and intellect does not allow these instruments to filter external experiences properly, so Puruṣa receives unfiltered, contaminated experiences and ignorantly thinks it is suffering the pain and misery reflected by the intellect.

Sāṃkhya views Prakṛti as a compassionate mother that provides everything to Puruṣa that he* needs to understand his true nature distinct from Prakṛti in her manifested and unmanifested states. Prakṛti manifests herself out of compassion for Puruṣa, just as a mother's milk is produced out of compassion for her child. Unless it is somehow contaminated, the milk from the mother's breast is always healthful to the child, and likewise the evolutes of Prakṛti are healthful to Puruṣa unless they are contaminated by the predominance of rajas and tamas, false identification, selfish action, possessiveness, or lack of discrimination.

Both Prakṛti and Puruṣa are infinite and eternal, and when Prakṛti is in her unmanifested state, she is so intermingled with Puruṣa that he becomes anxious to realize his own true nature. Puruṣa's anxiety allows him to come even closer to Prakṛti, and it is this move or intention toward her that inspires the latent forces in Prakṛti to function. Thus Puruṣa initiates the manifestation of the universe, and thus Prakṛti helps Puruṣa realize himself as distinct from her. But when through ignorance Puruṣa forgets his purpose in coming closer to Prakṛti, then instead of discriminating himself from the unconscious principle, he entangles himself with it. The moment he remembers his purpose and discriminates himself from this manifest world and from its cause, he realizes his true nature and recognizes his freedom.

Just as a chef continues cooking until the food is cooked and stops the moment it is ready, so Puruṣa continues to flow in the current of life until his purpose is fulfilled. The moment the highest goal of life—realization—is attained, he stops flowing in that current. Likewise, a dancer performing to entertain her audience

*Here for the sake of convenience the pronouns *he* and *she* are used in reference to Puruṣa and Prakṛti, although both are beyond gender.

continues to dance until the audience is satisfied. The moment the course of dance (which depends on the audience's duration of enjoyment) is fulfilled, the dancer stops her dance. In the same way, the great dancer Prakṛti continues her dance until her discriminating function is accomplished. The moment she accomplishes her job, she withdraws herself back into her unmanifested state. The purpose of the manifestation of Prakṛti is to show herself to Puruṣa so he can realize that he is distinct from her. The moment Puruṣa realizes that he is not the external objects, then the entire manifestation is withdrawn.

In actuality, pure consciousness, Puruṣa, is subject neither to bondage nor to liberation, because he is never really in bondage. The concepts of bondage and liberation, pain and suffering, are the result of ignorance or false understanding. Prakṛti binds herself with the rope of her own manifestation, and when Puruṣa recognizes her as distinct from him, she liberates herself. As has previously been stated, there are eight attributes of mahat or buddhi (the intellect), which is the prime evolute of Prakṛti. These eight are attachment and detachment, vice and virtue, nonmeritorious and meritorious actions, and ignorance and knowledge. Prakṛti binds herself with the first seven attributes and liberates herself with the eighth—the light of knowledge. Thus bondage and liberation are both concepts of the intellect. Through the practice of the yoga of discrimination—that is, the repeated affirmation of nonidentification with the body, senses, or mind (such as, for instance, "I am not the experiencer, I am not the doer; whatever is going on is in Prakṛti")—one polishes one's intellect and becomes more consciously aware of one's true nature. This type of knowledge or understanding leads one to the state of freedom from all confusions and false identifications, and thus one attains the knowledge of the true Self. After the Self realizes its true nature, all anxieties are dissolved. Then the Self becomes disinterested in seeing Prakṛti, and Prakṛti becomes disinterested in showing herself, because she has seen and her purpose has been fulfilled. Prakṛti and Puruṣa are both infinite and all-pervading and are therefore eternally together, like two sides of the same coin, but when their purpose is fulfilled the process of manifestation ceases.

In the Sāṃkhya philosophy, there are two kinds of liberation: *jīvana mukti* and *videha mukti.* The liberation attained in one's lifetime is called *jīvana mukti.* In this kind of liberation, a person continues his existence on this platform as a liberated being. He lives in this world and enjoys the worldly objects until he casts off his body. He continues his journey through worldly life just as a fan continues to revolve, due to its previously generated speed, for a short while after it has been switched off. When all the saṃskāras—the impressions of past actions—are finished, then he casts off his body and is said to enter into *videha mukti*, which is liberation after death.

The Concept of God

There is a great controversy among Sāṃkhya philosophers regarding the concept of God. The earliest available text, the Sāṃkhya Kārikā, does not discuss the existence of God. The absence of such a discussion led scholars to believe that early Sāṃkhya did not accept the existence of God. They argued that because the entire universe is a system of cause and effect, it could not be caused by God because by definition God is eternal and immutable. That which is unchanging cannot be the active cause of anything, so the ultimate cause of the universe is eternal but ever-changing. That cause is Prakṛti, the eternal and ever-changing unconscious material principle. Next, one could argue that Prakṛti is not intelligent and must, therefore, be controlled and directed by some intelligent principle in order to produce the universe. But because there are many Puruṣas, they cannot guide and lead the infinite, all-pervading Prakṛti, so one could therefore conclude that there is a God. But this is not possible, because the act of controlling or guiding Prakṛti means to *do* something or to be active. In addition, if God controls Prakṛti, then what inspires God to make her create a world full of pain and misery? Moreover, one cannot say that God has desires because desire implies imperfection, which is a quality God cannot have. Therefore, there is no such thing as God. Puruṣa is sufficient to inspire the unconscious Prakṛti to manifest herself in the form of the universe.

Later developments in Sāṃkhya philosophy, however, clearly indicate acceptance of the existence of God. These philosophers point out that in metaphysical discussions it is very difficult to explain the nature of the universe and of oneself without accepting a Supreme Being. For example, on the one hand, Sāṃkhya believes in the existence of many Puruṣas and only one Prakṛti. One Puruṣa or all the Puruṣas together may inspire Prakṛti to manifest. If one, then it is against the wish of the other Puruṣas; if all the Puruṣas then there must be some communication and agreement among the Puruṣas. But no one has any record of a cosmic conference of all the Puruṣas to make such a decision. Therefore, there must be one Supreme Being who could guide Prakṛti independently.

The *Bhagavad Gītā* states that the unmanifested Prakṛti issues forth the entire universe as guided and directed by God. But earlier scriptures of Sāṃkhya philosophy did not talk about God because they wanted to teach human beings to be independent and courageous so that they could explore all the potentials hidden within. Without proper understanding, the concept of God leads one to a state of inactivity, and then one becomes a burden for oneself and others. That is why the early Sāṃkhya philosophers did not talk about God, but this does not mean that they themselves denied the existence of God. The practical aspect of Sāṃkhya is the Yoga system, which unanimously recognizes the existence of God.

The Practical Teachings of Sāṃkhya

From earliest times, Sāṃkhya philosophy understood the basic problem of human life: that the mind turns one's bliss into misery by its projections, preoccupations, and identifications with noneternal things. As has been discussed, Sāṃkhya recognizes three functions of the mind: the lower mind, the ego, and the intellect. Whatever is sensed by the sense organs is received by the mind and transmitted to the ego and the intellect. The intellect presents this experience to the Self. However, the Self (Puruṣa), which falsely identifies itself with the intellect, enjoys or suffers that experience as the intellect does, even though actual enjoyment or suffering does not belong to the Self. The senses contact many objects, and in the process of receiving the experience of external objects there is a constant process of filtration. The mind transmits only those experiences that are profitable and desirable to the ego. The ego identifies with those experiences and filters them again, transmitting to the intellect only those that are related to the ego. Before the intellect forwards experiences to the Self, it also filters them, providing only those experiences necessary and beneficial to the Self.

This is the natural process, but because of the predominance of tamas and rajas in the personality and because of intense attachment to worldly objects, the mind, ego, and intellect lose their capacity of filtration. They accumulate unnecessary mental garbage, and it becomes a great burden for the intellect to discriminate good from bad, important from unimportant. Because of this lack of filtration, mind, ego, and intellect lose their strength and block the path for going inward. Thus one remains at the stage of the lower mind, whose very nature is to doubt, to suspect, and to vacillate. One becomes confused, and that confusion leads to frustration, which consequently leads to disappointment and complete destruction. For this reason, Sāṃkhya philosophy emphasizes polishing the mind so it can filter experience and provide valid knowledge with full understanding.

Sāṃkhya philosophy discourages external rituals because most of the time people don't understand their significance and so they perform them on only the grossest level. Therefore, Sāṃkhya instead emphasizes right knowledge of the external world and the Self. It does not advise a student to renounce the world but rather teaches one how to live in the world yet remain above. An adept of the Sāṃkhya system is called a *sthitaprajña*, which may be translated as "one who is established in wisdom, who has cut down all desires mentally, and who is self-satisfied within." Such a person is not distressed by unpleasant events and is not overpowered by pleasure; thus he remains free from attachment, fear, and anger. One who is free from all afflictions, who does not chase after the good and does not hate the bad, who has withdrawn all his senses completely from their objects and dwells within is *sthitaprajña*.

Sāṃkhya philosophy gives a complete method for attaining this state. First of all, one should control and purify his thinking process because thinking about a sense object produces attachment to it, and from attachment there arises desire to obtain it. When for some reason the desired object is not obtained, there arises anger toward the impediment, and this anger destroys one's patience and produces delusion. Delusion gives birth to confusion or loss of memory, and then one's intellect becomes disorganized. After the disorganization and contamination of the intellect, one becomes lost in the jungle of pain and sorrow.

The Sāṃkhya system reminds one to examine one's thinking process to purify it so that he can develop proper attitudes toward the objects of the senses. If one is aware of the very first flicker of an arising desire, it is easier for his intellect to discriminate and to make proper decisions. But if the thinking process is not examined in the very beginning and if it becomes caught up in the stream of attachment, desire, anger, and so on, then it becomes very hard to extricate oneself from this flow. However, a strong, positive thought led by discrimination does not permit the senses to wander blindly toward external objects. The enjoyment of external objects with full awareness and discrimination does not disturb one's internal state, but rather it provides great eternal peace and cheerfulness. This is the basis of the steadiness of intellect that reveals the true nature of the world and helps Puruṣa attain realization, the highest goal. Thus, Sāṃkhya philosophy advises a person not to run away from the world but to have perfect mental control so that he will not be agitated by the tides of the ocean of worldly objects. As the *Bhagavad Gītā* (Ch. 2, v. 70) states: "He attains peace into whom all sensual experiences enter, just as so many rivers flow into the ocean, which, though being ever filled, remains unaffected. But he who is desirous of enjoyments, never attains peace."

chapter

6

Yoga

Practical Disciplines for Knowing the Self

Yoga is the most practical school of Indian philosophy. The word *yoga* is derived from the Sanskrit root *yuj*, which means "to unite." The Yoga system provides a methodology for expanding one's individual consciousness to universal Consciousness. There are various schools of Yoga—for example, Bhakti Yoga, Jñāna Yoga, Karma Yoga, and Kuṇḍalinī Yoga. But here only Pātañjala Yoga will be reviewed because it is the most comprehensive school of Yoga. Patañjali was the first sage to systematize the philosophy and practice of Yoga. His work is known as *Pātañjala Yoga Sūtra*. There are various commentaries on this text, Vyāsa's being the most ancient and profound.

The Yoga system is highly practical; it discusses the nature of mind, its modifications, impediments to growth, afflictions, and the method for attaining the highest goal of life—*kaivalya* (absoluteness). Since this method is described in eight steps, it is also known as *Aṣṭāṅga* Yoga, the eightfold path.

The Yogic View of Mind

According to Patañjali, Yoga is the control of the modifications of the mind. He realized that it is the mind that leads a person to bondage or to liberation; that most human problems are mental and that the only remedy to solve them is mental discipline. The mind is the finest of all human instruments that serves one in attaining one's goals. The mind is also the link between consciousness and the physical body. For this reason, Patañjali places great emphasis on the study of the mind and provides all the possible means to control its modifications and unfold its great power for higher attainment.

Theoretically, the Yoga system is based on the same tenets as Sāṃkhya philosophy, and it also assimilates the teachings of Vedānta. In Sāṃkhya philosophy, the mind is categorized into three functions or parts (lower mind, ego, and intellect), but in Vedānta philosophy the mind is divided into four parts (lower mind, ego, intellect, and "mind-stuff" or *citta*, the storehouse of memories). In Yoga, however, the mind is studied holistically, and the term *citta* is used to denote all the fluctuating and changing phenomena of the mind. According to Yoga, the mind is like a vast lake, on the surface of which arise many different kinds of waves. Deep within, the mind is always calm and tranquil, but one's thought patterns stir it into activity and prevent it from realizing its own true nature. These thought patterns are the waves appearing and disappearing on the surface of the lake of the mind. Depending on the size, strength, and speed of the waves, the inner state of the lake is obscured to a greater or lesser degree. The more one is able to calm one's thought patterns, the more the inner state of the mind is unveiled. It is not very difficult to calm down the waves of thought patterns on the surface of the lake of mind, but it is very difficult to calm down those unrhythmic and destructive waves of thought patterns that arise from the bottom. Memories are like time bombs buried in the lakebed of mind that explode at certain times and disturb the entire lake.

There are two main sources for the arising waves of thoughts: sense perceptions and memories. When the waves of a lake are stilled and the water is clear, one can look deep down and see the bottom of the lake. Likewise when one's thought patterns are quieted, one can see one's innermost potentials hidden deep within the mind. Because the mind is an evolute of Prakṛti (see the previous chapter on Sāṃkhya philosophy), it is composed of the elements of sattva, rajas, and tamas. The relative proportions of these three qualities determine the different states of citta, the mind. The turmoil caused by the interaction of the guṇas is responsible for the arising thought patterns in the mind.

Five Stages of Mind

The mind is described in five stages, depending on the degree of its transparency: disturbed (*kṣipta*); stupefied (*mūḍha*); restless (*vikṣipta*); one-pointed (*ekāgra*); and well-controlled (*niruddha*). The predominance of rajas and tamas causes the mind to be disturbed (*kṣipta*). Because of the predominance of rajas, the mind becomes hyperactive; because of the predominance of tamas, it loses its quality of discrimination. Thus it flits from one object to another without resting on any. It is constantly disturbed by external stimuli, but it does not know how to discriminate what is beneficial from that which is useless. In the second stage (*mūḍha*), the mind is dominated by tamas, which is characterized by inertia, vice, ignorance, lethargy, and sleep. In this state, mind is so sluggish that it loses its capability to think properly and becomes negative and dull. In the restless stage (*vikṣipta*), there is a predominance of rajas. In this state, the mind runs from one object to another but never stays anywhere consistently. This is an advanced stage of the disturbed mind.

These first three stages of mind are negative and act as impediments in the path of growth and exploration. At this level, one experiences pain and misery and all kinds of unpleasant emotions, but the next two stages are more calm and peaceful. All the modifications are found in the earlier three stages. In the one-pointed and well-controlled states there are no modifications at all. In the one-pointed state of mind (*ekāgra*), there is a predominance of sattva, the light aspect of Prakṛti. This is a tranquil state near to complete stillness in which the real nature of things is revealed. This fourth state is conducive to concentration, and the aim of the Yoga system is to develop or to maintain this state of mind for as long and as consistently as possible. In the well-controlled state of mind (*niruddha*), there is no disturbance at all but a pure manifestation of sattvic energy. In this state, Consciousness reflects its purity and entirety in the mirror of mind, and one becomes capable of exploring one's true nature. Only the last two states of mind are positive and helpful for meditation, and many yogic practices are designed to help one attain these states. When all the modifications cease and the state of stillness is acquired, then Puruṣa (Consciousness) sees its real nature reflecting from the screen of the mind.

The Modifications of Mind

The Yoga system categorizes the modifications of mind into five classes: valid cognition, invalid cognition, verbal cognition, sleep, and memory. All thoughts, emotions, and mental behaviors fall into one of these five categories, which are further divided into two major types: those that cause afflictions (*kliṣṭa*) and those that do not cause afflictions (*akliṣṭa*). False cognition, verbal cognition, and sleep always cause afflictions and are in themselves afflictions; they are harmful modifications. Valid cognitions and memories (depending on their nature) are not considered to be causes of affliction and are not harmful for meditation.

The sources of valid cognition are perception, inference, and authoritative testimony, which have already been described in detail in the Sāṃkhya chapter of this book (see page 137). False cognition is ignorance (*avidyā*). Ignorance is mistaking the non-eternal for the eternal, the impure for the pure, misery for happiness, and the nonself for the Self. It is the modification of mind that is the mother of the *kleśas*, or afflictions. Ignorance has four offshoots: *asmitā*, which is generally defined as I-am-ness; *rāga*, attachment or addiction, which is the desire to prolong or repeat pleasurable experiences; *dveṣa*, hatred or aversion, which is the desire to avoid unpleasurable experiences; and *abhiniveśa*, fear of death, which is the urge of self-preservation.

Verbal cognition is the attempt to grasp something that actually does not exist but is one's own projection. An example of such a projection is the fantasy of marrying a gossamer-winged fairy and together flying through the empyrean to the most wondrous paradise. All such fantasies are mere verbal cognitions that do not correspond to facts and only cause the mind to fluctuate. Sleep is a modification of mind in which one's relationship with the external world is cut off. One might ask: If sleep is a modification of mind, aren't the dreaming and waking states also accepted as modifications? The answer would be no; the dreaming state is occupied with verbal cognitions, and the waking state is occupied mainly with valid cognitions and invalid cognitions. Memory, the fifth and final mental modification, is the recall of impressions stored in the mind.

Overcoming the Modifications

The modifications of the mind are caused by nine conditions or impediments, namely sickness, incompetence, doubt, delusion, sloth, nonabstention, confusion, nonattainment of the desired state, and instability in an attained state. These impediments disturb the mind and produce sorrow, dejection, restlessness, and an unrhythmic breathing pattern. Yoga provides a method for overcoming these problems and controlling the modifications of the mind. Patañjali states that the mind and its modifications can be controlled through practice (*abhyāsa*) and detachment (*vairāgya*). The mind is said to be like a river that flows between two banks. One bank is positive and is the basis for liberation, while the other bank is negative and is the basis for indiscrimination and infatuations with sense objects. When the current of the river is controlled by practice and detachment, it tends to flow toward the side of liberation. *Abhyāsa*, practice, means a particular type of effort or technique through which the mind maintains stillness. Practice does not mean engaging in mental gymnastics; it is, rather, sincere effort for maintaining steadiness of the mind. Perfection in practice is attained through sincerity and persistence. Methods of practice will be discussed in conjunction with the discussion of the eight limbs of Yoga. *Vairāgya*, detachment or dispassion, does not mean to renounce the world or to withdraw oneself from one's environment; rather it means to have no expectations from external objects. Detachment means to eliminate identification with the evolutes of nature and to understand oneself as pure Self, as a self-illuminating conscious being.

Patañjali also describes another method, called kriyā yoga, to help students attain a higher state of consciousness while dealing with a restless mind. Kriyā yoga, which means the yoga of purification, is a threefold discipline composed of the practice of austerity, study of the scriptures, and surrender to God. By practicing the path of kriyā yoga, students learn to perform their duties skillfully and selflessly while dedicating the fruits of their actions to others. Austerity or asceticism does not mean torturing the body or suppressing thought patterns; rather it means practicing choice or control in selecting actions that will be helpful in attaining liberation. The greatest of all austerities is to perform one's duty skillfully and selflessly for the sake of duty and in the service of others without any intention of enjoying the fruits of one's actions oneself. Study of the scriptures helps one discover ways he can deal effectively with himself and explore all his potentials within and without. It also includes self-study and *japa* (repetition of a mantra). Surrender to God is easy in concept but difficult in practice. When one can perceive all activities as part of a grand ritual that is being performed on the altar of life in the worship of the Divinity, the actual practice of surrender to God begins. There remains no place for hatred, jealousy, anger, greed, or any other negative feelings. There remains only love for all creatures, which radiates its light of bliss and knowledge in every mental and physical action.

The Eightfold Path of Yoga

All the various spiritual paths lead to the same single goal of Self-realization, but many methods are provided in order to accommodate people of varying temperaments and capacities. All the different paths—Karma Yoga, Bhakti Yoga, Jñāna Yoga, Kuṇḍalinī Yoga, Mantra Yoga, Haṭha Yoga, and so on—are not mutually exclusive but merely emphasize different aspects and are interconnected like the spokes of a wheel. Pātañjala yoga, a highly scientific path, combines many different practices in a systematic way through which one can develop voluntary control over one's body, desires, emotions, thoughts, and the subtle impressions that lie dormant in the unconscious mind. The eight components of this system (see chart) are: restraints (*yamas*); observances (*niyamas*); posture (*āsana*); breath control (*prāṇāyāma*); sense withdrawal (*pratyāhara*); concentration (*dhāraṇā*); meditation (*dhyāna*); and spiritual absorption (*samādhi*).

Realization of the highest state of consciousness requires a one-pointed and well-controlled mind free from all worldly desires. Attachment to worldly objects is the main cause of and is the direct evolute of ignorance, which produces all the modifications of the mind. According to Pātañjala yoga, attachment to worldy objects is the archenemy of the individual who wants to understand his inner self. The necessary qualities and conditions for reaching the subtler levels of consciousness include will power, discrimination, full control of the mind, conscious direction of one's potentials toward the desired end, a firm resolution to turn away from all worldly

The Eight Limbs of Pātañjala Yoga

Haṭha Yoga:

- *Yamas* (five restraints)
  - nonhurting (ahiṃsā)
  - nonlying (satya)
  - nonstealing (asteya)
  - sensory control (brahmacarya)
  - nonpossessiveness (aparigraha)
- *Niyamas* (five observances)
  - purity (śauca)
  - contentment (santoṣa)
  - Kriyā Yoga:
    - zeal (tapas)
    - study (svādhyāya)
    - surrender (Iśvara praṇidhāna)
- *Āsana* (posture)
  - cultural poses
  - meditative poses
- *Prāṇāyāma* (control of vital force)
  - prāṇa, apāna, samāna, udāna, vyāna

Pratyāhāra (withdrawal of the senses)

Saṃyama:

- *Dhāraṇā* (concentration)
- *Dhyāna* (meditation)
- *Samādhi* (spiritual absorption)

attachments, determination to obliterate the ego, control over all inharmonious processes, and constant awareness of the ultimate goal.

Yamas—Restraints

To fulfill the above conditions, Pātañjala Yoga begins by prescribing an ethical code designed to calm one's relationship with oneself and others. The first two limbs of Pātañjala Yoga—the yamas and niyamas—consist of ten commitments that constitute this code. The five yamas (restraints) are nonviolence (*ahiṃsā*), truthfulness (*satya*), nonstealing (*asteya*), continence (*brahmacarya*), and nonpossessiveness (*aparigraha*). They replace imperfections with virtues and together make up a code of social and moral laws that regulates one's relationships with others.

Ahiṃsā. *Ahiṃsā* literally means "noninjury" or "nonviolence." Generally, one thinks of nonviolence as merely restraining from the physical act of violence, but in Yoga scriptures nonviolence is to be practiced in thought, speech, and action. Actually, the real practice of nonviolence necessitates expressing a spontaneous flow of all-encompassing love. Thus, the core teaching of nonviolence reveals the light of unity in all creation and teaches one how to expand his personality.

Satya. *Satya*, truthfulness, is the most important goal of morality and social law. According to Pātañjala Yoga, one should be truthful to oneself and to others in thought, speech, and action. The field of truthfulness is very vast; it encompasses individual, family, social, national, and ultimately universal life. The Yoga student is taught to speak what he thinks and to do what he says. Sometimes one lies without awareness or sometimes just for fun or for the sake of creating gossip. These simple lies are like seeds that create habits that will one day become one's nature. Thus one cannot even trust in himself because of his untruthful nature. The day a person becomes totally truthful, his whole life becomes successful and whatever he says or thinks comes true. He gains inner strength through which he casts away the insecurity in his life.

Asteya. *Asteya*, nonstealing, provides a great opportunity for the practice of nonattachment and nonpossessiveness. Actually, nonstealing is a negative explanation of contentment, because when one is self-satisfied he is not tempted to desire others' things. Such a person considers whatever he has as sufficient, and he does not allow himself to disturb social peace and harmony in order to attain desired objects by illegitimate means. The Yoga system advises that nonstealing be practiced mentally, verbally, and physically. An honest author writes original thoughts, and if some material is borrowed from others, the author honestly and respectfully gives references. That is an example of nonstealing at the thought level. In the same way, nonstealing practiced at every level of the personality helps maintain purity of life, and purity of life allows one to shine and grow in all dimensions.

Brahmacarya. *Brahmacarya* literally means "to walk in Brahman." One who dwells in Brahman consciousness is called a *brahmacāri.* The word *brahmacarya* is commonly translated as "sexual abstinence," but celibacy is only a partial explanation of this word. Sexual continence in itself is not the goal; the goal is to control the senses in order to achieve deeper levels of inner awareness. Pātañjala Yoga takes brahmacarya in a wider sense to mean selectively performing only those activities that are helpful in achieving the highest goal of life. Such a state of consciousness is possible only if the mind is free from all sensuous desires, including the sexual urge, which is the most powerful and which can be most destructive if not directed and channeled properly. Sensual activity in excess also leads to the dissipation of vital energy that could be utilized for the attainment of higher consciousness. For achieving this goal, the Yoga system advises one to organize all his sensuous forces and to utilize them in a proper and beneficial way. It teaches control of sensuous cravings in order to attain that inner peace and happiness that is greater than all transient sensuous pleasures. Uncontrolled senses dissipate the mind, and a dissipated mind loses its capacity to concentrate in one direction or on one object. A person with a dissipated mind fails to think properly, to speak properly, or to act properly. For higher attainment, one therefore has to withdraw his energies from the petty charms and temptations of sensory objects and convert the flow of the life force toward higher consciousness.

Aparigraha. *Aparigraha*, nonpossessiveness, is generally misunderstood to mean denying oneself all material possessions, but the word actually indicates an inward attitude rather than an outward behavior. The feeling of possessiveness is an expression of dissatisfaction, insecurity, attachment, and greed. One who strives his whole life to gain more and more worldly objects is never satisfied because that desire can never be quenched. One who is constantly greedy for more forgets that it is impossible to eat more than the stomach can hold, to sleep on more ground than the body covers, or to wear more clothes than the body requires. Whatever one possesses that exceeds the essential requirements becomes a burden, and instead of enjoying it one suffers in watching and taking care of it. A person who desires more than that which is required is like a thief who covets that which belongs to others. Nonpossessiveness does not mean that one should not plan for the future or that one should give away all one's money; it simply means that one should not be attached to what he has. An attitude of possessiveness excludes one from all that one does not have, but the practice of nonpossessiveness expands one's personality, and one acquires more than he has mentally renounced.

Niyamas—Observances

The five niyamas regulate one's habits and organize the personality. They consist of purity (*śauca*), contentment (*santoṣa*), austerity (*tapas*), self-study (*svādhyāya*), and surrender to the

Ultimate Reality (*Īśvara praṇidhāna*). These observances allow a person to be strong physically, mentally, and spiritually.

Śauca. In the context of Yoga science, *śauca* refers to both physical and mental purity. Physical purity protects the body from diseases, and mental purity prevents mental energy from being dissipated. Physical purity can be achieved easily, but one has to pay close attention to purity of mind, which depends on positive thinking, mindfulness, and discrimination. The Yoga system places great emphasis on developing purity of the mind because concentration and inward exploration are impossible without it and because psychosomatic disease and emotional disturbance result from its absence.

Santoṣa. *Santoṣa*, contentment, is a mental state in which even a beggar can live like a king. It is one's own desires that make one a mental beggar and keep one from being tranquil within. Contentment does not mean one should be passive or inactive, for practice of contentment must be coordinated with selfless action.

Tapas. *Tapas*, austerity, does not mean the mortification of the flesh; it means the generation of heat. Heat is a symbol of strength, purity, knowledge, and light, and those actions that generate heat, strengthen will power, and enlighten the heart are known as tapas. The *Bhagavad Gītā* clearly states that Yoga is not for one who indulges the flesh nor for one who tortures it. In practicing tapas, one is advised to inspire oneself with spiritual warmth, to burn with zeal for enlightenment. All those activities that increase spiritual fervor constitute tapas. A simple life free from sensuous indulgences, a regulated diet, and the performance of all one's actions in the service of humanity are a part of the practice of asceticism. Tapas is the foundation of physical strength, mental growth, and blazing spiritual fervor.

Svādhyāya. *Svādhyāya* includes studying the scriptures, listening to saints and sages, and observing the lessons from one's own experiences. This niyama warns a student not to doubt too much and not to trust too much but rather to be very selective in studying the scriptures and listening to sages and scholars. One should select only the gems of the teachings from available sources and then assimilate them into his own philosophy of life. Without utilizing the quality of selectiveness, one may confuse himself with a variety of teachings from various scriptures and saints and thus create mental conflict. The skillful study of reliable scriptures enhances one's understanding and gradually leads to a broader unfoldment of his potentials.

Īśvara praṇidhāna. *Īśvara praṇidhāna*, surrender to the Ultimate Reality, is the highest method for protecting oneself from the archenemies of attachment, false identification, and the idea of doership. Surrender is possible, however, only with infinite faith and dedication. Ego is the greatest barrier resisting such complete surrender, but when one begins to feel and realize the everflowing knowledge and peace from the Ultimate Reality, he starts to surrender his ego and eventually become free from all passions. The moment one realizes why the air provides oxygen to all, why the rain moistens the earth, and why the sun gives light and heat, then he feels the everflowing love and compassion of the Supreme Being. At that moment one casts away his egoism, surrenders himself to the Ultimate Reality, discharges his duties selflessly, and enjoys worldly as well as eternal life.

The yamas and niyamas are simple in theory but difficult in application. The initial steps may be very hard, but a burning desire for growth and a constant awareness of one's capacity helps one to practice them in daily life. One should try to observe them to their fullest extent, but if he fails somewhere in doing so, he should not feel guilty. Even a small degree of success can reduce the intensity of his mental and emotional turmoil. The Yoga system does not suggest forcing oneself to master these restraints and observances but encourages one to be gentle in practicing them as sincerely as he can. The restraints and observances help modify and calm one's lifestyle, prevent the mind from being distracted, and help the body to regain its physical strength. They are in themselves sufficient means for revealing all of one's potential and leading him to the highest goal of life, but they are difficult to practice in and of themselves. For this reason the Yoga system places importance on them while advising the practice of other practical yogic disciplines as well.

Āsana—Posture

Āsanas, physical postures, ensure physical health and mental harmony. They are used in conjunction with the yamas and niyamas and the other limbs of Pātañjala yoga, for without the other elements of the system, mere physical exercise cannot provide the desired benefits. Nowadays, because many students do not understand the importance of coordinating the yamas and niyamas with the āsanas, the yogic postures have largely degenerated into a system of physical culture. Yoga, however, emphasizes āsanas not only as a means of improving physical beauty but as an important prerequisite for the attainment of higher spiritual goals. The aim of Yoga is to attain the highest state of samādhi. That is why it places the greatest importance on the meditative postures, which enable one to sit comfortably and steadily for a long time with the head, neck, and trunk properly aligned.

The postures are broadly divided into two major categories: postures for physical well-being and postures for meditation. The commentators on Patañjali's sūtras mention only a few postures that are helpful in meditation, but later Yoga scriptures describe a complete science of postures for physical and mental well-being. There are eighty-four classical postures, but only four of these are suggested for the practice of meditation. These are *sukhāsana* (the easy pose), *svastikāsana* (the auspicious pose), *padmāsana* (the lotus pose), and *siddhāsana* (the accomplished pose). In all meditative postures, the emphasis is on keeping the head, neck, and trunk straight. The spine being thus aligned provides steadiness and comfort in the posture and minimizes the consumption of oxygen and the production of carbon dioxide. The meditative postures coordinate the activity of the circulatory, respiratory, endocrine, and nervous systems. Thus the body becomes still and calm, which is helpful in keeping the mind tranquil and harmonious. The physical postures are designed to enhance physical well-being, suppleness, and control. They activate specific muscles, organs, glands, and nerves, and provide specific therapeutic effects. In the Yoga system, complete physical harmony is considered to be an essential prerequisite for achieving one-pointedness of mind. Thus, āsanas are preparatory training for the higher rungs of Yoga.

Prāṇāyāma—Control of the Vital Force

After practicing physical exercises, the student becomes aware of a deeper level of personality—prāṇa, the life force—functioning in the body. The word *prāṇa* is derived from the Sanskrit root *ana* and the prefix *pra. Ana* means "to animate or vibrate," and *pra* means "first unit." Thus the word *prāṇa* means "the first unit of energy." Whatever animates or moves is an expression of prāṇa—the life force. All the forces in the world, including individual beings, are different manifestations or expressions of this life force.

This vital force animates all the energies involved in the physical and mental processes, and thus it is prāṇa that sustains and activates the body and mind. Prāṇa is the basic principle underlying all biophysical functions. Later writings of Yoga explain a highly advanced science of prāṇa, which yogis claim establishes the link between body and mind and vitalizes both. Because the breath is the grossest manifestation of this vital function, the science of prāṇa is also called the science of breath. Continuous regulation of the breath strengthens the nervous system and harmonizes all mental activities.

Yoga texts say that prāṇa is the creator of all substances and the basis of all functions. The *Bṛhadāraṇyaka Upaniṣad* says that the thread of prāṇa (*vāyu*) runs through and holds together the whole universe. This thread is the cause of the creation, sustenance, and destruction of all substances in the world. The same life force on which humankind depends is also the cause of the animal and vegetable kingdoms. As long as prāṇa is in a normal condition, the cells and tissues remain healthy and perform their functions properly, but the moment its vitality starts decreasing, the cells begin to decay. The intrinsic nature of prāṇa is to be active and to move, and this is the very quality that distinguishes the organic world from the inorganic. Life begets life from the life force prāṇa; it is because of this life force that cells live and multiply, transmitting the same vitality to new cells and tissues. Food, water, temperature, and oxygen are the serving, preserving, and maintaining conditions of the life force in cells and tissues. Though bodily organs are working under various known and unknown principles—such as the physical, chemical, pranic, mental, and so on—the supreme force of life is the undefinable yet undeniable vital activity on which all other principles and laws are dependent. Because prāṇa establishes a link between human beings and the surrounding atmosphere, it is also the link between individual and cosmic beings. The breath is the thread through which prāṇa travels from the cosmos to the individual and from the individual to the cosmos.

Depending on its function in different organs, prāṇa is divided into ten types. The ten prāṇas are *prāṇa, apāna, samāna, udāna, vyāna, nāga, kūrma, kṛkala, devadatta,* and *dhanañjaya.* Of these ten, the first five are the most important.

Prāṇa. Prāṇa here is used to designate a specific type of prāṇa, the vital force of inspiration. In this context the word *prāṇa* (*pra* + *ana*) means "that which draws in or takes in." The life force that receives the fresh cosmic vitality from the atmosphere, activating the diaphragm, lungs, and nostrils, is called prāṇa. The head, mouth, nostrils, chest (heart and lungs), navel, and big toes are said to be the main centers of prāṇa. This important vital force resides in the brain and governs the functions of the senses and the process of thinking. Certain physical activities—such as the ability of the cerebrum to receive the sensations of smell, sound, taste, touch, and vision, the function of the cranial nerves, and the power that governs all mental activities—are the functions of prāṇa. Primitive instincts, emotions, intelligence, self-control, memory, concentration, and the power of judgment or discrimination are manifestations of prāṇa. As long as prāṇa is in its normal state, all the organs function properly. Bodily toxins, intoxicants, malnutrition, the aging process, frustration, fatigue, restlessness, and physical and mental shocks disturb the vital force. When the vitality of the mind starts to decay due to such conditions, then higher abilities such as intelligence, memory, concentration, discrimination, and patience start to diminish, and the lower instincts or emotions become predominant.

In the cosmos and in the body there is a continuous flow of solar and lunar energy, also referred to in Yoga texts as positive and negative energy, as *pitta* and *kapha*, bile and phlegm, fire and water, light and darkness, male and female, and so on. When prāṇa is predominated by solar energy, it is active and the right nostril is open. But when lunar energy predominates, it is passive and the left nostril is open. The flow of prāṇa through the right or the left nostril provides specific conditions and changes in mood and behavior.

Apāna. Apāna is the excretory vital force. Expulsive movements occurring in the bowels, bladder, uterus, seminal vessels, and pores during defecation, urination, menstruation, procreation, perspiration, and all other kinds of excretions are due to the function of apāna. The penis, anus, thighs, scrotum, ribs, root of the navel, and the abdomen are said to be the abode of apāna. When the excretory vital force, which functions through the thoracic and abdominal muscles, is disturbed, then symptoms such as sneezing, asthma, croup, or hiccups are observed.

Samāna. *Samāna* is the digestive and assimilating force that makes food suitable for absorption and then assimilates it. This vital force is seen in the entire body, not just in the digestive system. Because of samāna's presence in the skin, vitamin D can be absorbed from the ultraviolet rays of the sun. The region between the heart and the navel center is predominantly involved in the absorption and digestion of food, and this part of the body is therefore considered to be the main center of this vital force. This vital force is responsible for growth and nourishment. Abnormalities of the assimilating vital force result in nervous diarrhea, dyspepsia (impaired digestion), intestinal colic, spasmodic or nervous retention of urine, constipation, and the like.

Udāna. *Udāna* means "energy that uplifts." It is the force that causes contraction in the thoracic muscles, thereby pushing air out through the vocal cords. It is, therefore, the main cause of the production of sound. All physical activities that require effort and strength depend on this vital force. It is said to be situated in the larynx, the upper part of the pelvis, all the joints, and the feet and hands.

Vyāna. *Vyāna* is the contractile vital force. All rhythmic or nonrhythmic contractions take place because of this vital force. It pervades the whole body and governs the process of relaxing and contracting the voluntary and involuntary muscles. This force also governs movements of the ligaments and sends sensory and motor impulses through the nervous tissues. It is involved in the opening and closing of the eyes as well as the opening and closing of the glottis. The ears, eyes, neck, ankles, nose, and throat are said to be the main centers of this vital force in the body. Fibrosis, sclerosis, atrophy, and pain in muscular and nervous tissues are the result of abnormalities in the contractile vital force.

Food and breath are the main vehicles through which prāṇa enters the body. Food contains a grosser quality of prāṇa than does the breath; one can live for a few days without food, but without breath one cannot function normally for even a minute. This is the reason that the Yoga system places so much importance on the science of breath. The regulation of the movement of the lungs is the most effective process for cleansing and vitalizing the human system. It purifies and strengthens the nervous system, which coordinates all the other systems in the body. Yogis have developed a most intricate and deep science related to the nervous and circulatory systems, but this science goes beyond the mere study of nerves, veins, and arteries. The science of breath is related to subtle energy channels called *nāḍīs.* According to yogis, the body is essentially a field of energy, but only a very small part of that energy is utilized, and so a great part of it remains dormant. With the help of prāṇāyāma (the science of prāṇa), however, a student of Yoga can unveil that energy field, expand it, and channel it to explore higher states of consciousness. Yogic texts say, "One who knows prāṇa knows the Veda's highest knowledge," and one of the Upaniṣads proclaims that prāṇa is Brahman. The science of prāṇa and the science of breath are thus of central importance in the Yoga system.

According to Patañjali, prāṇāyāma means to refine and regulate the flow of inhalation and exhalation. When one can breathe deeply and noiselessly without jerks or pauses, one can allow one's prāṇa to expand and to be awakened for higher attainments. Patañjali does not advise the practice of prāṇāyāma until one has achieved a still and comfortable posture. Postures that remove physical tension and provide stillness are therefore the prerequisites to prāṇāyāma. Patañjali lists four kinds of prāṇāyāma: external (*bāhya vṛtti*), in which the flow of prāṇa is controlled during the exhalation; internal (*ābhyantara vṛtti*), in which the flow of prāṇa is controlled during inhalation; and intermediate (*bāhyā-bhy-antara-viṣayākṣepī*), in which the other two prāṇāyāmas are refined, and the fourth (*caturtha*), in which prāṇāyāma is transcended. The first three prāṇāyāmas must be regulated within space and time, but the fourth prāṇāyāma is highly advanced and transcends these limitations. When the external and internal prāṇāyāmas become very subtle, then, because of intense concentration in a perfect, relaxed state, one loses awareness of time and space, and thus the fourth prāṇāyāma happens automatically. In this prāṇāyāma, the breath becomes so fine and subtle that an ordinary breathing movement cannot be observed. Without practical instruction from a competent teacher, it is not possible to understand and apply this method of prāṇāyāma successfully. The practice of prāṇāyāma prepares fertile ground for concentration. The first four stages of Yoga discussed thus far—that is, yama, niyama, āsana, and prāṇāyāma—are sometimes collectively known as Haṭha Yoga.

Pratyāhāra—Withdrawal of the Senses

The fifth limb of Yoga is *pratyāhāra*, the withdrawal or control of the senses. In outward activities the mind contacts external objects through the five senses of sight, hearing, touch, taste, and smell. The interaction of the senses with their objects is like the blowing wind that disturbs the surface of the lake of mind and causes waves to arise. Withdrawal of the senses is a technique through which a student acquires the ability to voluntarily draw his attention inward and keep his mind from distractions.

Patañjali defines pratyāhāra as the withdrawal of the senses from their objects and their establishment in the mind. The senses are constantly wandering from one object to another, and the mind also wanders with them, although the mind is more subtle than the senses. The senses are the vehicles of the mind as it travels on its journey, but the mind is master of the senses because without it, the senses could not contact or experience any objects. Wherever there is contact of the senses with their objects, the mind is necessarily involved, so withdrawal of the senses actually means withdrawal of the mind. Vyāsa, the Yoga Sūtras' commentator, therefore says that when the senses are disconnected from their objects, they dwell in or dissolve into the mind. Once the modifications of the mind are controlled, it is not necessary to make any extra effort to control the senses. When the queen bee (mind) flies, all the bees (senses) fly, and when she sits, all the bees sit around her.

Relaxation is actually the practice of pratyāhāra. When one wants to relax a limb of his body, he simply disconnects the communication of the mind and the senses to that particular limb. This is called releasing tension, and when one has mastered voluntary relaxation in this way, he attains perfect control over the senses and mind and enters a state of concentration. The process of withdrawing the senses and the mind is actually the process of recollecting the scattered forces of the senses and mind. When these forces are no longer dissipated, concentration naturally takes place.

Dhāraṇā—Concentration

Having withdrawn the senses and the mind from external objects, the mind must then carry a single thought pattern in a desired direction. Concentration, the sixth limb of Yoga, is a process through which one withdraws the mind from all directions and focuses its powers for further journey inward. To facilitate this process, one selects a suitable object for concentration, such as a mantra, a form, or a center in the body, to name a few. In a relaxed state, past impressions accumulated in the mind rise to the surface, disturbing the mind's ability to stay on one thought pattern. In daily life, one unconsciously and involuntarily concentrates in many ways. In extreme happiness or sorrow, for example, the mind becomes concentrated on one single thought pattern. But such external concentration is motivated by emotion, instinct, or impulse, and is therefore not considered to be yogic concentration. According to Patañjali, concentration is an internal process that takes place in the mind and is volitionally directed by the will.

There are five factors that are helpful in bringing the mind to a state of concentration. One cannot focus the mind unless one has interest in the object on which one wants to concentrate, so developing interest is the first step. With interest, attention can then be developed. Voluntary focusing based on interest and directed by will power and strengthened by determination results in paying full attention to an object. Practice is the next requisite. Regular repetition of definite techniques and processes that help the mind to flow spontaneously without a break helps form the habit of concentration. For example, setting a specific practice time, creating a favorable environment, keeping a proper diet, regulating sleep and sex, and selecting a definite method make it easier to concentrate the mind. Next, using the same straight, steady, and comfortable seated posture every time one practices and using a smooth, deep, and regular diaphragmatic breathing pattern help one keep the mind and body calm, yet alert. Finally, a calm mind is necessary because an emotionally disturbed mind cannot concentrate. An attitude of detachment from external objects and of witnessing one's own physical and mental activity calms the mind and develops emotional maturity. When the student practices concentration, he is advised not to exert undue effort because effort leads to tension, and tension dissipates or disturbs the nervous system and senses as well as the mind.

There are various kinds of concentration: gross and subtle, outer and inner, subjective and objective, and so on. According to Vyāsa's commentary on the Yoga Sūtras, one can concentrate internally on some point within the body, such as the cardiac center, the base of the bridge between the nostrils, or the tip of the tongue; or one can concentrate externally on any selected object. If the object of concentration is pleasant, beautiful, and interesting, then it is easy for the mind to focus on it for a long time. Using a mantra or the breath for the object of concentration is considered to be the best method for learning to focus the mind one-pointedly in preparation for attaining a meditative state.

Concentration is the gateway through which one enters into meditation and attains samādhi. In the words of Swami Rama:

> Without concentration the energy of the mind is dissipated in vague thoughts, worries, and fantasies. A disciplined man expresses himself more clearly through concentration; a man of ordinary intellect with highly developed concentration is more creative than the highly intellectual man of poor concentration. Through concentration a direct link with the cosmic mind is established so that the mind can attend to several things simultaneously. Concentration is no substitute for labor or action, but it does assist the individual in gaining unique experiences and truths hidden in the deeper recesses of the mind.
>
> Patañjali gave elaborate treatment to the science of concentration, for he realized its utility in calming an agitated mind. Modern scientists now concur with this view and are convinced that only through concentration can one gather together scattered forces and emotions and resolve conflicts. With steady practice the nervous system and the mind are relaxed, and the mind then becomes steady, one-pointed, and free from the shackles of desire. The aspirant is thus led, through concentration, to the superconscious state where he experiences the bliss divine.*

Dhyāna—Meditation

The seventh step in the practice of Yoga is meditation. Meditation is an advanced state of concentration in which one single object of concentration flows without interruption. In this state, the mind becomes fully one-pointed, and this one-pointedness starts

*Swami Rama, *Lectures on Yoga* (Honesdale, PA: Himalayan International Institute, sixth edition, 1979), p. 118.

expanding into a superconscious state. Ultimately there comes a state of samādhi—complete spiritual absorption. This is a spontaneous expression of the unbroken flow of Supreme Consciousness.

The process of withdrawal of the senses, concentration, and meditation can be compared to a river that originates when many small streams gather and merge into one large flow of water. The river then flows through hills and valleys without being stopped by bushes and rocks, and it then finds the plains, where it flows smoothly and harmoniously, passing through forests and villages until it reaches its final destination and merges with the sea. So it is with the process of meditation. At the initial stage, the senses and mind are withdrawn and made one-pointed. Then that one-pointed mind flows constantly toward one object without being distracted by petty emotions, thoughts, memories, and anxieties. Then it enters into the smooth, uninterrupted flow of the meditative state in which *siddhis* (supernatural powers) are experienced. These are analogous to the villages through which the river flows undistractedly. At last the mind ultimately enters samādhi and merges with the ocean of Supreme Consciousness.

Samādhi—Spiritual Absorption

The word *samādhi* is closely related to the word *samāhitam*, which means "the state in which all questions are answered," or "the state in which one is established in one's true nature." Out of curiosity regarding the basic questions that the mind wants to solve, the mind flits from one thought to another and becomes restless. But the moment the mind resolves its curiosity, it has no reason to wander here and there, and thus it naturally establishes itself in its true nature. Then the mind is in a state beyond the concept of language in which it is accustomed to think or produce modifications. Samādhi is a state beyond thinking and feeling in which individual consciousness expands and becomes one with the Supreme Consciousness. In the state of samādhi, the individual soul merges into the Supreme Soul, casts away all limitations and causations, and enjoys eternal bliss and happiness. It is not a state of the dissolution of individuality but rather of the expansion of individuality. When individual consciousness expands to its fullest capacity, that is called samādhi.

In different Yoga traditions this state is called soundless sound, the state of silence, or the highest state of peace and happiness. There are two stages of samādhi: *sabīja* and *nirbīja*. Sabīja samādhi means samādhi "with seeds." In this state, the sense of individuality is retained and the seeds of desire and attachment still remain in latent form. Here the yogī realizes the Truth while a sense of "I" as different from that realized Truth is maintained. In the state of nirbīja or seedless samādhi, however, the individual consciousness is completely united with the Supreme Consciousness. Here the yogī expands the sense of "I" and becomes one with the realized Truth within. This state of samādhi should not be confused with the state of dreamless sleep or death. In dreamless sleep there is a predominance of inertia (*tamas*), but samādhi is a state beyond the concept of all three guṇas. In the words of Swami Rama:

> There may seem to be some resemblance between withdrawal from the external world in deep sleep and the highest state of nirvikalpa samādhi, but there is a vast difference between them. One is an unconscious state while the other is the height of consciousness. Suppose two people go to see a king. One goes and sleeps before the king while the other remains awake and enjoys the king's presence. The one who remains awake is like one in the blissful state of samādhi, while the other, being asleep, remains in the darkness of ignorance. In deep sleep, although very near to reality, one is not aware of reality.
>
> Even during sleep a yogi remains fully awake to

Brahman, and in the waking state he remains as if asleep to worldly attachments. In this divine union of lover and beloved, the subject and the object are dissolved in an ocean of supreme love. It is difficult to express the joy of this superconscious state. Personal experience is the only way to realize that eternal joy.*

Saṃyama

Patañjali uses the term *saṃyama* to describe the combined state of concentration, meditation, and samādhi. According to Patañjali, one can achieve whatever one wants to through the practice of saṃyama because it expands human potentials and allows one to explore higher and higher states of consciousness. Through the practice of saṃyama it is said that one can develop supernatural powers or perfections, called *siddhis*, which are described in the third chapter of the Yoga Sūtras. Because the body is a miniature presentation of the cosmos, whatever exists in the cosmos is present in the body. Microcosm and macrocosm being one, an individual can thus have access to the powers of the universe. The practice of saṃyama upon any object brings perfection regarding that object. By practicing saṃyama on latent mental impressions (saṃskāras), for example, one can realize their content and achieve knowledge of previous births. By the practice of saṃyama on the navel center, one can understand one's entire physiology. By the practice of saṃyama on the throat center, one can eliminate hunger and thirst. By the practice of saṃyama on the distinction between Puruṣa and Prakṛti, one can attain knowledge of Puruṣa, the Supreme Consciousness. Many other kinds of supernatural powers, such as super powers of sight, sound, smell, touch, taste, and the powers of minuteness, lightness, greatness, and lordship are also mentioned.

*Swami Rama, *Lectures on Yoga*, p. 157.

One who attains these partial perfections still has to go beyond their charms and temptations to establish himself in the state of perfect bliss and happiness beyond these siddhis. Constant awareness and the grace of the guru and God, who are one and the same in Yoga, help one to cross these stages. As Swami Rama says:

> The transition from the one-pointedness of the conscious mind to expansion into the superconscious is possible, however, only through the grace of the guru, and without such grace the aspirant who, through concentration, stills the conscious mind, becomes aware only of the murky depths of the unconscious. This is a maze of diverse impressions, and one can lose himself in it so that he cannot transcend the unconscious to attain the superconscious state. Occult sciences, black magic, and so on, are based on this experience of the dark shadows of the unconscious—a state which represents a fall from the conscious to the unconscious rather than an ascent from the conscious into the purity of the superconscious.*

The Concept of God

Patañjali accepts the existence of God. According to him God is a perfect supreme being who is eternal, all-pervading, omnipotent, omniscient, and omnipresent. God is a particular Puruṣa who is unaffected by the afflictions of ignorance, egoism, desire, aversion, and fear of death. He is also free from all karmas (actions), from the results of action, and from all latent impressions. This conception of God can give hope to human beings, for when one overcomes all afflictions (ignorance, egoism, attachment, aversion, fear of death) and does not allow himself to identify with his karmas or to reap their consequences, and when one becomes

*Swami Rama, *Lectures on Yoga*, p. 143.

free from all saṃskāras, then he becomes a liberated soul and merges into God-consciousness.

Patañjali views the individual in essence as God, but because of the limitations produced by afflictions and karmas, one separates oneself from God-consciousness and becomes a victim of the material world. There is only one God. It is ignorance that creates duality from the one single reality called God. When ignorance is dissolved into the light of knowledge, all dualities are dissolved and full union is achieved. When one overcomes ignorance, duality dissolves and he merges with the perfect single Being. That perfect single Being always remains perfect and one. There is no change in the ocean no matter how many rivers flow into it, and unchangeability is the basic condition of perfection.

chapter 7

Mīmāṃsā

Freedom Through the Performance of Duty

The word *Mīmāṃsā* means to analyze and understand thoroughly. The philosophical systems of Mīmāṃsā and Vedānta are closely related to each other and are in some ways interdependent and complementary. The teachings of Vedānta may be said to have their roots in the fertile soil of Mīmāṃsā. Mīmāṃsā emphasizes the teachings of the Veda in the light of rituals, while Vedānta emphasizes the teachings of the Veda in the light of knowledge. Traditionally, the Mīmāṃsā system is called *Pūrva-mīmāṃsā*, which means the earlier or initial teachings of the Veda, and Vedānta is called *Uttara-mīmāṃsā*, which means the later or higher teachings of the Veda. In progressive and integral study, Mīmāṃsā comes first and Vedānta later, just as youth comes before maturity. Mīmāṃsā is meant for householders, while the exclusive practice of Vedānta should take place after one has realized the facts of worldly life; Vedānta is therefore meant for retired life. In this context "retired life" does not mean quitting a job and going on a pension; rather it refers to the retirement from worldly charms and temptations, in which one receives a pension of perfect detachment and contentment. Without a positive view toward life, without understanding the importance of selfless action, without carrying out individual and social responsibilities skillfully, one can never retire but will simply become increasingly tired and frustrated in the emptiness of self-created tedium and pressure.

Mīmāṃsā teaches the yoga of action, while Vedānta teaches the yoga of knowledge. One should develop a lifestyle designed within the framework of the yoga of action while simultaneously internalizing and spiritualizing one's actions to realize the Vedāntic truths. Generally these two aspects combined are referred to as the yoga of action—Karma Yoga. The main goal of the Mīmāṃsā philosophy is to provide a practical methodology for interpreting the teachings of the Veda. In so doing, it also provides a philosophical justification for rituals and explains the meanings behind them. In the Veda, numerous gods and goddesses are invoked. The Mīmāṃsā system therefore deems it necessary to provide a clear explanation of their nature and purpose. The Mīmāṃsā system also discusses the science of sound and the science of mantra, but the major concern of the Mīmāṃsā system is to emphasize the use of meditation with rituals.

The first systematic work on this school is the Mīmāṃsā Sūtra of Jaimini, which is divided into twelve chapters. Sabara Swami wrote a major commentary on the Mīmāṃsā Sūtra, and many other commentaries and independent works on the Mīmāṃsā system exist. Kumārila Bhatta and Prabhākara, the pioneers of this system, founded two branches of Mīmāṃsā, although the major teachings of both branches are the same. Most modern scholars focus on the Mīmāṃsā theories of knowledge, metaphysics, ethics, and theology, but this review will discuss Mīmāṃsā from a different standpoint, focusing on the concept of duty and on ritual.

Many think that the rituals explained in the Veda, which are reestablished by the Mīmāṃsā system, are mere dogma and religious ceremonies, but this is not exactly true. Rituals are the beginning tools for going inward. Through them one learns how to organize his life and prepare a lifelong plan so that he can utilize his time properly and become creative. Another common misunderstanding of the Mīmāṃsā system concerns the concepts of *dharma* (virtue) and *adharma* (nonvirtue). According to Mīmāṃsā, activities that do not thwart the activities of others are dharma (virtuous deeds) and those that do thwart them are adharma (nonvirtuous deeds). To be more specific, all the actions and rituals prescribed by the Veda are virtuous, and those that are not in conformity with the rules of the Veda are nonvirtuous. It should be kept clearly in mind, however, that the Veda is not a mere manual or textbook. *Veda* means knowledge, and that which is realized, understood, or performed in the light of knowledge is dharma. The Veda specifically states: "One should follow only that advice of mine which is good and beneficial, and leave that which is not." Thus, the Veda never advises one to perform rote actions blindly in the name of dharma; rather it advises one to keep an open mind and to use discrimination and understanding to determine which actions are virtuous and which are not. The main message of the Mīmāṃsā system is to find happiness here and hereafter by allowing one's conscience to guide his actions and thereby to understand the real nature of his dharma.

Before discussing the major teachings of Mīmāṃsā, the following topics should be understood: the concept of duty; the concept of rituals; the divergent teachings of the Veda; the science of mantra; the concept of gods and goddesses; the concept of divinity within physical objects; the sources of valid knowledge; and the concept of soul.

The Concept of Duty

Many people are very concerned about their rights but little aware of their duties. There is a vast difference between rights and duties. Unless one knows what one's duties are, he cannot fully understand what his rights are. Demanding rights without accepting duty leads one to many problems. Duty is that for which one is responsible, that without which one cannot live a happy and peaceful life. Duty is the universal law that unites one person with another, that unites all the members of a family and maintains its peace and harmony. It is because of the law of duty that the family, society, the nation, and the entire universe continue to exist. The concept of duty is far superior to the instinctual urges. When one relates to family, society, and nation only because he is tied by the rope of attachment or fear, he is not following the law of duty. But when he acts with full knowledge and understanding, when all of his actions are performed for the sake of peace and harmony and are centered toward inner exploration, then he is following the law of duty.

The highest of all duties is to realize one's own inner Self in its purity and entirety while allowing others to do the same. All other duties are subservient to this central one. Following one's own dharma to attain the highest duty of Self-realization is the way of practice prescribed in Mīmāṃsā, but to do this, one must fully understand what dharma is. The term *dharma* is variously translated as "virtue," "duty," "morality," "righteousness," or "religion," but no single English word conveys the whole or the correct meaning of dharma. According to the Mīmāṃsā system, dharma is the intrinsic nature of *ṛta*, the breath of cosmic life. One who wants to breathe and live properly is not supposed to disturb the breath of cosmic life. Disturbing others disturbs the rhythm of the cosmic breath, and that is called adharma. But performing one's dharma establishes peace and harmony in the breath of cosmic life. All those activities that are helpful in coordinating individual life with cosmic life constitute one's duty or dharma.

The concept of duty is so vast and deep that it is very hard to specify what one's duty is in every case. First of all one has to develop insight into the real nature of duty so that he can correctly understand his own individual duty and thus follow his dharma. There is always a hierarchy in one's duties. Everywhere and at every moment some kind of duty is involved, and one has to be very discriminating to understand the appropriate duty that is to be performed at a particular time and place. Knowing one's role in life can help him realize his primary duty. For example, it is the highest duty of a mother to take care of her small baby, while the highest duty of a teacher is to teach, that of a student is to study, and that of a doctor is to take care of his patients. But even an appropriate action is not truly dutiful if it is performed under pressure or with the intention of earning reward.

Mīmāṃsā proclaims that the Vedic rituals are the highest duties one has to perform, but it also explains and demonstrates that while one Vedic command may be comparatively more important than others in one context, other commands may be more important in other contexts. All duties are one's highest duties in some regard, but they must be thought of and performed in the proper time and place or else they lose their validity.

The Concept of Rituals

Many regard the trappings of ritual—burning candles, sprinkling water, offering flowers, reciting mantras, performing certain gestures, and so forth—as the ritual itself, but these acts are only the external appearances of the actual ritual. When one understands the inner meaning of these externals, he can start enjoying the divine grace that flows through the practice of rituals. Rituals provide a context in which one receives full opportunity to understand the value of action. Most people lack a positive, productive attitude toward their daily activities or jobs, performing them only to earn money or status. But practicing rituals can help one be more aware and understand a higher viewpoint.

Everyone has a morning routine composed of various steps. For example, a working man awakens early, goes to the bathroom, brushes his teeth, washes his face, shaves, takes a shower, dresses, and finally eats breakfast. He does none of this with any sense of consecration—his actions have no higher end or aim than simply to reach the office at exactly nine o'clock. As a result he does not enjoy the activities he performs from bathroom through breakfast, and his whole life rotates in a similar mechanical framework because of his mundane view of existence. But viewing the daily, unexceptional routines of life as rituals to be performed with awareness provides a way to spiritualize and enjoy all activities in order to expand the center of consciousness while performing necessary actions. The true role of rituals is to spiritualize all actions for higher attainments. In short, a ritual is a mental attitude. When one decides to make breakfast an offering or oblation to the gastric fire in the service of the Divine Being within, then the whole process is transformed, although the activities are the same as always. If one analyzes the inner nature of rituals as explained in the Brāhmaṇa literature, one will realize that those rituals and sacrifices provide training for daily living.

In regard to this claim, two of the *yāgas* (rituals) mentioned in the beginning of the *Śatpathabrāhmaṇa—darśa* and *pūrṇamāsa*—can be studied. One who intends to perform these rituals starts the mental preparation one day in advance, taking only a light meal the night before and sleeping in a devotional and positive mood. Then one arises early in the morning, performs one's usual ablutions, gets some water and food, and prepares a meal. In performing these activities as part of a ritual, one develops the attitude of living in God-consciousness so that every moment and action in life can be experienced in God-consciousness. In this divine frame of mind, the person performing the ritual brings water in which divinity is contained, and God-consciousness is maintained as the person cleans the rice, burns the fire, cooks the rice, and finally serves it and offers it to the Divinity. The participants of darśa and pūrṇamāsa transcend the physical plane and interpret ordinary physical activities in a subtle and divine light. They have a specific concept in mind. For example, in the ritual of cleaning rice, they think, "Who can separate dirt or pebbles from rice but the almighty discriminating agency that is God? Though it seems that I am performing these actions, it is not because of me; it is God who is allowing me to do so."

Rituals are performed not to worship or please any deity but rather simply because the Veda commands one to perform them. Thus, they are practiced for the sake of duty. Ultimately the food is cooked and served, and through the use of mantras, the Divinity is invited to partake. One mentally feels the presence of the Divinity, offering food and water exactly as it would be offered to a physical being. One then bids the Divinity farewell and enjoys the food as well as the blessings or grace the Divinity has bestowed. This entire process is an unbroken meditation in action in which one's body and mind are perfectly harmonized. In the scriptures, all processes—physical, mental, and spiritual—are considered to be essential aspects of ritual. During the whole procedure, the mind does not have time to be dissipated because of the intense feeling of the presence of the Divinity.

The scriptures say that one who performs darśa or pūrṇamasa enjoys the celestial pleasure of heaven. When one is depressed, frustrated, dejected, or emotionally disturbed, he lives in the fierce darkness of hell, but when one is cheerful, positive, and compassionate, he enjoys the celestial joy of heaven both within and without. The highest goal of ritual is not to enjoy a distant future heaven but to be free from all bondages here and now. Actions that are not performed selflessly for the sake of duty and as a part of ritual are like thorny trees that produce the poisonous fruits of pain and misery. But actions that are performed selflessly for the sake of duty and as a part of a grand lifelong ritual in the service of Divinity are like beautiful trees that produce the nutritious fruits of love and joy. They destroy all the poisonous shrubs and clear out all the thorny bushes in the garden of human life. Thus actions performed for duty's sake are rituals, but actions performed without proper understanding are mere actions. The Mīmāṃsā system believes that one can cut one's own poisonous plant of past karma with the powerful ax of present karma, and performing rituals helps in this process. Rituals are designed to train the mind and to provide a lifelong schedule for one to follow that does not allow one to feel lonely or forsaken by God. This lifelong routine, designed in a framework of positivity and God-consciousness, enables one to enjoy this very life here and now and to simultaneously explore the inner avenues of being.

The Divergent Teachings of the Veda

Just as one has to understand the real nature and appropriateness of duty before he can perform his duty properly, likewise he needs to understand the real nature and appropriateness of the Vedic teachings before he can follow these teachings properly. To do this, he first has to resolve all the conflicts that arise from the diverse teachings found within the Veda. The methodology employed in the Veda to describe the different levels of truth is very strange to the modern mind. The teachings of the Veda were compiled when society was first being formed, when culture and civilization were first being established. It was very important then for the Vedic sages to introduce their teachings with strong emphasis so that individuals and society as a whole would welcome them. The method they therefore applied is called *stutivāda*, which means "to state with strong emphasis and admiration." In studying the Veda, one should therefore use discrimination. He should understand that many teachings have been glorified to impress the reader, and he should be careful to select only the gems of real teaching for personal practice. Just as in English there are various types of sentences—interrogatory, declarative, imperative, exclamatory—so too the Veda is composed of various types of sentences. These include *vidhi* (imperative), *niṣedha* (negative), and *stuti*, which are the admirational sentences of exaggerated praise. Just as any language can be analyzed and understood by the nature and structure of its sentences, Mīmāṃsā studies the Veda according to the nature of its sentences. Having analyzed them, it states that imperative statements are more valid than admirational sentences. The teachings of imperative sentences can therefore be accepted and practiced, but the teachings of admirational sentences must be further analyzed to determine their implied core meanings.

Thus the Mīmāṃsā system provides a technique for studying the Veda, understanding its real meaning, and selecting the gems of knowledge hidden in its depths. There is no real conflict in the divergent sentences of the Veda; it is merely defective analysis that fails to discern their true knowledge. The methods for knowing the actual meaning of the Veda is provided in Mīmāṃsā texts, such as *Mīmāṃsā-anukramaṇikā* of Maṇḍana Miśra, but as this study is not within the scope of the present survey, it will not be further described.

The Science of Mantra

The generic term for all Vedic verses and sentences is *mantra*. The Veda is the embodiment of knowledge expressed in the form of sound and symbolically represented in script. Mīmāṃsā posits the theory that sound is eternal, and it provides the most ancient as well as the deepest study of sound. Mīmāṃsā places greater emphasis on mantras than it does on gods and goddesses because it believes in the validity of the science of sound on which the science of mantra is based. This belief accounts for Mīmāṃsā's trust in the efficacy of systematic rituals. Mīmāṃsā states that the Vedic rites are grounded in verifiable truth rather than blind faith; it does not view the performance of rituals as a means for imploring favors from a deity.

Mīmāṃsā does not study sound only at its articulated level but explores the subtle levels of sound by delving into its origin and realizing its various vibrational patterns. Sound is called *vāk* in Sanskrit, but this word cannot be translated merely as "sound" or "speech." *Vāk* refers to both thought and expression, while speech is the communication of thoughts and feelings through spoken words. *Vāk śakti*, the power of speech, is actually a law of communication that is responsible for conveying thoughts and concepts, both individually and collectively. When one talks with someone else, the law of communication (vāk śakti) is already present before one speaks and after one has spoken. Vāk Śakti is the force flowing from a higher level of consciousness through the articulated level of speech, which is its gross expression. Following thorough analysis, Mīmāṃsā categorizes vāk śakti on four levels: *parā* (transcendent), *paśyantī* (concentrated thought pattern), *madhyamā* (formulated thought pattern ready for expression), and *vaikharī* (expression with the help of words).

According to Mīmāṃsā there are two universally intertwined factors in manifestation: *śabda*, the sound; and *artha*, the object denoted by that sound. One signifies the name, and the other signifies the form. They are inseparably associated; there can be no śabda without artha, no artha without śabda. Together, they are the self-existent reality which is not subject to change, death, and decay. As they manifest, a double line of creation—words and objects—is formed.

External sound, sensed by hearing, is of two types: sound with meaning and sound without meaning. Sound with meaning consists of the phonemes and words that make up language, but sound without meaning is not formulated into words and is not recognized as an element of communication. According to Mīmāṃsā, external sound is transient, but it is also a manifestation of the eternal Logos. The Nyāya school does not accept the Mīmāṃsā theory of sound; it holds that words are transitory in every regard. Mīmāṃsā counters that the perception of sound that begins when vibrating air contacts the ear drums must be distinguished from the sound itself. For sound to exist, one object must contact another, and that is an external event. But the Mīmāṃsā theory of sound with meaning goes beyond this, including also the internal mental movement of ideas that seeks outward expression through audible sound in phonemes, letters, words, and sentences. Thus the perception of sound is transient, but sound itself is eternal. The moment at which sound can be perceived is not the same moment at which it is produced; sound is manifested prior to being audible.

The finest state of sound, called *parā vāk*, is perfect. The ultimate sound, or Supreme Consciousness, manifests in various grades and degrees that are distinguished from each other by their differing rates of vibration. Any vibration that can be perceived by physical instruments, such as the ears, is only a gross manifestation. The Mīmāṃsā system views the study of sound on a physical level as inadequate for solving the perennial questions concerning the Ultimate Reality. The subtlest state of sound vibration is known as *paśyantī vāk* in Mīmāṃsā. There is only a slight difference between the state of parā and that of paśyantī. Both are transcendent states, but in paśyantī, the Supreme Consciousness sees the entire universe as its primeval desire; thus this state is called *paśyantī*—"one who sees." In this state the power of desire still remains dormant, but it is nonetheless the direct cause of the universe, which will be manifested as both idea and speech. This language of silence is a universal language; it is the source of all language and speech. The third state of vāk is called *madhyamā*, meaning "that which is intermediate." This state of speech is neither transcendent, as in paśyantī, nor completely manifest, as is *vaikharī* (the grossest state of sound); it is between these two stages. Finally, the fourth state of speech is completely manifest and audible. At this stage, a sound that belongs to a specific language can be perceived through the sense of hearing. This state of sound is always accompanied by geographical, cultural, and social diversities and distinctions that form different languages composed of articulated and distinguishable sounds.

The origin of speech is transcendent and eternal, and the flow of paśyantī, madhyamā, and vaikharī from the state of parā is also the flow of the forceful stream of energy from vāk śakti. Like a river hidden in the mountains that comes gurgling forth as it rushes to the valleys where streams merge with it and then flows on to the plains before finally dissolving its identity into the ocean, similarly speech emerges from its hidden source in the state of silence (parā), flows downward into more and more manifested stages, and then at last dissolves into infinity, its origin. This is the process of the unfoldment and enfoldment of vāk śakti.

All speech that passes through the human mind becomes contaminated with the limitations of time, space, and causation. Divinity, or truthfulness, is therefore veiled in everyday speech, but this is not the case with mantras. Mantras are not mere words but are specific sound vibrations that have been experienced by sages in the deepest state of meditation. They are said to be the sound-bodies of certain aspects of the cosmic forces. A mantra is therefore referred to as a *setu*, a bridge, that the student can use to cross over the mire of delusion and reach the other shore of Supreme Consciousness. Mantras are capable of lighting in every human heart the eternal lamp of love that does not flicker with the severe winds of worldly charms and temptations.

The potential of a mantra lies in a dormant state until it is awakened. The secret of awakening and utilizing mantras lies in the rhythmic vibrations in which the mantra is meant to be pronounced and repeated. The proper use of mantras, with their prescribed rituals, is designed to lead one to experience the bliss and happiness contained within the mantra itself. The power of mantra and its awakening can be explained by the following analogy: In the rainy season in some tropical countries the humidity may be one hundred percent, but one cannot quench his thirst with atmospheric water alone because it is not concentrated in usable form. Likewise the great potential of mantras is hidden and diffuse. One must therefore learn how to awaken, concentrate, and utilize their potential.

The Concept of Gods and Goddesses

Modern scientists have developed mathematical equations and scientific laws to describe the order and lawfulness of the universe and thereby increase man's power and control over its phenomena. Likewise, the Vedic sages developed immense powers of introspection and discovered form equations that express the underlying order, lawfulness, structure, and dynamics of the phenomenal world. The forms of expression and sound patterns are known as deities and mantras, respectively. These forms contain a profound symbolic meaning that must be understood to comprehend the concept of deity.

The deities or gods are the personified forms of those equations that originate in accordance with the vibrating sound patterns of mantras. For an uneducated person, the equation $E=mc^2$ is just a meaningless arrangement of lines on a piece of paper. But for those with a sufficient understanding of physics, this formula can help one to comprehend the nature and dynamics of the universe.

The critics of Mīmāṃsā philosophy state that the Mīmāṃsā system believes in many different gods and goddesses. But when one analyzes this further, he finds that within this apparent diversity, there is an underlying unity. The all-pervading consciousness manifests itself in different stages, each of which has a different form (deity) and sound vibration (mantra). Thus exists the apparent diversity of deities and mantras to represent the unitary consciousness. The process of manifestation begins with the emergence of the most subtle forms, from which the grosser or more delineated forms are then manifested. This process has been described and symbolized in various ways in the different mythologies and physical sciences that try to account for the origin, form, and lawfulness of the universe. In the Vedic tradition, prototypic forms have been conceptualized as deities—gods or goddesses—each characterized by a particular set of divine qualities. The Vedic deities provide a metaphorical representation of the progressive stages of manifestation. Though the modern mind usually prefers the term "archetype" rather than "deity," both terms are essentially synonymous in usage.

The Vedic deities radiate from the source of energy that generates all forms and names. They are thought-forms that represent the cosmic powers and are therefore the central points that control all the potentials of manifestation and are the main cause of the universe. Deities are capable of transforming and directing one's pranic and psychic energies to reveal the inner avenues of human potential that make one blissful, radiant, and perfect. The forms of a deity contain unimaginable powers that are behind and involved in manifestation, but a deity is not limited to any specific anthropomorphic form. If it were, it would not be possible for a single deity to be present at many different rituals being performed in different places at the same time.

Deities are not imagined by the human mind, but rather are known through intuition by great sages in the deepest state of meditation. The deities emerge as primal forms and sound-bodies (*mantras*) endowed with perfect bliss and happiness beyond all mundane experiences. Though it seems that deity and mantra are two distinct principles operating on two different levels, in reality they are one and the same. A deity is a gross physical form of a mantra, and a mantra is a subtle form of a deity. When the sequence of vibration of a mantra is materialized into a particular form or shape, that is called a deity. Likewise, a materialized form can be dematerialized and reduced to certain frequencies of vibration that will be heard as a mantra.

There are certain rules by which a mantra converts into a deity and a deity converts into mantra. Both deities and mantras operate on a principle similar to the conversion of energy into matter and matter into energy in physics. Wherever a particular ritual is performed with the proper utilization of mantras, the deity related to those mantras is present because when the vibration is concentrated, the materialized form of the deity appears. According to the Mīmāṃsā system, the vision of a deity does not therefore depend on the grace of that deity. Rather, the deity, or form, is manifested wherever the mantra related to it is pronounced in a prescribed manner, and it then has to yield the desired objects that are believed to be provided by it. The history of the Vedic sages gives repeated examples of such occurrences. The Mīmāṃsā system does not rely on the grace of God for attaining worldly things or achieving liberation. Adepts of Mīmāṃsā philosophy and practices have full confidence that their individual and cosmic powers can be utilized at will, and they know how to use rituals as the methods for controlling such powers.

The concept of ritual is misunderstood in modern society, but Mīmāṃsā identifies two purposes of ritual: to attain and expand one's own inner potential and unite it with the cosmic force; and to pay respect and show gratitude to the cosmic forces that are constantly supplying light and life to all living beings. It is through rituals that human beings express reverence and gratitude to the cosmic forces that control this universe and maintain its peace and harmony. The *Bhagavad Gītā*, which synthesizes all systems of Indian philosophy, says that human beings should honor those cosmic forces that provide for humanity. This is one of the foremost duties of human beings and should be an inseparable part of everyone's life. "Ritual" is meant in the broad sense here. Pouring purified butter in the ceremonial fire and reciting mantras verbally is not the only ritual. Giving up one's own desires and attachments, renouncing the fruits of one's actions in the service of humanity, helping those who are in need and carrying out one's responsibilities happily, are the real meaning of the word *ritual.*

The Concept of Divinity Within Physical Objects

The human mind is so engrossed in its own sensory experiences and limited world view that it seldom allows one to feel the presence of divinity in every walk of life. But Mīmāṃsā is highly practical, and it applies the theory of the all-pervading presence of divinity by providing specific practices designed to remind the student of this truth.

For example, the use of common objects such as water, fruit, incense, grass, stones, and fire in rituals links the mundane with the spiritual. There is a prescribed way for gathering these items for the ritual and for handling and using them during the ceremony. For instance, before a blade of grass is uprooted, one is to recite a specific mantra to revere and glorify the divinity within the grass and to ask permission to uproot the grass and use it in the ceremony. When the grass is uprooted one recites another mantra, explaining the process in the following sense: "I am uprooting my negativities symbolized by the grass. Even within negativities, there is divinity. I am uprooting it for use in the ritual, in which the real nature of divinity is going to be unveiled."

Vedic sages and the masters of Mīmāṃsā philosophy are not

materially oriented, but they use material objects in a skillful way to realize the nonmaterial conscious principle. They allow themselves to feel the presence of divinity even in grass, stones, or trees. This is not the worship of grass, stones, or trees themselves, but rather the worship of the divinity manifested in them. The concept of divinity as existing in both living and nonliving beings enables the human mind to expand its individual consciousness to universal consciousness. It prevents the mind from being overcome by hatred, jealousy, anger, greed, and all other negative attitudes. This practice thus helps one to understand the great Vedāntic truths: "The whole universe is Brahman" and "Thou art That."

The Sources of Valid Knowledge

Mīmāṃsā, like many other philosophical systems, places great importance on the study of nature and the sources of valid knowledge (pramāṇas). According to Mīmāṃsā there are six different sources of valid knowledge: perception, inference, comparison, testimony, postulation, and nonperception. (Nonperception is recognized as a source only by the school of Kumārila Bhaṭṭa and not by that of Prabhākara). Mīmāṃsā emphasizes testimony as a source of knowledge because it believes exclusively in the authority of the Veda. The Mīmāṃsā theories of perception and inference are very similar to those of the Nyāya system, but the Mīmāṃsā theory of comparison is quite different from that of Nyāya, although both ultimately base their theories on the similarity of two things, of which one is already known.

Postulation (*arthāpatti*) is the necessary supposition of an unperceived fact to explain some apparently conflicting phenomena. For example, a person who does not eat during the day but constantly grows fat can be suspected of eating at night. One cannot solve the contradiction between fasting and growing fat unless he assumes that the person eats at night. Knowledge of the person eating at night cannot come under the category of perception or inference, nor can it be reduced to testimony or comparison. Nonperception (*anupalabdhi*) is the source of one's immediate cognition of nonexisting things. One can know the nonexistence of a thing by the absence of its cognition, that is, if it is not present in the senses and it cannot be understood by any other source of valid knowledge. For instance, one can feel the absence of a jar that does not exist because it is not perceived by the senses, but one cannot say that the nonexistence of a jar is inferred by its nonperception, because an inference is based on the universal relationship between middle and major terms. And in this case there is no universal relationship between nonperception (middle term) and the nonexistence of a jar (major term). Therefore direct knowledge of the nonexistence of a jar can be explained only if nonperception is recognized as a separate and independent source of knowledge.

The Concept of Soul

Mīmāṃsā does not entangle itself in the discussion of metaphysics but instead emphasizes the practical approach of Karma Yoga, the Yoga of action. Rituals, or actions, have three components: the performer, the object of the action, and the process of performing it. The main doctrine of Karma Yoga is: "As you sow, so shall you reap." Accordingly, one is the master of his own destiny and is free to enjoy his karma as either master or slave. Mīmāṃsā therefore considers the soul to be an eternal, infinite substance with the capacity for consciousness.*

*Regarding the nature of the soul, the two subschools of Mīmāṃsā (Kumārila Bhaṭṭa and Prabhākara) differ slightly, but as no practical lesson would ensue from a discussion of these differences, they will not be considered here.

Major Teachings of the Mīmāṃsā System

Selfless Action

In an historical debate with Śaṅkara, Maṇḍana Miśra, a great pioneer of Mīmāṃsā, verified that knowledge alone liberates. This liberating knowledge can be achieved only through the yoga of action. Knowledge does not nullify action, it only burns the binding power of those actions. Knowledge allows a person to understand the nature of action and to pave the way for a life of skillful action. Running away from the duties of the world does not solve the problems of life. There is no way that these problems can be avoided; they must be accepted as challenges.

One is bound in the rope of one's karma from time immemorial. It is possible, however, to live freely in this world and to find joy in meeting all of life's challenges. Knowledge, spiritual strength, and skillful action done selflessly form the entrance way to the kingdom of eternal life. Inner strength is the driving force necessary for both temporal and spiritual success. This strength comes only from selfless service expressed through mind, action, and speech. No one can live in this world without performing actions. From birth to death the entire body/mind organism is geared to perform some sort of action continuously. Inaction leads a person to inertia, and selfish action serves as a rope of bondage; it is selfless action alone that helps one gain release from the bondage of karma.

Mīmāṃsā teaches the art of living and performing selfless action. When the human mind understands the purpose of life and one expands one's personality while realizing the presence of divinity within and without, one moves to higher dimensions of awareness, expanding one's love for all creatures of the world. Through the expansion of the center of love and the performance of selfless action, a person becomes free from all residue of the past (samskaras).

Selfless action done to the best of one's ability is the finest of all sources of tranquility. It allows one to experience higher levels of consciousness and cast away all the boundaries created by karma. No one can be free without paying the karmic debts remaining from what was done in past lives. These karmic debts can be paid only through the performance of selfless action. It is the ultimate responsibility of all human beings to discharge their duties faithfully, skillfully, and selflessly, so that they can be freed from the obligations of their own karmic debts. Selfless action in the service of humanity is the real implication of the Vedic rituals.

Nonattachment

When one learns to love others—not just human beings but all creatures of the universe—one is learning to love. There is only one force, called life. By loving all, one loves the life force itself. One should learn to express love through mind, action, and speech. Of these, action is the most important; selfless action done skillfully is the highest of all expressions of love. If one really wants to learn to love others, he will have to surrender the desire to enjoy the fruits of his actions. Actually, universal love means nonattachment. Attachment is an expression of the ego, which identifies itself with the external objects of the world. Through this identification, one excludes himself from many things that should be integral parts of his life. Attachment is an attitude of mind that binds the personality to the petty objects of desire that one longs to achieve. Attachment to any object creates the fear of losing it. Nonattachment does not mean not to strive to be successful in whatever one is attempting to do; nor does it imply that one should be lackadaisical in his actions. On the contrary, true nonattachment frees one to be fully enthusiastic, which inspires his will power to grow.

For the practice of nonattachment, one has to develop a proper philosophical attitude. He must consider himself to be a traveler in the cosmic city of life and must view this present life as a brief stopping place in his journey. Nothing here is one's own; everything—including the body, mind, and all external objects—is on temporary loan. One should not identify himself with these tools; he should neither grieve over loss nor be overjoyed with gain. One should always remember that these objects are borrowed for a particular purpose, which is enjoyment. One should learn how to use these objects and enjoy every moment of being alive without forgetting the highest goal of life. While living in the world and enjoying its objects, one should not forget that sooner or later one will leave all this behind. Thus the principle of nonattachment provides a constant awareness of truth. It does not imply non-enjoyment, but is the process of applying oneself toward the highest goal of life instead of involving oneself in the whirlpool of desires.

Most spiritual practices and rituals are concerned with making demands. Many of the prayers ostensibly devoted to the Supreme Being are actually laden with selfish wishing: "O Lord, you are Emperor of the universe. You are the richest, kindest One. Please grant me a wonderful job, a loving spouse, two beautiful children, and a nice house." According to the Mīmāṃsā system, these are man-centered prayers. Such prayers are not capable of leading one to the highest goal of life. There is a higher kind of prayer, called God-centered prayer, that is meant for leading one to enlightenment. Prayers that are not free from the bondage of attachment and desire cannot provide the highest goal of life, but even the most common activities involved with worldly objects and people, if driven by the motor of nonattachment, can lead to the attainment of liberation, or self-enlightenment.

Normally one is a slave to one's duties and actions, but when those duties and actions are performed with perfect detachment, one becomes their master and is no longer bound to receive their fruits. Rather one is free to receive or reject what he chooses from them. An action in itself never binds one; it is the fruit of that action that binds. One can therefore find joy in renouncing the desire to enjoy the fruits of his actions. Action performed with attachment makes one helpless; he has no choice but to enjoy or suffer the fruit of that action. The action performed with nonattachment, however, benefits all without creating any bondage to the performer. If one thinks it proper to receive some fruits for a particular purpose, then he can accept that which is necessary and distribute the remaining fruits to others.

Nonattachment should not be confused with either complacency or indifference. Complacency does not allow a person to improve further, whereas nonattachment inspires a person actively to seek higher attainments. Indifference is usually indulged in as a mere escape: when one finds himself unable to cope with a situation or to solve a problem, he assumes an attitude of apparent indifference toward it. This form of escapism is the negative property of a weak and forlorn person, while nonattachment is a positive quality of a strong and inspired soul. One who is nonattached meets all the challenges that come his way without allowing them to disturb his equilibrium and tranquility. Such a person remains unaffected by both failure and success.

The concept of nonattachment can be better understood through the example of the manner in which an oblation is offered in the ritualistic fire. The performer of the ritual takes the oblation (clarified butter, sesame seeds, rice pudding) in his hand, recites a mantra while holding it, and then says, "This oblation is offered to the deity; it does not belong to me anymore (*idam na mama*)." In this way, he expresses his resignation of ownership over the object. Offering oblations in the sacrificial fire symbolizes mental training for renouncing attachment to worldly objects and sharing one's possessions with all, just as the fragrant smoke of the burned oblation is enjoyed by all.

Self-control and Self-discipline

Although it is true that one is the master of his life, most of the time one allows himself to live as a slave of his environment. This slavery manifests itself in all aspects of personality—on the physical, mental, and energy levels. One suffers because he has not learned how to control the tools and instruments provided by God. The body and mind are great instruments for higher attainment if they are disciplined and under control. When the body, breath, and mind are out of control, however, they create great problems and do not allow one to concentrate within to explore his inner potentials. No external agent can impose the kind of discipline that is needed to be able to control the body, mind, and senses. This discipline must come from within. It must be self-discipline, arising from a commitment to improve oneself and a belief in one's ability to do so.

Everyone knows that in the long run self-control and self-discipline are helpful, but most people hesitate to put forth the necessary effort and instead want to lean on others. But in order to improve, one has to build a firm pillar of practical self-training and self-discipline on the foundation of self-observation and a commitment to personal growth. No one can help a person who is not committed to self-improvement.

Daily Schedule for Psychophysical Well-being

As training for self-discipline, Mīmāṃsā emphasizes the importance of having a well-organized daily schedule. This daily schedule must be designed in such a way that it does not conflict with one's external or internal life. This schedule should be able to help one to spiritualize all the actions that must be performed in daily life. Life itself does not have to be changed; only one's attitudes do. Mīmāṃsā therefore provides techniques for improving one's attitudes toward the elements of daily routine. For instance, everyone eats and breathes; no one can refrain from these activities, and both are natural processes for a living being. Mīmāṃsā therefore advises saying grace before meals to soothe the mind and make the flow of the breath more regular—both of which are essential for the proper enjoyment and digestion of a meal. When one says grace as a prerequisite to eating, one calms the breath by withdrawing the mind and senses from all outward directions and concentrating within. When one remembers the presence of divinity during grace, this harmonious state of mind reflects onto the body. It stimulates the secretion of saliva and gastric juices and thus inspires a good appetite. As a result, one enjoys his food and digests it properly.

Once faith in God is established in a person's unconscious mind, it cannot easily be removed; faith in God becomes a part of human understanding and an inseparable part of a person's makeup. Mīmāṃsā understands this inner inclination of the human mind and formulates all its beneficial teachings within the framework of religion and in the name of God. An idle mind is the devil's workshop; so the mind must be kept occupied. Mīmāṃsā provides a schedule for one's whole life and divinizes all activities through ritualistic philosophy. Then the mind does not have time to brood on the past or to fly ahead into idle speculation concerning the future. Rather, the mind is trained to occupy itself with the performance of the present ritualized action.

This philosophy advises one to consider all his activities as part of the cosmic ritual. The entire universe is an altar, and each individual life is a miniature representation of that cosmic altar, which should shine and radiate the light of the life force for the benefit of all humanity. This altar should be full of the fragrance of positivity, love, compassion, and happiness. One should know how to pour the water of love, bliss, and happiness on this altar and how to offer the oblations of selfless service in the fire of knowledge. One should learn how to enjoy the blessings of divinity in all the circumstances of life.

Social Awareness

When one becomes self-controlled and self-disciplined, he gradually expands his's awareness and eventually finds himself in perfect resonance with society. He yearns to be a citizen of a well-civilized society and nation and dissolves all conflicts between his individual personality and social life. He becomes a dynamo that radiates love and compassion and follows an inner discipline as a spiritual seeker.

Sense of Equality

In order to experience this growth, one has to learn how to dissolve the inferiority and superiority complexes in which he is entangled and because of which he suffers. These complexes and conflicts are the main problems in human life; they serve as barriers that check the everflowing current of love through the human heart. To remove these obstacles to growth and thus experience an expanded sense of self, one needs to establish and nurture a feeling of equality with others. Through its ritualistic approach, the Mīmāṃsā system establishes a theory of equality and removes the complexes of inferiority and superiority. In some of the most holy and sacred rituals, people from higher and lower castes, male and female, old and young, warriors and intellectuals, and even the animal and plant kingdoms, are necessary participants. The absence of a representative from any one of the groups vitiates the efficacy of the ceremony. The Mīmāṃsā system understands that without establishing a sense of equality, the theory of love cannot be practiced.

Unity Within Diversity

To see the basic unity that underlies and suffuses the apparent diversity of this existence is a very important factor in being able to resolve the conflicts, confusions, and contradictions everyone experiences in life. These inner and outer problems must be resolved for one to be able to realize his potentials. An average human being is engrossed in the external objects of the material world, and his ego, with its false identification with the body, mind, and senses, causes him to lose his capacity to see the one single Reality that manifests in different forms. The outward flow of mind becomes so accustomed to dealing with the diversities of life that the individual becomes oblivious to the underlying unity.

It is very difficult for an untrained mind to experience this essential oneness of the universe. To assist one in doing so, Mīmāṃsā teaches that the ultimate Reality, called Indra, manifests himself in the form of the moon, the sun, fire, wind, and all other cosmic powers, which are personified as individual deities. Partially informed scholars generally think that Mīmāṃsā is polytheistic, but this is not exactly true. Polytheism is an initial stage of the Mīmāṃsā philosophy that is applied to reach the state of monism. The Mīmāṃsā system states that all the things of the world have an essential potential, Śakti, which is the power by virtue of which everything comes into existence, remains for a period of time, and returns again into its origin. This all-pervading potential is one and the same in all the divergent objects of the universe; it only appears to be diverse with many names and forms, just as water appears to be different colors depending on the colors of the vessels in which it is contained. When viewing the objects of the external world, one should be aware of the divinity of all things, and one should learn how to tie all his experiences together with the thread of divine unity.

Selectiveness

Novices are sometimes confused by Mīmāṃsā's varied teachings, spiritual practices, rituals, and concepts of gods and goddesses. Mīmāṃsā therefore advises one to be selective and conscious of his own interests, inclinations, attitudes, capacities, and circumstances when deciding which particular spiritual practice and lifestyle to adopt. This process of discrimination, self-examination, and introspection consists of listening to various teachers and studying diverse scriptures, but selecting only those that are helpful and beneficial for personal growth. Without first developing this quality of selectiveness, one will waste his time and instead of progressing will gradually lose his own faith, love, and other higher qualities.

Every teaching is not meant for every human being. One should study as much as possible, but as far as his spiritual practice is concerned, he should incorporate into his schedule only that which suits his own personality and which does not create any internal or external conflict. That is why great masters say, "You should do what I say, but you should not do blindly what I do." This selectiveness also implies broadmindedness. One who is on the path of spiritual progress must open his heart and mind to listen to others and at the same time be selective so that he can choose the gems of teachings from sundry sources and integrate them properly within the framework of his personal philosophy of life.

Seeing Eternity in the Noneternal

Oftentimes one may not understand the inner meanings of certain rituals and the external objects used in their performance. One might then perform them blindly without understanding their deeper meaning, or become disgusted with the religious beliefs associated with these rituals. Neither reaction is beneficial. Many people think that establishing a relationship between divinity and a symbol (such as the Jordan River or the Ganges; trees, stones, or animals) is a primitive way of thinking. To these people, it is a primitive philosophy or religion that advocates the worship of animals and nonliving things. Actually, these critics do not understand the inner meaning of such beliefs. Because of their egos and sense of self-importance, many people do not recognize the presence of divinity in other living and non-living things. To gain a proper understanding and appreciation of any kind of worship, ritual, faith, or devotion, one must first understand and appreciate the importance of love.

Love and reverence cannot be separated from each other; love without reverence is lifeless and empty. When one learns to love another human being, he also learns to love the life force itself. How can one then separate from himself the animal, plant, and mineral kingdoms, in which the same life force as his own is manifesting and dwelling? Love is the Lord of life. Therefore, it should be revered in all its forms. One should be aware of extending his love not only to human society but to all the creatures of the world, as well as plants and minerals. This makes an aspirant aware of that universal consciousness that manifests itself in the form of love and unites person to person, the human kingdom to the animal kingdom, and the world of animals to plant and mineral life.

This divine love is the inner light of the inner heart and is omnipresent and omnipotent. Why should human beings be sensitive to their species only? The worship of animals simply means to see divinity in the animal kingdom. The omnipresence and omniscience of divinity, which pervades the entire universe, including both organic and inorganic principles, can be realized in any place at any time. This realization of the omnipresence of divinity is possible only when one withdraws his narrowness and expands his God-consciousness within and without. Gratitude is the best way to express one's love and sincerity. The sun provides light. If one does not express his gratitude for this, he is surely blocking his natural flow of love. A plant gives fruit, a river gives water, and neither asks for anything in return from human beings. How can mankind be ungrateful for these phenomena? The expression of gratefulness and appreciation is not worship of plants and animals, it is worship of that all-pervading consciousness that is in oneself and in all other beings and objects.

chapter

8

Vedānta

The Philosophy of Monism

The Mīmāṃsā and Vedānta systems are closely allied; Mīmāṃsā is known as *Pūrvā-mīmāṃsā* , and Vedānta as *Uttara-mīmāṃsā*. Pūrva-mīmāṃsā developed out of the ritualistic teachings of the Veda, while Uttara-mīmāṃsā developed from the Upaniṣads and is the culmination of Vedic thought. In fact, *Vedānta* literally means "the end of the Vedas." In ancient times, an Indian student's education was not considered complete until he or she received instruction in the Upaniṣads, but it is said that mere study of the Veda is not sufficient to enable one to reach his goal. Rather, a student needs to realize its teachings experientially.

The methodology used to describe the subject matter of the Upaniṣads is unique. Most of the Upaniṣads are written in symbolic language. One should not depend entirely on grammatical and linguistic knowledge to comprehend the real meaning of the Upaniṣads, for it is not possible to unravel their terse metaphorical teachings without the guidance of an accomplished master. The meaning of *upaniṣad* is "a scripture that can only be studied and properly understood while sitting closely to the teacher." One must have direct instruction from qualified teachers (*Brahmaniṣṭha*) to understand the subject matter and symbolism hidden beneath the surface language of the Upaniṣads.

The subject matter of the Upaniṣads is not clearly organized in the texts, but Vyāsa—also known as Bādarāyaṇa—systematized the Upaniṣadic concepts in the Brahma Sūtras. The Upaniṣads are rife with discrepant passages. Bādarāyaṇa was the first scholar to attempt to clarify and reconcile the apparent contradictions in the teachings of the Upaniṣads. The Brahma Sūtras are divided into four chapters: *Samanvaya*, which deals with the coherence of the Upaniṣadic teachings; *Avirodha*, which deals with noncontradiction in relation to established theories and logical rules; *Sādhana*, which describes the means of realization; and *Phala*, which deals with the goals of Vedānta philosophy. The sūtras are very terse, and because elaborate interpretations are not provided, their meaning is extremely difficult to understand. Various commentaries have consequently come into existence to explain them. Each commentator has tried to justify his own position through profound reasoning and argument. In this way over the course of centuries many schools have developed, the most famous among them being founded by Śaṅkara, Rāmānuja, Madhva, Vallabha, and Nimbārka. Each of these schools has a long tradition. Even today their original teachings, as described in innumerable subcommentaries, are faithfully followed throughout India and abroad.

Views Common to All Schools of Vedānta

All the schools of Vedānta consider and try to resolve the following major questions: What is the ultimate Reality? From where do all physical and mental phenomena originate? What is the nature of the state in which all phenomena dissolve? What is that reality through which everything is known? What is that which makes an unknown known? What is the means for attaining immortality? What is the nature of the Self? What happens after death? What is the importance of the body, mind, and senses? All the Upaniṣads share a common understanding regarding these questions and their resolutions. For example, the Upaniṣads unanimously maintain the existence of an all-pervasive Reality, called Brahman or Ātman. They also all analyze the Self as distinguished from the body, breath, mind, and intellect, which cover the Self like veils or sheaths (*koṣas*). The pain and pleasure one experiences are considered to be the passing and changing modes of the body, senses, and mind, born of ignorance and not ultimately real. The Self is considered to be eternal and to have the essential nature of bliss and knowledge. Whatever seems to be pleasant is so because of the existence of the pure Self in that object; the pure Self is the ultimate source of all joy. This Self is to be realized with the help of a sharp and penetrating intellect. This Self-realization is the highest goal of life. To achieve this goal, the Upaniṣads do not encourage external rituals but instead emphasize the internalization of awareness.

The Upaniṣads uniformly deny the ultimate existence of the multiplicity of objects, holding that all diverse names and forms are unreal and that only the underlying unchanging eternal Reality can truly be said to exist. This is analogous to saying that golden ornaments with diverse names and forms are only temporary appearances of the essential element, gold. The ornaments are derived from gold, and when they are melted down, they become gold again. Likewise, life emerges from the eternal and dissolves into it again. The underlying Reality remains essentially the same regardless of the various forms it exhibits.

After the Upaniṣadic teachings were systematized in the Brahma Sūtras, a flood of commentaries and interpretations ensued. These vary greatly in approach, but the commentary of Śaṅkarā is outstanding. His commentary is so elaborate and profound that sometimes only his philosophy is considered to be

Vedānta. However, there are also many schools based on the Brahma Sūtras of Bādarāyaṇa that uphold various theories of monism, qualified monism, or dualism.

None of the schools of Vedānta agree with Nyāya, Vaiśeṣika, Sāṃkhya, Yoga, and Buddhism regarding the theory of the manifestation of the universe. Vedāntins do not consider the universe to be the transformation of an unconscious nature. All the schools of Vedānta hold that without the guidance of the conscious principle, unconscious matter could not produce this world, which adheres to certain rules and laws. Such order and regulation, they argue, cannot be the attributes of an unconscious principle. The schools of Vedānta also unanimously agree on the existence of God. They view Reality as Supreme Consciousness, which is simultaneously involved in the phenomenal world and transcendent. To avoid confusion, Vedāntins use the term *Brahman* to denote the transcendent aspect, and the word *Iśvara* to denote that aspect of the ultimate Reality that oversees the phenomenal world. All the schools of Vedānta philosophy agree that the existence of God cannot be proved or known by reasoning and logic alone; God's existence can be established only through direct experience or by testimony. Reasoning is, however, necessary to justify faith, to understand the real teachings, and to remove all doubts.

Monism—the School of Śaṅkara

According to tradition, the school of pure, unqualified monism is the most ancient in Upaniṣadic thought. The founder of this school is said to be Vyāsa, who systematized the teachings of the Upaniṣads. The teacher/student lineage of this school progresses from Vyāsa, to Śukadeva, to Gauḍapāda, to Govindapāda, to Śaṅkara. This progression is confusing in the light of historical dates, however. Vyāsa was both father and teacher of Śukadeva, and they probably lived between 1,000 B.C. and 500 B.C., whereas Śaṅkara's time was somewhere between the sixth and ninth centuries A.D. Thus there is a gap of at least one thousand years between Śaṅkara and Vyāsa. One traditional explanation for this chronological lacuna is that Gauḍapāda was initiated by Śukadeva in divine form, not as a living human entity. According to another tradition, when Śaṅkara met his teacher Govindapāda, that great yogi had already been living on the banks of the river Narbadā in southern India for a thousand years. Followers of this tradition staunchly maintain that Govindapāda's body had been made immortal through his mastery of the science of alchemy. There are still sages in the Himalayas and even in the plains of India who have not aged in hundreds of years. Devarahavā Bābā, a famous dark-haired yogi, still lives on the bank of the river Ganges and is considered to be ageless, as are many sages of the Himalayas who live apart from the crowd and are known only by a few fortunate ones. This may be the secret of Śaṅkara's tradition.

Śaṅkara was ordained a monk by the sage Govindapāda, who instructed him in the teachings of the Brahma Sūtras as explained by Vyāsa. Govindapāda's teacher, Gauḍapāda, had also written a few books, among which his *Māṇḍūkya-kārikā* is the most famous. No works of Govindapāda are extant, but both Gaudapāda and Govindapāda are very much respected in the tradition of Śaṅkara. Śaṅkara was the first philosopher and teacher to establish a formal school of Advaita (monistic) Vedānta. He based his theory on three great landmarks of Indian philosophy and culture: the Upaniṣads, the Brahma Sūtras, and the *Bhagavad Gītā*. These three together are called the *Prasthānatrayī*. Śankara wrote profound commentaries on these three scriptures. From the Upaniṣads, he selected only eleven for his commentary. They are very profound and valuable and form the greater body of Vedānta. He also produced many other works that are major contributions to the formulation of the nondualistic theory of Vedānta.

Śankara accomplished two main missions through his nondualistic theory of Vedānta. First, he reformed the society of the time, which was polluted by unworthy religious preceptors, and second, he provided a concrete philosophy and spiritual practice for those who were prepared to explore the innermost avenues of human life. His teachings can be divided into two major parts: social, ethical, and moral teachings; and metaphysical and spiritual guides. The concepts of Self (Ātman), the Supreme Consciousness (Brahman), cosmic illusion (Māyā), the universe, God, human life, and liberation are the major topics discussed in Śankara's writings.

The Concept of Ātman, the Self

The concept of Self in Advaita (monistic) philosophy is quite different from that of the concept of Self in the Nyāya, Vaiśeṣika, Sāṃkhya, and Buddhist philosophies. According to Śankara, Self is the all-pervading, self-illumined Consciousness. It is the highest truth, the absolute; it is beyond all phenomena in existence, beyond time, space, and causation, and it cannot be experienced by the senses or the mind. The entire phenomenal world is confined by time, space, and causation, and as long as one remains bound by these concepts, his experience is limited. But beyond the realms of time and space, there is an absolute unconditional Reality that has no beginning and no end. That is called Ātman, the Self.

The Self is within the body, it is also outside it, and at the same time is separate from it. The body is composed of matter, and it therefore deteriorates and decomposes, but the pure Self is beyond any such death and decay. The Self is the fountainhead of the life force, which animates and motivates the entire body/mind complex. It is the eternal source of intelligence and wisdom and is completely untouched by any external changes and mutations. The source of consciousness, the Self, is always the same, unchangeable and immortal. It flows from eternity to eternity and from infinity to infinity. A person's body passes from childhood to youth, from youth to maturity, and from maturity to old age, but the inner being of a person remains essentially the same. This sameness belongs neither to matter nor to energy, both of which are constantly changing. This sameness is the transcendent absolute Reality.

One's finite state of consciousness occurs because his infinite inner essence manifests on various levels or gradations. A person passes through many degrees and stages and ultimately merges again into infinity. Ātman, the pure Self, ever witnesses all the changing phenomena within and without. One after another there arises an ever-changing flow of thoughts and emotions, but underlying this, there exists a permanent and unchanging Reality that remains constant and that is witness to all these mental phenomena. Thoughts, passions, emotions, and moods arise and go away, to be replaced by others, which also pass away. But the witness who eternally watches all inner and outer changes is beyond the realm of sense perception; it is beyond the reach of mind, ego, and intellect. It is the very source of consciousness; it provides vitality and energy for the functions of all energies, senses, mind, and intellect. Scientific observation depends entirely upon sense perception and is not capable of providing a method of understanding or experiencing the Reality that is the witness. The power of witnessing dwells in the innermost chamber of everyone's heart. An external object can be studied when it is illumined by light, but light itself cannot be illumined through any external objects. Likewise, the senses and their perceptions are experienced in the light of Ātman (consciousness), but Ātman itself cannot be experienced through the senses. The senses are known as senses because of Ātman, but Ātman is revealed by itself. In daily experience one says, "I have a body, a brain, and a mind." This implies that one is not body, brain, and mind, but something separate and different from all of these.

When brain and mind are at rest during deep sleep, there remains a self-illumination that experiences the resting state of mind. In deep sleep the self is established in its pure nature, which is beyond the grasp of the mind and senses, but when a person wakes up he is able to remember that he slept deeply and enjoyed a good sleep. It is the never-changing Self, shining and permanent, that experiences its own state of dreamless sleep and remembers it during the waking state. But no scientific or parapsychological research will ever be able to study the Ātman, because the very nature of the Self is beyond the constructs of time, space, and causation. Ātman is the inherent essence of all beings; it is eternal, beginningless, and endless. Perfection is its vital stuff, but lack of insight prevents a person from seeing the truth of his immortal nature. Vedānta philosophers often give the following analogy to describe the nature of Ātman. Ātman is like an ocean of bliss and consciousness, and the physical appearance of an individual is like a wave in the ocean of bliss. When the wind of saṃskāras and desires blows, the waves appear and disappear. Those who think that the waves are different from the ocean are ignorant. The rising and falling of waves in the ocean does not affect the existence of the ocean. Such is the case with birth and death, which cannot create any difference in the essential nature of the Ātman. The physical and mental lives of human beings are blown away by death, but death does not affect Ātman. Death is nothing but returning to the origin from which one has come and from which one will emerge again. Life does not begin in the ovum, and its end is not the grave. There is a continuous existence from eternity to eternity in the beginningless and endless journey of the Self. It is the physical body alone that is circumscribed by life and death. The *Bhagavad Gītā* says that the Self cannot be born and cannot be killed. If one thinks that he kills and if the other thinks that he is being killed, both of them are ignorant because they do not know that the real Self can neither kill nor be killed. Indestructibility is the essential nature of the Self.

The Concept of Brahman, the Supreme Consciousness

According to Śaṅkara, Brahman is the ultimate Truth within and without. Whatever exists is Brahman; and whatever does not exist in the manifest world is also Brahman. Whatever is seen and whatever is known is Brahman. Brahman is all-pervading and self-illumined Consciousness. Śaṅkara says that there is only one Reality, and that is Brahman; nothing exists separate from Brahman. If one perceives something as different from the Real (Brahman), it is due to ignorance, but this does not mean that ignorance exists separately from Brahman. In its cosmic sense, ignorance is known as Māyā, the cosmic illusion. The concept of Māyā makes Śaṅkara's theory unique, and it will be discussed separately.

Brahman and Ātman are identical, exactly as the forest and the trees are identical. One cannot prove the existence of a forest by analyzing the different kinds of trees and plants, but the conglomerate of trees, plants, and bushes is still a forest. Likewise, there are numerous individual souls (*vyaṣṭi*), but this does not alter the fact that their conglomerate nature (*samaṣṭi*) is Brahman. The concept of names and forms does not belong to Brahman because Brahman is the all-pervading infinite absolute Reality, while names and forms denote finite things that are limited by time, space, and causation. All things that have name and form are transitory, but the absolute Brahman is permanent existence that swallows up all the names and forms of the transitory plane. All things with name and form can be destroyed by death, but Brahman is the state of reality that destroys even the concept of death. Brahman is the very source of existence, from which springs the entire universe qualified by name and form. It is only the imagination that gives color, touch, smell, and sound to worldly sensations. The real nature of Brahman in worldly objects is hidden from the ignorant, but those who see things as they really are, as reflections of Brahman, live in Brahman-consciousness. The absolute Brahman is like the self-effulgent sun, from which radiates the light of knowledge, bliss, and consciousness. It is because of that radiation of light from Brahman that all the names and forms of the world are perceptible to the senses.

Brahman is the resplendent, unaffected, and unchanged Absolute.

The entire universe emanates from Brahman, exists in Brahman, and at the time of dissolution returns into Brahman. Thus, nothing exists separately from Brahman. Brahman is the only existence, and all other relative realities exist because of Brahman. The concept of duality, or the relationship between the manifold universe and the singular Brahman, is a projection of the cosmic power of illusion. Vedānta actually does not recognize the concept of bondage or the concept of liberation because the soul (Ātman) and Supreme Consciousness (Brahman) are one and the same and remain always unaffected by changeability and partiality. When the sun is concealed by clouds, a learned person knows that in actuality the sun is not covered or destroyed by the clouds but that the clouds merely obstruct the sun from one's sight; the sun is never really affected or disturbed by clouds. In a comparable way, the absolute Self remains embedded with its perfect effulgence and glory in the innermost chamber of the heart. Nothing exists except Brahman, and Brahman is ever-free.

The Concept of Māyā

If, as Vedānta posits, Brahman alone exists as the absolute self-shining Consciousness, then what is this universe? If there is only one single Reality called Brahman, then why do human beings perceive diverse worldly phenomena and behave according to the dictates of their environment? Advaita philosophers explain the existence of the universe with the help of the concept of Māyā, which is found in the Upaniṣads. The Ṛg Veda states that Indra (a term used for absolute Reality) assumes various forms through Māyā.

The Upaniṣads state that the face of Truth is veiled with the golden disc of Māyā, which must be removed for one to realize the ultimate Truth. The concepts of time and space that veil the face of Truth are evolutes of Māyā. Beyond Māyā there is no time or space, and there is no universal cause because only Brahman—the absolute

Reality—remains. According to the Upaniṣads, Brahman is the only Reality, and the world is ultimately false. The entire universe is the projection of Māyā. Because Māyā veils the Truth, the individual self misconstrues both the world and itself as being different from Brahman. In the cosmic sense, ignorance is called Māyā, but in reference to individual misconceptions, it is called *avidyā*. The words *avidyā, ajñāna, adhyāsa, adhyāropa, anirvacanīya, vivarta, bhrānti, avyakta, nāmarūpa, bhrama, mūlprakṛti,* and *bījśakti,* are often used as synonyms of Māyā.

Description of Māyā

The following characteristics clarify the nature of Māyā.

1. Like Prakṛti, Māyā is unconscious and is opposed to the conscious principle Brahman, but it is neither real nor independent.

2. Māyā is an inherent power of Brahman, through which Brahman veils itself. It is inseparable and undifferentiated from Brahman. Māyā is neither identical with Brahman, nor different from Brahman, nor both.

3. Māyā is beginningless.

4. Māyā is both positive and negative, though it is not real. It is positive because it projects the world of plurality, and it is negative because it conceals the real, nondual nature of Brahman that is perfect knowledge and bliss. These two aspects of Māyā are known respectively as *āvaraṇa-śakti*, the power of concealment, and *vikṣepa-śakti*, the power of projection. In other words, through its aspect of concealment Māyā hides the purity and originality of Brahman and Ātman, and through the power of projection it produces the world qualified by names and forms. Thus Māyā can be said to be noncomprehension as well as miscomprehension.

5. Māyā is indescribable because it is neither real, nor unreal, nor both real and unreal. It is not real because it does not have any independent existence apart from Brahman. It is not unreal because it is the actual power by which Brahman manifests itself as this apparent universe. It is also not both real and unreal because the conception of real and unreal in the context of one thing at one time is self-contradictory. From the standpoint of the world, Māyā is comprehended as real, but from the standpoint of the absolute Reality it is unreal. Thus it is neither real nor unreal, nor both real and unreal. Because of its complex nature, it is indescribable.

6. Māyā is relative. The one absolute Brahman appears in many forms, and its power of becoming finite is called Māyā.

7. Faulty cognition or mistaking one thing for something else is a form of Māyā (*bhrānti*). Seeing a snake in a rope or silver in a shell are examples of this.

8. Māyā is removable. By right knowledge or proper understanding, the misunderstanding called Māyā can be removed. Confusing a rope for a snake is rectified through a correct apprehension of the rope.

9. The substratum of Māyā is Brahman, yet Brahman is untouched by it. Thus Māyā is the power of the absolute Brahman. It has no independent existence, but rests in Brahman. From the practical point of view, however, it is not totally illusion. There are certainly some differences between hallucinations, illusions, dreams, and the experiences of the waking state. Compared to the experiences of dreams, the experiences of the waking state are more real, but from the absolute point of view, hallucinations,

illusions, dreams, and the experience of the waking state are all equally unreal.

Māyā and Brahman

In summary, Māyā is tangibly existent, but it cannot be described either as being or as nonbeing. The existence of the universe cannot be called unreal. Māyā's power of concealment hides the absolute state of Brahman, just as sleep obscures knowledge of the waking state. By the power of the projection of Māyā, the entire universe is created, exactly as the objects of dreams are created in the dreaming state. Māyā's powers to conceal and project function simultaneously. The state in which Brahman is consciously associated with Māyā to create the universe is called Īśvara, God. This combined state of Māyā and Brahman appears as the creator, preserver and destroyer of the universe. In the same manner, Ātman appears as Jīva or the individual self. From the cosmic point of view Māyā is one, but from the individual point of view it is many.

Māyā can therefore be studied in two different ways: cosmically and individually. The Brahman associated with cosmic Māyā is called Īśvara or Saguṇa Brahman or God, and the individual self associated with Māyā (*avidyā*, ignorance) is called *jīvātman*. Both the cosmic and individual levels of Māyā hide the true nature of Brahman and the Self. The limitation of Brahman and the Self, therefore, is only apparent and unreal. The limitation produced by Māyā is called *upādhi*, meaning "condition," but false conditions cannot make a difference to the Reality, just as a mirage of water cannot convert a sandy desert into a lake. Ultimately, all projections of Māyā are unreal, being illusory in nature. The entire universe is expanded from Brahman with the help of Māyā, just as a magical illusion is projected by the magician. In actuality, the Absolute is not touched by it at all, just as a magician is not tricked by the illusions of his own magic.

Brahman associated with Māyā is the material cause of the universe, and Brahman unassociated with Māyā is the efficient cause of the universe. These causal relationships between Brahman and the universe are analogous to those between a spider and its web. When the spider wants to weave its web, it utilizes its own inherent potential to produce filament. The spider, being a conscious creature, is the efficient cause of the web. Because the filament is an inseparable and intrinsic property of the spider, the spider itself is also the material cause of the web.

The Concept of the Universe

According to Śaṅkara there is only one Reality, and that is Brahman. He does not totally deny the existence of the world but emphasizes the ultimate Reality for a particular purpose. The world is only an appearance; it is not the ultimate Reality. As long as one is in the world, however, he cannot take it to be entirely unreal. Even Śaṅkara accepts that some degree of error and illusion exists. The objects of dreams last as long as a person is dreaming. Likewise, as long as one mistakes a rope for a snake, he is frightened and reacts to the rope exactly as if it were a real snake. But when one realizes that it is a rope and not a snake, he may laugh at his own folly. In a like manner, as long as one is engrossed in the ignorance of relative consciousness, this world is indeed quite real. But when true knowledge dawns, one becomes aware that the world is sublated, that the world does not exist independently from the cause, Brahman. Śaṅkara states that once the self is entangled in the creation of Māyā, it has to receive help from Māyā to overcome Māyā. When someone is sunk in mud, he can get out of it only with the help of mud because there is nothing supporting him except mud.

Opponents of Śaṅkara's theory inquire, "If the world is completely unreal, how is it possible to feel the existence of the world as real? How is it possible to be affected by worldly objects? If no snake exists in a rope, then that imaginary snake cannot bite; one cannot die from a rope bite. By the same token, if the world is completely unreal and imaginary, then one cannot continue practical behavior in the world." Śaṅkara replies by stating that the imagination creates the presence of a snake in a rope, and that imagination is so strong that a person can die from an imaginary snake bite. Thus, wrongly perceived situations may result in physical or psychological reactions.

It is not the intention of Śaṅkara to refute the existence of the universe. In actuality, Śaṅkara holds two different views of reality: apparent and absolute. All external and internal phenomena belong to the apparent reality, and Brahman alone is the absolute Reality. As long as one is entangled in the miscomprehension of physical and mental phenomena, apparent reality seems to be real. From the plane of this apparent reality, one cannot see or realize the absolute Reality; one thinks that this apparent reality is all there is. But from the heights of absolute Reality, one clearly sees and realizes both sets of reality—apparent and absolute. For him, only absolute Reality exists, and apparent reality seems to be completely illusory. In general, Śaṅkara presents his monistic philosophy from the standpoint of absolute Reality. That is why apparent reality is posited to be illusory and unreal throughout his system.

The Theory of Causation

Śaṅkara accepts the theory of causation, but his version of the theory differs somewhat from the version accepted by Sāṃkhya philosophers. Śaṅkara's theory of causation, known as *vivartavāda*, states that an effect is merely an illusory appearance of the reality that is the cause. When the world is experienced as having qualities of multiplicity and changeability, these qualities are mere appearances of the ultimate Truth, which is always and ever nondual and immutable.

The aspect of reality that remains unchanged and that cannot be annihilated is known as the Self. In actuality the entire universe is the illusory manifestation of the Self, but as long as one is in the world, he cannot totally discard the objects of the world as being unreal. Certainly there must be some levels of reality in the illusion. Even objects of a dream, which last for only a few moments, release a deep impression in the personality. Likewise the worldly objects related to the waking state have great impact on human personality and behavior. Thus they cannot be thought to be simple illusion. For practical application, Śaṅkara provides a specific method of *sādhanā* and a world view to deal with this relatively real or unreal physical and mental world. This method consists mainly of meditation and contemplation and is described briefly in a later section. The process of manifestation of the universe as described in Vedānta indicates that the universe is an orderly system. In the grand cosmic illusion, the whole universe operates according to fixed rules and laws. The epistemological explanation of the universe is also helpful in understanding the role of a human being on this platform and his quest to realize his essential eternal nature.

The universe is described by Vedānta as being composed of many gradations and stages of descending and ascending forces of Brahman associated with Māyā. Even in the field of illusion there are various gradations, with some illusions seeming to be more real than others. This relativity is also Māyā. In the material world some objects last longer than others—a stone lasts longer than paper. But that which truly exists can never really be destroyed, just as that which does not exist can never be produced. Paper exists only relatively; its name and form eventually change into something else. The entire universe of apparent existence will be destroyed when the cosmic illusion is eventually withdrawn to the ultimate Reality in the final dissolution of the cosmos. However, even in this state of complete dissolution, Māyā will remain as an essential potential of the ultimate Reality called Brahman. That is why Vedānta claims that Māyā is inseparable from Brahman.

Prāṇa, The Life Force

Another Vedāntic view holds that all animate and inanimate objects of the world are the results of the vibration of prāṇa, the life force, which is not different from Māyā. The vibration of prāṇa is at the root of the entire universe and is the prime cause of all events occurring in the world. Prāṇa is the cosmic life principle; it is the breath of the ultimate Reality. Because of this life force, living beings animate and produce vibrations. Likewise, all gross elements are the materialized forms of vibrating patterns of prāṇa. Thus the entire universe is a pattern of vibrations and movements. With this vibrating energy, the smallest atoms as well as the biggest planets are held together in a state of continuous vibration. Electricity, gravity, magnetic force—all these are different states of vibration. Even the sensations of color, smell, sound, touch, and taste are vibrational patterns. Intellectual faculties are also the result of vibrations, and the very force of vibration is also prāṇa. Individual beings and the entire cosmos are manifestations of the infinite cosmic life force.

In Vedānta, the entire universe is considered to be the derivative of Brahman associated with Māyā, which is termed Iśvara. Therefore there is no such thing as dead matter in the universe. The universe, in its entirety, is a living organism. The Veda says that the cosmic life force, prāṇa, existed before the beginning of evolution. Before the manifestation of the universe, there was neither existence nor nonexistence, space nor time, light nor darkness, death nor immortality. The eternal supreme Being was breathing without breath and was one with the cosmic energy. From that mighty source—Brahman and Māyā—the entire universe came into existence.

Prāṇa, the potential of consciousness, is the eternal, infinite source of individual and cosmic life. Although this universe of appearances is noneternal, Reality itself is eternal. One grieves over the loss of an external object because he does not fully realize this truth. When one perceives the gross world without understanding the universal life force by which the entire universe is governed, he sees this world as ever-changing and as subject to death and decay. But the moment he truly comes to know the universal governing force of prāṇa, he is liberated from the laws of the world that are responsible for his misunderstanding.

In truth, nothing is ever lost and nothing is gained. What is seen as creation or destruction is merely the appearance of something changing form. When a form passes through an unknown and unseen period of time, that state is called death. When this process is scientifically analyzed, it is found that life and death are only different vibrational states of prāṇa. When one understands the secret of these cosmic variations of the life force, he mourns no death nor loss, for he comprehends the falseness of these concepts. From the standpoint of gross matter, the universe and everything in it is subject to decay and death, and therefore everything is ultimately a source of pain and misery. But from the standpoint of universality, or the cosmic life force, or absolute Reality, this universe is as real and eternal as Reality itself. From an elevated vantage point, nothing is lost and nothing is gained, but from a lower outlook, everything is lost and nothing is gained.

The Process of Manifestation

Vedānta explains manifestation as being a systematic process. It maintains that the physical universe is composed of five gross elements: earth, water, fire, air, and space or ether. In each element all the other elements are contained, so no element is pure. An element is differentiated from the others by a predominance of a particular element in it. Vedānta states that all five elements are produced in a quintuplicated manner referred to as *pañcīkaraṇa.* The following diagrams depict the makeup of the five constituent elements of the universe.

The Five Elements

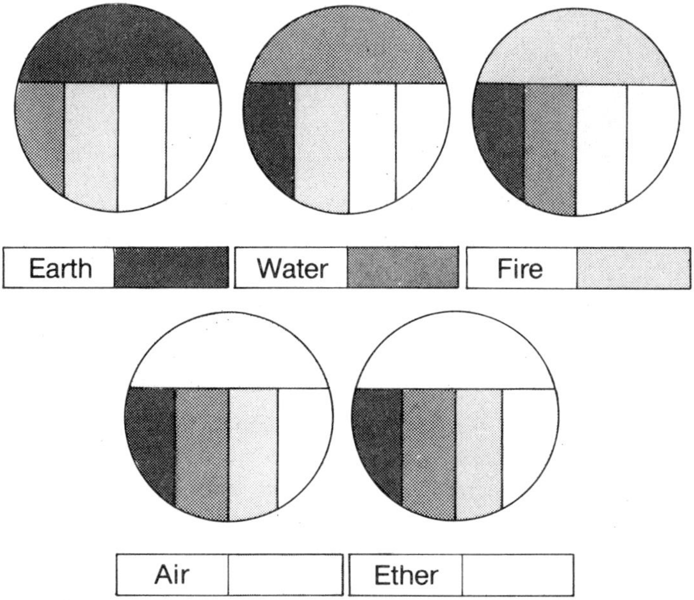

Vedānta borrows much from the Sāṃkhya explanation of the nature of the universe. In Sāṃkhya there are three inner instruments (intellect, ego, and mind), but according to Vedānta there are four inner instruments for cognition. These are intellect, ego, mind, and *citta* (mind stuff or memory bank). The ten senses, the five subtle elements, and the five gross elements are the same in Vedānta as they are in Sāṃkhya. Vedānta also describes prāṇa, the life force, as having ten varieties: *prāṇa, apāna, samāna, udāna, vyāna, nāga, kūrma, kṛkala, devadatta,* and *danañjaya.* Among these, the first five are the most important.

The Relationship Between the Absolute and the Universe

The reality or unreality of the universe depends on one's

conceptualization of the truth. When one is not conscious of the ultimate Truth, the apparent world seems real. When one forgets the ultimate goal of life, he identifies with the objects of the world and tries to possess them. Thus he becomes dependent on them and suffers pain and misery. But the moment one understands the law of cosmic life and comprehends the reality behind transitory things, he sees the unreality of this projected universe and knows the reality of Brahman behind the curtain of Māyā. Brahman-consciousness swallows up all names and forms, frees one from the fear of death, and opens the door to eternal life. The moment one succeeds in dissolving the plurality of names and forms and detaches himself from the external world, he is in oneness with eternal life. The Vedāntic view of the relationship between the Absolute and the universe indicates that enlightenment or liberation is not an external achievement, but rather an unfoldment of the inner potential that had become veiled by the darkness of ignorance. Dissolving illusory names and forms and realizing the true single divinity hidden within the diversity is the goal of Vedānta. In short, the Vedānta system affirms the divine link between the external world and the absolute Reality.

The Concept of God

The concept of God in the Vedānta system is unique; it is not found in the other systems of Indian philosophy. Because of Vedānta's complex concepts of Brahman, Māyā, and the universe, its concept of God is also complex. If Brahman alone is real, it is very difficult to convince an intellectual mind of the reality of the existence of the universe. From a certain standpoint Śaṅkara establishes the unreality of the universe, but from another point of view he establishes the reality of everything, including both this universe and that which is beyond.

To understand the concept of God, a student of Vedānta must first be very clear whether he is taking the standpoint of apparent reality or absolute Reality. According to Śaṅkara, if the universe is real, then the concept of God is also real because God is that state of consciousness that is united with Māyā, its essential potential. From a worldly point of view, God is real, but from the standpoint of absolute Reality, God is as unreal as this universe. Although Śaṅkara talks about God with the analogy of a magician, he is not talking from a worldly standpoint when doing this. His view is that God is a magician who allows his magical powers to create illusory objects in order to show a play to the audience of individual souls. A magician is never affected by his own magical powers, but the audience does not know the secret of the play and so confuses the illusory for the real.

Devotion to God is very important in order to become liberated from the mire of illusion. But for those who have already risen from the mire of multiplicity and have stepped onto the marble platform of nondual knowledge, there is no need of pursuing a god who is involved in spreading Māyā's net of illusion. Vedānta provides a means for establishing oneness between jīva (the individual self plus ignorance) and Īśvara (Brahman plus Māyā) and ultimately reaching a state beyond, *turīya*, the supreme Consciousness.

The Self and Human Life

A human being is a combined state of Self, mind, prāṇa, and body. The body is the dwelling place of the Self. It can be compared to the innermost palace of the city of life, in which dwells the Lord of life called the Self. The *Śrīmad Bhāgavatam* explains this concept beautifully. It states that there was once a prince of eternity who searched for a suitable kingdom with the necessary wealth, luxury, and subjects for him to enjoy his sovereignty. He saw a beautiful city with nine gates about its outer boundary that was protected by a cobra with five hoods. There were countless numbers of chambers within the city's walls, inside each of which there was ceaseless activity directed toward making the city flourish and prosper. Inside the city was a splendid, opulent palace. The gatekeeper of the city greeted the prince cordially and welcomed him into the city. The prince went to the palace, where he saw an elegant and lovely princess walking in the garden. Their eyes met, he immediately fell in love with her, and shortly thereafter they were married. As the story goes, they had many children and grandchildren, but in the process of raising his family and ruling his kingdom, the prince completely forgot his physical, mental, and spiritual health.

The prince of the story is the individual self (Ātman) born of the cosmic Self, the supreme Brahman. Because of ignorance the prince has separated from the emperor Brahman. In order to enjoy his sovereignty, the prince uses his magic power and projects an imaginary kingdom outside himself. The city represents the body, and the nine gates represent the eyes, nostrils, ears, mouth, anus, and urethra. The five hoods protecting the body-city are the five gross elements: earth, fire, water, air, and space. Inside the body there are numberless chambers or cells that ceaselessly carry on the activities of life. The princely Self sees the princess of intellect wandering in the garden of desire, and attraction and attachment born of ignorance lead him to identify himself with her. Thus the Self marries the intellect in order to enjoy the objects of the senses. But the Self becomes so involved with the world that he loses his peace and forgets his essential infinite nature and his magical powers. He becomes deluded by his own illusory creation, and instead of enjoying sensory objects as a master, he becomes their victim and performs his actions solely to satisfy his sense cravings. The charms and enjoyments start sapping his vitality, and he becomes weak and overwhelmed with self-generated problems.

One day an old spinster, the daughter of Death, whose name was Old Age, entered the city. She had been wandering throughout the universe to find an appropriate mate. Whenever she began to court anyone, he would faint in her embrace, and unable to maintain his physical existence, would fall into the mouth of Death, her father. Old Age started to seduce the prince, and because of his habit of indulgence in sensory pleasures, the prince could not resist her embrace. As was her nature, she began sapping all his strength and energy, and having lost the capacity to tap his inner strength, the prince quickly fell prey to weakness, frustration, dejection, loneliness, and disappointment. Many opponents, such as disease, sorrow, and other physical and psychosomatic illnesses, then attacked the city of life under the leadership of the great warrior Death. The poor cobra (the elements), who had been ignored for a long time, was very weak; he tried his best to protect the city of life for the prince, but he could not. The enemies threatened to enter, and the old prince called his ministers and commanded his army and all his subjects to defend him, but it was too late. Because of fear none of them would respond to his commands. Ultimately, the poor prince surrendered himself into the hands of Death without ever understanding his true invincible nature and immense power. As he surrendered, he looked pitiably at his wife, and was shocked to see her unconcernedly waving good-bye. Then he realized that the intellect is unconscious and that it is not her nature to think when she is deprived of the presence of her Lord of life. Now he knew that it had always been his power of consciousness that had made her appear to be conscious, and that he had been a fool to waste his life chasing after unreal sense pleasures. Such is the case with a human being. Too late, he realizes his faults and his misunderstandings regarding his relationships with his intellect and his other faculties.

The Five Sheaths, or Koṣas

The Self is hidden in the innermost chamber of the heart, and five sheaths veil it. Human life is a composite of these five sheaths and the Self. The five sheaths are the physical sheath, the energy sheath, the mental sheath, the sheath of wisdom, and the sheath of bliss. The physical sheath, which includes the skin, blood, flesh, bone, marrow, and ligaments, is composed of the five gross elements. It is also called the food sheath because it depends on food and is made of food. This is the grossest and outermost veil of the soul. The next sheath, the energy or prāṇa sheath, is more subtle. The gross manifestation of the energy sheath in a human being is the breath. There are ten subtle levels of prāṇa on which human biochemical functioning depends. More subtle than the energy sheath is the mental sheath. It comprises four inner instruments of cognition: lower mind (*manas*), ego (*ahaṅkāra*), intellect (*buddhi*), and mind stuff (*citta*). Beyond this sheath is the sheath of wisdom, through which knowledge from eternity transmits into the intellect. The last sheath is the sheath of bliss. This sheath should not be confused with Brahman, whose essential nature is pure bliss. Compared with that bliss, this sheath is merely pseudo-bliss predominated by ignorance. The Self at this level is very close to realization of its essential nature but is not yet free to see its glory and perfection.

The Self has a body, but the body is not the Self. The Self becomes a slave of the senses and their objects because of its identification with the body, senses, mind, and the other sheaths. The moment the Self remembers its real nature and understands that the five sheaths are provided for its enjoyment, it detaches itself from them and is no longer affected by the charms and temptations of the world. The Vedānta system does not deny the importance of the sheaths, but it makes one aware that he should not identify himself with them, that he should go beyond them to enjoy eternal life.

These five sheaths (see diagram) are also studied in terms of three types of bodies: gross (*sthūla śarīra*), subtle (*sūkṣma śarīra*), and causal (*kāraṇa śarīra*). The gross body is the same as the food sheath. Consciousness engrossed in this body corresponds to objects in the waking state. The subtle body is a combined state of the energy, mental, and wisdom sheaths. Consciousness engrossed in

The Five Sheaths, or Koṣas

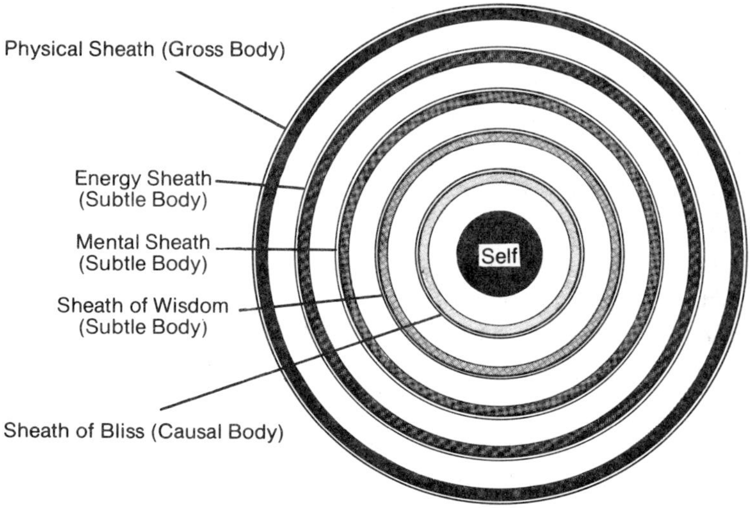

this body corresponds to the world of ideas and dreams. The causal body is the same as the bliss sheath, which corresponds to the state of deep sleep. In the Upaniṣads, Consciousness enveloped in these three types of bodies is termed *vaiśvānara*, *taijasa*, and *prājña*, respectively.

Four Aspects of Being for Practical Study

For practical application, the human being can be studied in four major parts: body, prāṇa, mind, and Self. (See diagram p. 238.)

The Body. The body, composed of the five gross elements, is the grossest instrument for progressing toward the goal of life. But unless it is healthy and in good condition, it is a great barrier in the way of one's growth. Its physical health depends on a subtle force by which it is governed, regulated, and nourished. That finer force that sustains the body is called prāṇa.

Prāṇa. The sustenance of all the levels of personality depends on the proper functioning of prāṇa. That life force is also the link between the body and mind, and its grossest manifestation is the breath. All physical phenomena reflect on the breath and, through the breath, on the mind. Likewise, all mental phenomena reflect on the breath and, through the breath, on the body. The breath therefore plays a vital role in the interaction of body and mind, and both body and mind and their functionings are vitalized by prāṇa, the very source of life. When the breath ceases, then all physiological and mental functions cease. In the Upaniṣads, prāṇa is compared to the queen honey bee. When she flies away, all the other bees (all psychophysiological energies and functions) fly away also, and when the queen bee prāṇa sits, all the other bees sit around her. Thus the functions of body and mind depend on the functioning of prāṇa. If there is a harmonious flow of prāṇa, then there will be harmony in

Four Aspects of Being

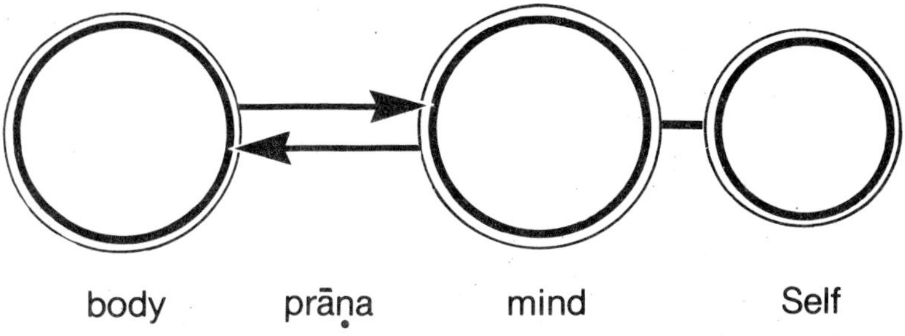

body and mind too. Breath is therefore considered to be the key for unlocking the secrets of the body and mind and for opening the final gate to go beyond all the mental states.

Mind. The next level of a human being is the mind. The Vedāntic concept of mind is quite different from those of the other systems of Indian philosophy. According to Vedānta, the mind serves as an inner instrument (*antaḥkaraṇa*) for receiving external experiences and transmitting them to the Self. Yoga provides only one term—*citta*—for this inner instrument, while the Sāṃkhya system studies the mind in three parts: intellect, ego, and lower mind. But in Vedānta the mind is divided into four parts or functions: lower mind, ego, mind-stuff, and intellect. The lower mind (manas) is the importer and exporter of feelings and sensations from the external world through the intellect to the Self. Ego (ahaṅkāra) is the faculty that is responsible for the sense of I-ness. It relates dualistically to the external world, identifying with the objects of the world and developing attachment or aversion to them. Mind-stuff (citta) is that faculty in which all memories—whatever passes through the lower mind, ego, and intellect—are stored and are occasionally recalled to the surface of the lower mind. Intellect (buddhi) is the decision-making faculty. It is the aspect of mind nearest to the Self and is predominated by sattva, the quality of brightness and lightness. In terms of modern Occidental psychology, the lower mind, ego, and intellect are the conscious mind, and the mind-stuff is the unconscious.

In daily life, sensory experiences come to the intellect in a specific manner. First of all, there is contact between a sense and a sense object. That experience is then carried by the sense to the lower mind. The lower mind determines and analyzes that experience in order to transmit it to the ego. Then the ego establishes a particular relationship with the experience, either rejecting or clinging to it. If the worldly experience is pleasant, the ego identifies itself with the object and transmits the experience to the intellect after coloring it with acceptance and attachment. If the worldly experience is unpleasant, the ego still identifies itself with that object and transmits the experience to the intellect, coloring it with rejection and repulsion. The intellect analyzes the transmission from the ego and makes the final decision to accept or reject. Intellect is the highest mental faculty. It decides what to do with the information provided by the ego and the lower mind, and thus controls the entire personality.

Every step of the transmission of experiences from the senses to the intellect is imprinted on the vast screen of the unconscious mind, called citta. The lower mind, the ego, and the intellect function in the waking conscious state, while the vast field of the unconscious mind is hidden behind it. Here all experiences are stored, in much the same way as information is stored in a computer. The unconscious mind also serves another function. When the conscious mind is relaxed and the senses are not in contact with external objects, many impressions of past physical and mental actions arise from the memory bed called citta. Most memories and anxieties are related to the unconscious mind. It is said that information regarding the entire universe is stored there; thus the Vedāntic saying, "That which is outside is also inside; the microcosm and the macrocosm are one and the same." The Vedānta system gives equal importance to controlling the flood of improperly analyzed feelings and sensations from the outside and from the inside. Unanalyzed and misunderstood sensations from worldly objects do not allow one the freedom to explore the inner avenues of life or to understand one's own real nature within. Likewise, sensations and feelings in the form of memories arising from the citta do not allow one to delve inward.

The Self. All these faculties become conscious because of the association of consciousness, the Self, with them. Without consciousness they are inert and lifeless. Intellect gets its intelligence from this source, prāṇa receives its vitality from this source, and the body grows and becomes active by virtue of this source. The realization of one's unity with this source is the very goal of life.

Liberation and the Means for Attaining It

In actuality, there is no place for bondage or liberation in the Vedānta system. There is only one existence—the Self. There is nothing outside the Self that can tie it with the rope of bondage. The Self is all-pervading and eternal, and it is therefore a misunderstanding or false apprehension to perceive multiplicity and transitoriness. This misunderstanding does not make any difference to the Self, which is pure and unaffected by the laws, rules, and regulations of the world. But it causes one to lose one's awareness of perpetual happiness and bliss. In the Vedānta system, liberation merely means to cast away the veils of ignorance and realize one's own essential nature, which is bliss, knowledge, and consciousness. Liberation is not an achievement; it is simply realization of the Truth that already abides within. This is not a mere intellectual understanding of the fact of one's true nature but rather an actual realization and transformation of inner attitudes.

Once one has accepted the existence of bondage, then the concept of liberation certainly exists. Bondage and liberation imply each other, and one is dependent on the other. Śaṅkara followed the view of his teacher's teacher, Gauḍapāda, according to which no one is perfect or imperfect; no one is accomplished, unaccomplished, or on the path of accomplishment; and there is no such thing as bondage and liberation. This is the absolute Truth, for all these words and their concepts imply duality, which itself is invalid. The very concept of duality is itself bondage, and the state beyond dualism is the absolute Truth, the goal of the human quest.

Vedānta philosophers use the following story to illustrate the nature of bondage and liberation. Once there was a washerman who had a donkey. One day he pretended to tie the donkey to a stake by showing the donkey the loose end of the rope around its neck and then only ostensibly tying it to the stake. The poor donkey thought that he was tied and stayed by the stake. The next day the washerman sent his son to bring the donkey to him, but when the boy tried to get the donkey to move, it would not budge. He even started beating the donkey, but still it would not move. The boy could not understand why the donkey would not move, and he went back to tell his father what had happened. Upon receiving his son's report, the washerman laughed and went to the donkey himself. He took the rope and moved his hand around the stake as though he were untying a knot. Only then did the donkey at last start moving.

Similarly, many people do not budge from their positions, even though they experience life as a series of pains and miseries, because they ignorantly think that they cannot move from where they are. In actuality all of us are ever-free, but our imaginations often create bondage for us and then prevent us from releasing our self-tied bonds. All spiritual practices are like the process that the washerman demonstrated in order to release the donkey and take him from the place of assumed bondage. Vedānta provides a systematic method of spiritual practice (*sādhanā*), which helps one to gain release from the self-created imaginary rope of bondage. The means described are *śravaṇa*, *manana*, and *nididhyāsana*. Śravaṇa entails studying the scriptures and listening to the learned teachers so that one can understand the validity of external objects and the essential nature of the Self and thereby discriminate the real from the unreal. In this way one can lead himself from darkness to light and from mortality to immortality. Manana is contemplation—repeatedly analyzing particular concepts. This is a process of pondering the truths received directly from teachers and through the study of the scriptures. Nididhyāsana is the process of applying those truths in one's daily life. One must form a lifestyle in which he can maintain his true consciousness.

Vedānta is the path of knowledge, and only serious and emotionally mature students are advised to follow it, for there are many delicate points where a student can fall from the path. Indeed, treading the path of Vedānta has often been likened to walking on the edge of a razor. This path of knowledge requires great concentration and good balance; these qualities are acquired through study, mental resolve, and withdrawal of the mind and senses from all their objects. When a person has understood the invalidity of external objects and has detached himself from them, then he can tread this path. To do so, purification of heart and mind and balance between intellectual and emotional activities are essential. This path is advised only for those who can trod it fearlessly. It is the path to be practiced by those who are like young elephants who walk without being disturbed by the barking dogs of unresolved conflicts and questions. These must be left behind. This is the path of mighty-hearted people.

People misunderstand this path and think that it is the path of renunciation, but it is actually the path of conquest. The student of Vedānta renounces the world not as a failure but as a conquerer. He conquers the negativities related to external objects, and for him nothing bad remains; everything becomes good and auspicious. According to Vedānta, birth and death are the two gates of the kingdom of eternity; from one gate a human being comes into the world, and from the other he enters into eternity. For a realized soul, death is not a source of fear but rather is a necessary vehicle for the journey of eternity.

Four Stages of Self-realization

The Vedānta system is based totally on the Upaniṣads. These works contain several great statements called *mahāvākyas* that serve as strong pillars to support the entire Vedāntic philosophy. Four of them are: (1) Brahman alone is real and the universe is unreal; (2) There is only one Brahman without second; (3) This

Self is Brahman, or I am Brahman; and (4) This entire universe is Brahman.* Some scholars charge that these four sentences are contradictory, but Śaṅkara's arguments resolve the apparent conflicts they contain. The four mahāvākyas cited here actually explain the states of realization that an aspirant of Vedānta experiences in the inward journey. The problem of contradiction arises because the mind by its nature is extremely limited and can in no way grasp the transcendent, multifarious truth of reality, and so it perceives contradictions among the necessarily incomplete verbal expressions of the various states of realization. An analysis of Śaṅkara's interpretation of these mahāvākyas will help unravel their inner meaning and reveal their essential harmony.

Brahman alone is real and the universe is unreal. The student's first step in the spiritual journey is to intellectually cancel the existence of the external world and accept the existence of one single Reality, called Brahman. All worldly thoughts and desires lead to transitory results because the entire universe and everything in it is ephemeral. Even virtues and right acts cannot produce everlasting results. An absolutely unchangeable result cannot be obtained by anything perishable and transitory. Worldly objects always pull one down unless they are properly analyzed by the faculty of discrimination. Vedānta therefore advises one to realize the unreality of the external world so he can control his worldly desires. Discrimination is the only means one has to cast away the net of duality and multiplicity, and discrimination cannot be strengthened without full determination and dedication. For this reason, the Vedānta system first of all emphasizes learning how to discriminate worldly transitory objects from the permanent reality. It then advises one to determine fully to dedicate his whole life to the search for knowledge.

*Scholars differ in the number and content of the mahāvākyas.

For full determination in the search for knowledge, renunciation and detachment are the most effective tools. They make one's mental resolves strong so that he will have a stable and secure basis on which to build his philosophy of life. On such rock-like resolve, one can practice visualizing and feeling the presence of divinity in every aspect of life instead of pursuing transitory and imperfect worldly objects. According to Vedānta, knowledge that is not capable of teaching the real value of external things, knowledge that does not help to free one from the bondage of the world, is not knowledge at all but is merely worldly information that burdens one's life. Data received from the senses and mind without proper analysis will cause one to flounder in an ocean of pain and misery. Knowledge that comes from the depths of consciousness, however, helps one to discriminate the real from the unreal. Unless one purifies his thoughts and mind, he cannot understand the real nature of the external world or hear the voice of conscience and intuition that is constantly speaking to him from the depths of his consciousness.

One comes to this world to learn through experience, which should be based not on foolish desires but on skillful experimentation that leads to understanding the reality of life. All those experiences that do not help a person gain mastery over his mind and skillfulness in his actions are a waste of time. A wise person turns his mind away from all worldly charms and temptations and redirects it toward Self-realization. If one allows himself to be attracted by the charms of petty things, he will not have time to explore the inner avenues of life. Thus, this first great statement of the Upaniṣads is meant to increase one's inner strength by emphasizing the reality of the divinity within and denying the reality of the external world. This is not a way of escaping from the world but rather is a way to become inward and thereby begin dissolving the multiplicity of external objects into a state of oneness.

There is only one Brahman without second. In the second

stage of realization, the student becomes aware of only one principle throughout the universe. His consciousness expands, and he does not allow his mind to waste energy in denying the existence of the world. In the first state of realization, there are two processes: accepting the existence of Brahman and negating the existence of the universe. But in the second state, there remains only the positive aspect: "There is only one Brahman without a second." This stage of realization resolves the seeming conflicts between the inside and the outside worlds and helps the aspirant realize the presence of divinity in external objects.

I am Brahman. Realization of the oneness of the truth outside is not sufficient for a spiritual seeker. Even though the first two stages establish peace and harmony in relation to the outside world, still there remains a subtle difference between the outside and inside worlds. Through the continuous practice of contemplation, a student of Vedānta starts thinking, "If there is only one Brahman without a second, then who am I?" Through deep contemplation, he dissolves the duality between inside and out and realizes that the Self that shines within him is the same as the all-pervading Brahman: "I am Brahman." This is the third stage of realization. Nothing is outside—everything is inside. Brahman and Ātman are one and the same.

All is Brahman. Eventually, the student transcends the feelings and attitudes of "I," "mine," "thy," and "thine" and no longer sees any difference in these concepts. His little ego expands into a higher ego; the limited "I" expands into the higher "I." In this state one fully understands that an individual "I" is the appearance of that highest "I." At this stage, one completely overcomes all passions, desires, and emotions such as attachment, hatred, jealousy, fear, delusion, and so on. One's heart starts beating with compassion to help those who are suffering. For such a person the entire universe becomes Brahman, and he finds himself in the universe and the universe in himself. He lives in Brahman-consciousness. This is the fourth and highest state of realization.

In this state ultimate bliss and happiness are expressed in the form of divine love for all. One's whole being becomes a center of universal love that radiates life and the light of knowledge and peace. In this state all words become mantras, and all actions are performed selflessly in the service of humanity. Such a person lives beyond the concepts of life and death; for him death and birth are as insignificant as a change of clothing.

Contemplation and Meditation

Vedānta is generally known as Jñāna Yoga, the path of knowledge. Jñāna Yoga is practiced through two different means: contemplation and meditation. In the classical texts of Vedānta only śravaṇa (study), manana (pondering), and nididhyāsana (application) are mentioned as methods for attaining the goal of life. The proper method for practicing contemplation and meditation is not described clearly in the texts of Vedānta philosophy; rather it is directly taught by the teacher to the student. The mahāvākyas mentioned previously are the guidelines for contemplation and the stages of inner realization. Through proper understanding of the mahāvākyas and through incorporating the techniques of meditation, a student can attain success in his quest.

Contemplation and meditation are complementary practices. Without contemplation, meditation becomes a mental exercise, and without meditation, contemplation becomes mere imagination. With the help of contemplation a person comprehends reality intellectually, and with the help of meditation he experiences the Reality within. Through contemplation one comes to know, and through meditation one comes to realize. Contemplation is a prerequisite for meditation, for unless one knows intellectually that there are higher levels of reality beyond mundane phenomena, he will not begin his quest to experience those levels of reality.

The Vedāntic method of contemplation is completely

different from the Christian method of contemplation. In Vedāntic contemplation, a student reflects on the transitoriness and hence ultimate invalidity of the experiences of external objects and looks beyond the ever-changing phenomena of the world to search for that which is real. In his contemplation, awareness of the highest goal of life, Self-realization, is always maintained. Questioning and analysis are the chief modes of Vedāntic contemplation. The student uses rigorous logic and close reasoning to realize the truth of his subject of contemplation. Faith and dedication are then employed to accept the truth, and strong determination is brought to bear to bring that truth into practice in daily life. Reliance on religious and theological concepts of God and on the practice of rituals is discouraged in Vedānta. Religious contemplation is viewed by Vedānta as actually a kind of daydreaming because such contemplation utilizes a set pattern of thinking based on mere belief. For example, a religious devotee may contemplate the life of Kṛṣṇa or Christ by remembering various stories that have been handed down recounting incidents in the life of the object of his veneration. Such an exercise may increase his piety, but it will not bring him closer to the goal of Self-realization.

Vedāntic contemplation, on the other hand, focuses on discriminating the real from the unreal in order to know the absolute Reality. The eternal sound Oṃ, which both symbolically and actually describes the absolute Reality, is used as a primary object of contemplation in the Vedānta system. On this point, Pātañjala Yoga and Vedānta are very similar to each other. Rājā Yoga also prescribes contemplation on the meaning of Oṃ and clearly states that Oṃ is the name of the supreme Reality. Both systems teach how to use the eternal sound Oṃ as an object of meditation while coordinating its mental repetition with the flow of the breath. The sound Oṃ comprises three simple phonemes, A-U-M, and a fourth state, silence. This fourth state is called *turīya*, the superconscious state, the absolute Brahman. The three sounds, A, U, and M, denote respectively the states of waking, dreaming, and deep sleep, and the aspects of divinity that are involved in the processes of manifestation, preservation, and annihilation. The Upaniṣads say that Oṃ is the bow, the individual self is the arrow, and the supreme Consciousness, Brahman, is the target. One should shoot carefully, like a skilled archer, while being completely absorbed in the goal—Brahman-consciousness.

The Vedānta system considers the possible difficulties on this path. No undeserving student is allowed to be initiated into this discipline. Vedānta requires that a few prerequisites be fulfilled by the student before starting the practice of this system. Those who have calmed their minds, mastered their senses, purified their emotions, prepared themselves to follow the commands of Vedāntic teachers, acquired positive thoughts, and have a burning desire to liberate themselves from the rope of bondage are deserving to be admitted as students. These prerequisites to practice the path of knowledge are in some ways the same as the yamas and niyamas of the Yoga system.

Unless the student understands the meaning of Oṃ as described in the Māṇḍūkya-kārikā and in many other Upaniṣads, its mere repetition in meditation becomes mechanical and boring. If the meaning of Oṃ has been properly contemplated and if the student has become attuned to the sound, then during meditation this sound leads him to the realization of higher dimensions of life. Success on this path is not easy. Constant awareness, guidance from a competent teacher, and faith in and total surrender to the absolute Reality lead the aspirant to the highest goal of life.

Index

(continued)

The main building of the national headquarters, Honesdale, Pa.

The Himalayan Institute

Since its establishment in 1971, the Himalayan Institute has been dedicated to helping individuals develop themselves physically, mentally, and spiritually, as well as contributing to the transformation of society. All the Institute programs—educational, therapeutic, research—emphasize holistic health, yoga, and meditation as tools to help achieve those goals. Institute programs combine the best of ancient wisdom and modern science, of Eastern teachings and Western technologies. We invite you to join with us in this ongoing process of personal growth and development.

Our beautiful national headquarters, on a wooded 400-acre campus in the Pocono Mountains of northeastern Pennsylvania, provides a peaceful, healthy setting for our seminars, classes, and training programs in the principles and practices of holistic living. For two decades students from around the world have been joining us here to attend programs in such diverse areas as biofeedback and stress reduction, hatha yoga, meditation, diet and nutrition, philosophy and metaphysics, and practical psychology for better living. We see the realization of our human potentials as a lifelong quest, leading to increased health, creativity, happiness, awareness, and improving the quality of life.

The Institute is a nonprofit organization. Your membership in the Institute helps to support its programs. Please call or write for information on becoming a member.

Institute Programs, Services, and Facilities

All Institute programs share an emphasis on conscious, holistic living and personal self-development. You may enjoy any of a number of diverse programs, including:

- Special weekend or extended seminars to teach skills and techniques for increasing your ability to be healthy and to enjoy life
- Holistic health services provided by our Center for Health and Healing
- Professional training for health professionals
- Meditation retreats and advanced meditation instruction
- Cooking and nutritional training
- Hatha yoga and exercise workshops
- Residential programs for self-development

The Himalayan Institute Charitable Hospital

A major aspect of the Institute's work around the world is its construction and management of a modern, comprehensive hospital and holistic health facility in the mountain area of Dehra Dun, India. Outpatient facilities are already providing medical care to those in need, and mobile units have been equipped to visit outlying villages. Construction work on the main hospital building is progressing as scheduled.

We welcome financial support to help with the construction and the provision of services. We also welcome donations of medical supplies, equipment, or professional expertise. If you would like further information on the Hospital, please contact us.